CAR

D0322926

An Introduction to Metaphysics

This book is an accessible introduction to the central themes of contemporary metaphysics. It carefully considers accounts of causation, freedom and determinism, laws of nature, personal identity, mental states, time, material objects, and properties, while inviting students to reflect on metaphysical problems. The philosophical questions discussed include: What makes it the case that one event causes another event? What are material objects? Given that material objects exist, do such things as properties exist? What makes it the case that a person may exist at two different times? *An Introduction to Metaphysics* makes these tough questions tractable by presenting the features and flaws of current attempts to answer them. Intended primarily for students taking a first course in metaphysics, this lucid and well-written text is also an excellent introduction for anyone interested in knowing more about an important area of philosophy.

JOHN W. CARROLL is Professor of Philosophy at North Carolina State University. He is the author of *Laws of Nature* (Cambridge, 1994).

NED MARKOSIAN is Professor of Philosophy at Western Washington University.

An Introduction to Metaphysics

JOHN W. CARROLL

North Carolina State University

NED MARKOSIAN

Western Washington University

 CAMBRIDGE
UNIVERSITY PRESS

CAMBRIDGE UNIVERSITY PRESS
Cambridge, New York, Melbourne, Madrid, Cape Town, Singapore,
São Paulo, Delhi, Dubai, Tokyo

Cambridge University Press
The Edinburgh Building, Cambridge CB2 8RU, UK

Published in the United States of America by Cambridge University Press, New York

www.cambridge.org
Information on this title: www.cambridge.org/9780521533683

© John W. Carroll and Ned Markosian 2010

This publication is in copyright. Subject to statutory exception
and to the provisions of relevant collective licensing agreements,
no reproduction of any part may take place without the written
permission of Cambridge University Press.

First published 2010

Printed in the United Kingdom at the University Press, Cambridge

A catalogue record for this publication is available from the British Library

Library of Congress Cataloguing in Publication data
Carroll, John W.
  An introduction to metaphysics / John W. Carroll, Ned Markosian.
    p. cm.   (Cambridge introductions to philosophy)
  ISBN 978-0-521-82629-7 (hardback)
  1. Metaphysics.   I. Markosian, Ned.   II. Title.   III. Series.
  BD111.C335 2010
  110–dc22   2010001514

ISBN 978-0-521-82629-7 Hardback
ISBN 978-0-521-53368-3 Paperback

Cambridge University Press has no responsibility for the persistence or
accuracy of URLs for external or third-party internet websites referred to in
this publication, and does not guarantee that any content on such websites is,
or will remain, accurate or appropriate.

Contents

Preface

The aim of this book is to introduce the philosophically curious to the central topics of contemporary metaphysics.

We expect that our audience will include undergraduate philosophy majors who have maybe already taken an introductory survey course in philosophy or a first course in symbolic logic, and who are now enrolled in a course devoted solely to topics in metaphysics. We also expect that our audience will include graduate students in philosophy who are either getting their first opportunity to tackle contemporary metaphysical issues or are looking for a book to keep on hand as a useful resource as they undertake a rigorous research seminar on some specific metaphysical topic. We hope that many more reflective minds, ranging from the contemplative layperson to sages of the philosophical professoriate, will find our text valuable as a source of sober reasoning and at least the occasional insight.

We have written this book as teachers. Though we realize that there is no way to keep our own philosophical commitments from seeping into our arguments and our choice of topics, we have tried not to make the book a forum for advancing metaphysical doctrines. We have gone out of our way to introduce topics and arguments without pressuring the reader to settle on any definite conclusions. In fact, the reader will find scattered about lots of spots where we cut off the discussion in order to identify the pros and cons of a particular thesis and then move on to another issue. In no case do we take what we say here to be the final word on a topic.

To help make the book accessible and engaging, we have not burdened it with extensive references. So, for example, we have made no attempt to identify everyone who has defended compatibilism about freedom and determinism or to reference all the possible criticisms of compatibilism.

We focus our discussion only on the most important formulations and criticisms of the view. Our annotative approach has been to include references to a few excellent and central works that would be a good next stop for readers on their way to further knowledge of metaphysics, whether they are needing sources to write a term paper or just want to find out what else David Armstrong, David Lewis, or Peter van Inwagen – three philosophers who figure centrally in this book – has to say.

It is rare that a philosophy teacher takes a class from the beginning to the end of a single metaphysics book. So each chapter of our book is self-contained; a teacher can assign any subset of the chapters. We should say, though, that we think all students planning to read any of the main topic chapters will benefit from having read Chapter 1. There we introduce our conception of metaphysics, introduce some basics about necessity and ontology, and explain why we set aside a certain common sort of skeptical question that can get in the way of thinking about metaphysical topics.

Although we write in the first person plural and have both been involved at least a little in writing each of the chapters, it will be obvious to those familiar with our other work who did the bulk of the writing in each of the eight main topic chapters. For those not so familiar: Ned was the primary author on "Freedom and determinism" (Chapter 3), "Personal identity" (Chapter 5), "Time" (Chapter 7), and "Material objects" (Chapter 8); John was the primary author on "Causation" (Chapter 2), "Laws of nature" (Chapter 4), "Mental states" (Chapter 6), and "Properties" (Chapter 9). (Chapter 1 was closer to being a joint project than any of the others.) Basically, each of us focused on the topics with which we felt the most comfortable. Fortunately, our own philosophical views are compatible enough – and the nature of the text is sufficiently devoid of specialized judgments – that it has not been difficult for either of us to live with the words put in our mouths by our co-author.

Thanks to Hilary Gaskin at Cambridge University Press and to Mark Heller for getting us started on this project. Additional thanks to Hilary for guiding us to publication; this includes arranging for a helpful review editor who provided comments on a nearly final draft. Funding to support preparation of the index by Ann Rives was provided by the Department of Philosophy and Religious Studies at NC State. Our thanks also go to the many colleagues and teachers who have discussed the central issues with us or who have otherwise provided crucial support over the years. These include David Auerbach, Randy Carter, Catherine Driscoll, Ron Endicott, Doug Jesseph, Michael Pendlebury, Ann Rives, Stephen Schiffer, David Robb, Melissa Schumaker, and David Sipfle, as well as Mark Aronszajn, Greg Fitch (RIP), Ed Gettier, Robert Grimm, Fred Feldman, Hud Hudson, Gary Matthews, Sharon Ryan, Tom Ryckman, Ted Sider, and Ryan Wasserman. We hope we haven't forgotten any teachers or colleagues who should be on this list. We certainly won't forget our immediate families. They are our greatest source of support. Thank you wives and children. Ned lost both his parents during this project. John's are doing well but have had their own serious health challenges to deal with. For getting us on the does-exist list and for decades of nurture and guidance, most of all, thank you moms and dads.

1 Introduction

1.1 What is metaphysics?

Since this book is called *An Introduction to Metaphysics*, it makes sense to begin with a short, simple, and clear definition of the word 'metaphysics'. If only it were that easy.

Part of the problem is that it's practically impossible to get any two philosophers to agree on a single definition of 'metaphysics'. (And the book is, after all, written by two philosophers.) But there are also issues relating to the strange etymology of the term 'metaphysics', and further complications arising from the fact that 'metaphysics' has one meaning in ordinary English and another meaning within (academic) philosophy. Nevertheless, we'll do our best in this section to offer the reader what we take to be a reasonable characterization of the field of metaphysics. In fact, we'll offer three different but mutually compatible characterizations.

Let's start with what metaphysics is not. Metaphysics – as we are using the term – is not the study of the occult. Nor is it the study of mysticism, or auras, or the power of pyramids. Although the word 'metaphysics' may indeed have all of those connotations in ordinary English, the word is used within academic philosophy in an entirely different way. And this book, as it happens, is meant to be an introduction to the branch of academic philosophy that is known as metaphysics.

What about the etymology of the word 'metaphysics'? Can that shed some light on our subject? Well, the current usage of the word has its origins in the ancient world. It seems that during the first century CE, some of Aristotle's works were being collected and published in Alexandria. (Aristotle had died 300 or 400 years earlier, around 322 BCE.) Among these was a collection of Aristotelian writings that was given a name in ancient

Greek that is normally translated into modern English as *Physics*.[1] (But the name is misleading: Aristotle's *Physics* is not mainly about physics. In fact, ironically, it is mainly about metaphysics.)

Shortly after the publication of Aristotle's *Physics*, another batch of Aristotle's writings was ready for publication. The editor in charge of the project gave this other work a title in ancient Greek that means, literally, *After the Physics*. (This was the equivalent of calling it *The Book We Published after We Published Aristotle's Physics*.) Moreover, it just so happened that this other book of Aristotle's contained discussions of such important but disparate philosophical topics as existence, identity, actuality, potentiality, time, change, causation, substance, matter, form, and universals (among others). Despite the fact that they were all discussed by Aristotle in other works of his (including his *Physics*), these topics (and others more or less closely related to them) eventually came to be associated with that particular book of Aristotle's in which they featured so prominently – a book whose Greek name is *Metaphusika* and whose English name is (you guessed it) *Metaphysics*.

If we take an etymological approach to characterizing metaphysics, then, we will say that metaphysics is the branch of philosophy concerned with a disparate collection of topics that happen to be associated with one particular collection of writings by Aristotle, namely, the collection that was published after Aristotle's *Physics*.

Unfortunately, this etymological approach doesn't give us a very satisfying account of what many take to be the most central branch of philosophy. It would be nice to be able to give a more conceptual, big-picture account of metaphysics. And indeed, as most metaphysicians will tell you, it's hard not to have the sense that the various topics within metaphysics do have something essential in common with one another, in much the same way that the various topics within ethics, or the topics within epistemology, have something essential in common.

Attempts to capture in a definition this something essential that most metaphysicians feel unifies the various topics of their field often result in somewhat elusive pronouncements like the following: metaphysics is the branch of philosophy concerned with fundamental questions about the nature of reality.

---

[1] All of the works of Aristotle discussed in this chapter can be found in *The Basic Works of Aristotle*.

This big-picture approach, unfortunately, is not without its own problems. One main difficulty is that most branches of inquiry, including biology, economics, and history, are also concerned with reality. Perhaps, however, there is an easy way to deal with this problem: let us assume that we all have at least a rough idea of what philosophy is, and that we can safely assert that other reality-based fields, such as biology and so on, are not branches of philosophy.

That still leaves the problem of distinguishing metaphysics from other branches of philosophy, such as ethics and epistemology, which are after all also concerned with reality. But now we might be able to take a contrastive approach. Here's the idea. Suppose (as we have already) that we possess a rough idea of what philosophy is. Then we can add some helpful context to our big-picture approach to characterizing metaphysics by saying that there are three main branches of philosophy: ethics (the branch of philosophy concerned with fundamental questions about right and wrong and good and bad); epistemology (the branch of philosophy concerned with fundamental questions about knowledge and justification); and metaphysics (the other main branch of philosophy). In other words, we can characterize metaphysics as what is left over when you subtract ethics and epistemology from the core area of philosophy.

But what exactly is left over when you subtract ethics and epistemology from the core area of philosophy? We think a good way to answer this question is with specific examples. Here, then, are some of the topics that metaphysicians deal with: ontology (roughly, the study of being, including the attempt to come up with a list of all the main categories of things that exist); the nature of time; the Mind–Body Problem (roughly, the problem of understanding the relationship between mental phenomena and the physical basis of those phenomena); the problem of personal identity (roughly, the problem of identifying the conditions under which an earlier person and a later person are one and the same person); the problem of freedom and Determinism (roughly, the problem of specifying what is required in order for a person to be acting freely); the nature of the laws of nature; the nature of causation; and the nature of material objects (including questions about the relation between an object and the matter it is made of, and the conditions under which two or more objects compose a further object).

If the topics on this list aren't yet perfectly clear to you, do not despair. We will explore one example of an ontological issue (the existence of properties) in some depth in Chapter 9 of this book. Each of the other topics on the list is the subject of its own chapter. So by the end of the book you should have a much clearer conception of what each of these topics amounts to. And then you will be in a position to appreciate our third approach to characterizing metaphysics, according to which metaphysics is the branch of philosophy concerned with topics like those listed in the previous paragraph.

Let us summarize our discussion so far. We have identified three different approaches to characterizing metaphysics. One is *the etymological approach*, according to which metaphysics is the branch of philosophy concerned with a disparate collection of topics that just happen to be associated with one particular collection of writings by Aristotle, namely, the collection that was published after Aristotle's *Physics*. Next there is *the big-picture approach*, according to which metaphysics is the branch of philosophy concerned with fundamental questions about the nature of reality. And finally, there is *the definition-by-example approach*, according to which metaphysics is the branch of philosophy concerned with such topics as ontology, time, the Mind–Body Problem, the problem of personal identity, the problem of freedom and Determinism, laws of nature, causation, and material objects (all of which will be discussed extensively in this book).

For the remainder of this chapter, our plan is to do three things. First, in 1.2, we will begin our metaphysical investigations with some basics about modality, especially the concept that philosophers call *metaphysical necessity*. This will permit us to discuss a topic that plays some role in almost every chapter of the book, and that also serves as a nice illustration of a conceptual problem in metaphysics. Then, in 1.3, we will introduce some basics about ontology. These two sections of this first chapter will let us demonstrate in a very introductory way some of the methods of the metaphysician. And finally, in 1.4, we will end the chapter by trying to set aside a common skeptical intrusion that you, the reader, would do well to resist.

1.2 Modality

Let's begin with a short list of some propositions that are widely accepted as being metaphysically necessary.[2]

---

[2] We 'list' propositions by displaying sentences that express the relevant propositions.

Kant is wise or it is not the case that Kant is wise.

$2 + 2 = 4$.

Red is a color.

All bachelors are unmarried.

It would be helpful if we could give you a definition of 'necessity' that would make it crystal clear why these are fairly uncontroversial. That's not so easy to do. About the best we can do is to say that these propositions are metaphysically necessary because they *can't* be false, because they *have* to be true. No matter how our world might be, these four propositions would be true.

Propositions that are *not* metaphysically necessary are ones that are either *metaphysically impossible* or *metaphysically contingent*. The metaphysically impossible propositions include:

Kant is wise and Kant is not wise.

$2 + 2 = 5$.

Red is not a color.

Not all bachelors are unmarried.

These propositions can't be true; they have to be false. They would be false no matter what. The metaphysically contingent propositions include:

Kant is wise.

There are four oranges in the refrigerator.

Red is the color of some fire engines.

Asia is the smallest continent.

Metaphysically contingent propositions can be true and also can be false. Whether they are true or false does depend on what the world is like. As you may have already inferred, the *metaphysically possible* propositions are the ones that are either metaphysically necessary or metaphysically contingent; they are the ones that are not metaphysically impossible.

Metaphysical necessity is one concept of necessity. There are others. For example, there is an important class of metaphysically contingent propositions that are *physically* (i.e., *lawfully*) *necessary*. For example, it is not uncommon to hear someone say, "It is impossible that there be a perpetual motion machine." But when this is said it is not meant that such a machine is metaphysically impossible, that it is somehow contradictory in the way that, say, Kant's being wise and not wise is. What is meant is that the existence of a perpetual motion machine would contradict some law of nature (e.g., The Second Law of Thermodynamics). For a quite different sort of example, there is *epistemological necessity*. Certain propositions are said to be possibly false that in fact are metaphysically necessary. For a long time, it was common to hear mathematicians and others say things like, "It is possible that Fermat's Last Theorem is false – there has been no proof."[3] Prima facie, what they said was perfectly true. Nevertheless, in the mid-1990s, thanks to the mathematical work of Andrew Wiles, Fermat's Last Theorem was proven. So, like other mathematical truths, it is metaphysically necessary – and always has been. Evidently, those who said it might be false were not saying that it wasn't metaphysically necessary. All they were saying was that, for all they knew, or for all anyone knew, Fermat's Last Theorem was false. They were reporting the *epistemological possibility* that it was false.

There is another epistemological notion worth mentioning here. Considering how it is characterized, you wouldn't think that there was much chance of confusing it with metaphysical necessity. But in fact it is easy to do, because the two notions in question share many important instances. Many metaphysically necessary propositions are *a priori true*. That means, very roughly, that they are such that, once the proposition is grasped, it can be known to be true based solely on reason.[4] Some perception might be required to grasp the proposition, to acquire the concepts involved, but with a priori true propositions, there is no further need to rely on perception in order to know that the world matches up. The a priori true propositions contrast with propositions that are *a priori false* (the propositions that can be known to be false by reason alone) and with the propositions that are *a posteriori* (the ones that are neither a priori true nor a priori false).[5]

The four examples of metaphysically necessary propositions listed above are all widely accepted as a priori true. The idea is that, if you understand logical terms like 'and' and 'not', you are already in a position to figure out

---

[3] Fermat's Last Theorem is the proposition that $x^n + y^n = z^n$ has no integer solutions for $n > 2$ and $x, y, z > 0$.

[4] 'A priori' is Latin for prior to. The idea is that a priori truths can be known independently of (prior to) experience.

[5] 'A posteriori' is Latin for behind; a posteriori propositions can be known only with the benefit of experience.

in your head that Kant is either wise or not wise. You don't have to have read the *Critique of Pure Reason* to find that out! Similarly, if in addition to being familiar with some logical concepts, you know what it is to be a bachelor and what it is to be unmarried, then you are already in a position to figure out by reason alone that all bachelors are unmarried. Parallel points could be made about the propositions that 2 + 2 = 4 and that red is a color.[6] So the a priori and metaphysical necessity seem a lot alike. Given only the examples we have introduced up to this point, these two philosophical concepts apply to exactly the same propositions.

But in other ways these concepts are very different. In particular, though we have given no formal definition of either, the differences in the rough characterizations we have given are pretty severe. Metaphysical necessity was characterized only in terms of having to be true, yet a distinctly epistemological concept – knowledge – was brought in to characterize the a priori. On the face of it, that seems to leave open that these two concepts, the a priori and metaphysical necessity, might not match up about every case. Maybe there are some propositions that are metaphysically necessary but not a priori true. Maybe there are some a priori truths that are not metaphysically necessary.

For a long time, the presumption was that these concepts don't come apart. The thought was that, though they are different concepts with different definitions, they have all the same instances. The reasoning behind this traditional presumption goes something like this: the truth of metaphysically necessary propositions doesn't depend on how the world is – they have to be true, they are true no matter what – and so their truth must be a purely conceptual matter. If their truth is a purely conceptual matter, then it can be known by reason alone. Meanwhile, if a proposition's truth is knowable by reason alone, if you don't need to interact with the world to know that it is true, then its truth must be a purely conceptual matter, and thus it must be necessarily true.

Many philosophers have been rethinking the traditional presumption. Saul Kripke offers that water is H_2O is an example of a proposition that is necessarily true but not a priori true.[7] It does seem to be necessarily

---

[6] To extend the parallels, our examples of metaphysically impossible propositions are all generally taken to be a priori false, and the examples of metaphysically contingent propositions to be a posteriori.

[7] Kripke, *Naming and Necessity*, pp. 116 ff.

true. How it could be false? Anything that wasn't composed of two parts hydrogen and one part oxygen just wouldn't be water. But it also seems clear that it is a posteriori true. The discovery that water is H_2O was not reasoned from reflection on the conceptual natures of water, hydrogen, and oxygen. This was an important scientific discovery made at the end of the late eighteenth century based on experiments that composed water from hydrogen and oxygen. It is hard to see how anyone could have come to know the molecular structure of water based only on reason.

The lesson we are trying to impart here is not that Kripke is right. Maybe he is and maybe he isn't. There is lots of interesting discussion of this example and other examples that Kripke and others have proposed.[8] Our point in discussing the water-is-H_2O example is to show that you should not simply assume that the metaphysically necessary propositions and the a priori true propositions match up exactly.

We hope we have helped you understand metaphysical necessity better just by citing examples of necessary truths and distinguishing metaphysical necessity from some ordinary notions (physical necessity and epistemological necessity) and an important philosophical one (the a priori).[9] But there is more that might be done. When seeking understanding, philosophers often try to provide a philosophical account or theory of the concept in question. A philosophical account can include something like a definition, a full characterization of the concept that is usually reported by a biconditional (an 'if and only if') sentence; such an account states a necessary and sufficient condition for the concept to apply. Often, however, philosophical accounts aren't that ambitious; some theories include only some plausible principle that describes some important feature of the concept.

You will run into several philosophical accounts in this book. Here is one simple example about moral freedom from Chapter 3:

Stacean Compatibilism
An action is free if and only if it is unconstrained.

And here is another:

Alternative Possibilities
S does A freely only if S could have done something other than A.

---

[8] See, for example, Sidelle, *Necessity, Essence, and Individuation.*

[9] Our approach has been similar to the approach taken by Alvin Plantinga in the first chapter of *The Nature of Necessity.*

All the theories we will consider will be subjected to scrutiny, and we will often find disagreement among philosophers about whether the account succeeds.

What about necessity? Is there some philosophical account of metaphysical necessity, something that might go beyond what we have done so far by way of introducing you to this crucial concept? There is actually a lot of agreement on one simple treatment. All metaphysicians will accept that something is metaphysically necessary if and only if its negation is not metaphysically impossible. Indeed, this account is already implicit in our discussion above.

Necessity in Terms of Possibility
P is metaphysically necessary if and only if not-P is not metaphysically possible.

All metaphysicians will also agree that, though this account is true, it is no great philosophical achievement in an attempt to provide understanding of metaphysical necessity. Notice that one can equally well explain possibility in terms of necessity:

Possibility in Terms of Necessity
P is metaphysically possible if and only if not-P is not metaphysically necessary.

Were a metaphysician to accept both the two preceding accounts with no further account of metaphysical necessity or metaphysical possibility, there would be a disappointing circle in his or her philosophy of modality. Also, it would be pretty unusual for someone to perfectly well understand metaphysical necessity and not understand metaphysical possibility. That's because metaphysical possibility and metaphysical necessity live very close to each other in conceptual space; they are both modal concepts. It is not exactly clear who would be helped by either theory.

Is there an account of either metaphysical necessity or metaphysical possibility that would be more illuminating, one helpful to someone who didn't have any prior understanding of either of these modal concepts? David Lewis took on the challenging task of providing such an account.[10] He thought that our world, the universe around us, is one of many. In our world, pigs don't fly, Rome is the capital of Italy, and no signals travel faster

---

[10] Lewis, *Counterfactuals*, especially pp. 84–91, and *On the Plurality of Worlds*.

than light. But, as he saw it, there are other worlds, ones where pigs do fly, Beijing is the capital of Italy, and superluminal travel is commonplace. Take all these other worlds together with our world (the actual world) to comprise *the possible worlds*. This permits accounts of both metaphysical necessity and metaphysical possibility:

> *Lewis on Necessity*
> P is metaphysically necessary if and only if P is true in all the possible worlds.

> *Lewis on Possibility*
> P is metaphysically possible if and only if P is true in at least one of the possible worlds.

Thinking of possibility as truth in a possible world is a picturesque and useful way of thinking of possibility, one that we will occasionally adopt when proposing and considering hypothetical examples. Indeed, to introduce a possibility for consideration, philosophers often start by saying, "Consider a possible world where ..." Thinking of necessity as truth in all possible worlds is just as picturesque and useful.

Lewis, however, did not intend to just be describing an effective manner of doing and delivering metaphysics. He took himself to be providing conceptual understanding of metaphysical necessity and metaphysical possibility. Despite how it might look, the biconditionals displayed above are not put forward to account for metaphysical necessity or metaphysical possibility in terms of metaphysical possibility (or any other kind of possibility). For Lewis, there is no circularity in his overall philosophy of modality. 'The possible worlds' is just a name for a certain collection of things – big universe-size things, admittedly – that Lewis assumes are just as much part of reality as you are and we are. Indeed, we could have just called them *the worlds*, and left the word 'possible' out of the explanatory parts of the accounts altogether. For a proposition to be metaphysically necessary is for it to be true in all those things, all those worlds. For a proposition to be metaphysically possible is for it to be true in at least one of them.

As is true of all the theories that are presented in this book, there are lots of questions that can be asked regarding Lewis's accounts of metaphysical necessity and metaphysical possibility. There is the question whether his accounts are true, whether they count exactly the propositions they should as metaphysically necessary and metaphysically possible. Even if true, we would also want to investigate whether the truths stated describe suitably crucial features of metaphysical necessity and metaphysical possibility rather than unimportant or accidental features of these concepts. We won't pursue either of these questions here; we have discussed Lewis's accounts mainly in order to provide some useful background and as an illustration of what a conceptual issue in metaphysics is like. Nevertheless, we are not done with another question that needs to be asked regarding Lewis. The question is whether we should accept Lewis's ontology of possible worlds. In 1.3, we introduce the topic of ontology.

1.3 Ontology

Besides seeking conceptual understanding, another basic way to engage in metaphysics is to do ontology. Traditionally, ontology is said to be *the theory of being* or *the study of existence.*

Given those descriptions, one might think that ontologists engage in a conceptual investigation parallel to how the metaphysician tries to better understand metaphysical necessity or moral freedom. If this were so, the ontologist would try to figure out what it is to exist. To begin such an investigation, one might compile a list of clear cases. Here's a start:

Does exist	*Does not exist*
Mars	Vulcan
New York City	Atlantis
Pedro Martinez	Sidd Finch
Oxygen	Phlogiston
Secretariat	Pegasus

Then one might go on to ask: What do the things on the first list have in common that all the 'things' on the second list lack? What is it to exist? One idea: to have a location in space. Another idea: to have causes or effects. Both proposals work pretty well for the two lists just given. Still, there are some hard cases that will raise difficult questions. With the first idea, both God and numbers would turn out not to exist, since (traditionally anyway) they are thought not to be located in space. With the second idea, assuming for the sake of illustration that God exists and caused the universe, God would be in but numbers would still be out. Are these acceptable consequences? Maybe. Maybe not.

In any case, understanding the concept of existence is *not* a focus of contemporary metaphysics. Since at least the mid-twentieth century, ontologists have not primarily studied or tried to characterize the concept of existence, at least not directly. It would be more accurate to describe them as trying to complete the does-exist list. They have not primarily addressed the question, "What is it to exist?"; they have primarily addressed the question "What exists?" So do not think of ontology as starting with some pre-theoretic judgments about what exists and what doesn't, and then trying to formulate a description of the crucial differences. Better to think of ontologists as doing inventory.

While that's an improvement by way of an accurate description of what ontologists do, it is still a little misleading. We have made it sound like an ontologist should have an observatory to use in discovering some undiscovered planets, or at least a snazzy pair of binoculars to help catalogue a description for each robin that happens by. But that's not what ontology is like either.

First, in general, ontologists are not interested in identifying entities one by one. They tend to do their work with much broader brush strokes. They aren't concerned with specifying that one specific robin exists or in counting all the planets. They aren't much concerned even with the broad categories of birds or celestial bodies. Ontologists generally work at a much more general, abstract, and, as they see it, fundamental level. They want to know: Are there any material objects at all? Do events exist? Do facts exist? Are there any immaterial souls? What about properties and relations? Do any (non-actual) possible worlds exist? Do numbers exist? Do sets? If any of these things do exist, the ontologist will also want to know something about what they are like.

Second, while doing ontology is quite different from trying to provide conceptual understanding of existence, it is much more theoretical and much less empirical than astronomy or making a bird list. The contemporary ontologist begins with some propositions, and then figures out what those propositions entail about what exists. Oftentimes, not wanting to deal with too many issues at once, the propositions will all come from a single subject matter. So, for example, an ontologist might start with the truths of mathematics, maybe even just the truths of arithmetic, and then ask what follows from these truths about what exists. Does it follow from the fact that 2 + 2 = 4 that 2 and 4 exist? Does it follow from this fact that the relation of identity or the operation of addition exists? For a slightly less abstract example, we could start with some claims of biology, and ask whether those propositions entail that species exist (over and above the members of species). What must exist in order for some proposition to be true has come to be known as that proposition's *ontological commitment*.

W. V. O. Quine is famous for describing and advocating this approach to ontology, though he advocated a somewhat formal and language-based version. Quine thought that one important task for philosophers was the translation of natural language sentences into the language of predicate logic. The notation of predicate logic includes quantifiers like '$(\exists x)$' for 'there exists an x such that' and '$(\forall x)$' for 'for any x'. The quantifiers always include a variable that can play a role in a subsequent formula. So, for instance, '$(\exists x)Wx$' might represent 'There is an x such that x is wise' or more colloquially 'Something is wise;' '$(\forall x)(Rx \supset Bx)$' might represent 'For any x, if x is a raven, then x is black' or more colloquially, 'All ravens are black.' Part of doing the translation is to specify a certain element of the semantics of predicate logic known as *the domain of quantification*, the entities that the quantifiers range over, all the things that the variables in the sentences of predicate logic might stand for. For Quine, once the translation is done, then the true sentences are committed only to the existence of members of the domain of quantification. Thus, Quine has famously concluded, "To be is to be a value of a variable."[11] There is plenty of room for disagreement with Quine over details. Fortunately, for us, more important than the Quinean details is the general Quinean strategy.

Ultimately, to carry out a successful ontological investigation, to determine what does exist, one starts from a list of propositions that are true. It also helps to begin with truths of great importance. This doesn't mean, however, that the truths should be restricted to, say, mathematical and scientific theories. That is a common practice, but often ontological investigations start from some common-sense truths, some claims of *folk theory*. What is the ontological commitment of the common-sense fact that Plato and Socrates have something in common? Does it commit us to, say,

---

[11] Quine, *Methods of Logic*, p. 224.

wisdom or some other property shared by Socrates and Plato? What of the fact that humility is a virtue? Does it commit us to such a thing as humility?

We will also engage in a (perhaps) surprising amount of discussion of some propositions put forward as part of philosophical theories. It is common to find philosophers arguing that certain entities exist because they must exist for these philosophers' philosophical theories to be true. Lewis's accounts of metaphysical necessity and metaphysical possibility, discussed in 1.2 above, provide a good example. Lewis was prepared to believe that the ontological commitment of the truth that it is possible that pigs fly includes that there are non-actual possible worlds. David Armstrong's theory of laws of nature,[12] a theory to be discussed in Chapter 4, is another important example; it says that there must be a relation of necessitation that holds between F-ness and G-ness for it to be a law that Fs are Gs.

Even the general Quinean strategy is not as simple as it first looks. Consider this simple truth: the average American family has 1.81 children. Naively paying close attention to its grammar, it looks as if the sentence reporting this truth is saying that there exists a family, it's American, it's average, and it has 1.81 children. So its truth seems to require that there exists a family with 1.81 children. This would be a pretty fishy start to our inventory of the contents of the universe. Where do you think such a family might live? What are eighty-one hundredths of a child like?

This is a good (and common) illustration of why ontology is not to be done uncritically. Careful consideration has to be given to one's starting point. Sentences reporting the important truths can't always be taken at face value. In the case of 'The average American family has 1.81 children,' clearly what is being said, and so all that is required for it to be true that the average American family has 1.81 children, is that the average number of children in families (i.e., the total number of children in families divided by the total number of families) is 1.81. Quine discussed a different example.[13] Consider the sentence, 'Pegasus does not exist.' That sentence is true. But philosophers have wondered how that could be the case if Pegasus doesn't exist. The worry is that there would be nothing for the name 'Pegasus' to mean, and, if the sentence isn't meaningful,

---

[12] Armstrong, *What Is a Law of Nature?*
[13] Quine, "On What There Is," especially p. 27.

then it is not true. Proceeding hastily in this manner, one might draw the paradoxical conclusion that Pegasus does not exist only if Pegasus does exist. Instead, relying on Bertrand Russell's theory of descriptions,[14] Quine argued that, in the sentence 'Pegasus does not exist,' the meaning of the name 'Pegasus' is not Pegasus, but is instead given by a description. For example, the meaning might be given by 'The winged horse captured by Bellerophon.' So, according to Quine, the sentence could be synonymous with something like 'The winged horse captured by Bellerophon does not exist,' which is true if and only if it is not the case that there exists one (and only one) winged horse that was captured by Bellerophon. If so, then there is no need to put Pegasus on the does-exist list. In both the case of the average American family and the case of Pegasus, a *paraphrase* is devised for the sentence expressing the truth under consideration that arguably better reveals the truth's ontological commitment.

We have to keep in mind that a genuine paraphrase preserves the meaning of the original sentence. So finding one is not always easy. As Quine was aware, it is doubtful that 'Pegasus does not exist' is synonymous with 'The winged horse captured by Bellerophon does not exist.' We bet that most of you perfectly well understood 'Pegasus does not exist;' we also bet that most of you had no idea that, according to legend, Pegasus was captured by Bellerophon.

Even granting that the ontologist has given a genuine paraphrase, there is still more work to be done. One has to defend the claim that it is the paraphrase and not the original sentence that better reveals the ontological commitments of the sentence in question. Two philosophers might well agree that *it is possible that* the Red Sox will win the 2090 World Series. They might also agree that *there is a possible world in which* the Red Sox will win the 2090 World Series. They might even agree that these two claims are synonymous. But they may disagree about which claim best reflects their ontological commitment. Someone like Lewis would claim that it is the latter, and put possible worlds on his does-exist list. But others might claim that the former is more basic, denying that our ontology need include possible worlds. So using paraphrase to avoid commitment to some entity requires taking a stand on something like the correct order of explanation: is it possible that the Red Sox will win the 2090 World Series *because*

---

[14] Russell, "On Denoting," especially pp. 487–8 and p. 491.

there exists a possible world in which that is the case? Lewis thought so. But it could also be that to say that there is a possible world in which the Red Sox win the 2090 World Series is just a nice, alternative (though potentially misleading) way to express the more basic fact that it is possible that the Red Sox will win that series, whose expression includes no apparent reference to possible worlds. Possible-worlds talk could be like our talk of families with 1.81 children.

We do not intend to diminish the importance of paraphrase to metaphysics. One just needs to be aware that, when one identifies a paraphrase as such, a meaning claim is being made, and that another substantive claim is being made when one identifies the paraphrase as the more basic rendering of the proposition in question. Those claims have to be judged in the light of what we know about the semantics of natural language, together with any reasons one might have for thinking that some ontological commitments are more acceptable than others. Ontology, like all interesting philosophy, is hard theoretical work.

1.4 Skeptical attacks

So far, we have taken a preliminary look at one main conceptual matter of metaphysics, namely (metaphysical) necessity, and we have also introduced the subject area of ontology. In this final section of Chapter 1, we consider a certain sort of skeptical challenge that can arise for a wide range of metaphysical views. It is one about which we otherwise will not have much to say.

Someone who raises this sort of skeptical challenge to a metaphysician basically says this: your theory tries to say what it is to be F, but if your theory is right, then we do not know that there are any Fs. What the challenger has in mind is that this consequence is big trouble for the theory because we obviously *do* know that there are Fs. A classic case of this sort of challenge is the Problem of other Minds. It is often offered as a challenge to *Substance Dualism*, the view that minds are immaterial souls that are thoroughly distinct from any human body or behavior. On such a view, it can appear that no one could know that anyone else's mind exists since we have introspective access only to our own minds and perceptual access only to what are merely the bodies and behaviors of others. How could you know whose soul was controlling the body of that friend you had lunch with yesterday? Maybe it was your friend's soul, but then again maybe it was Madonna's or Michael Jackson's. So, if Substance Dualism is true, then you don't know whether you were talking to your friend, the Material Girl, or the King of Pop! Such a crazy-sounding conclusion about what you know could easily lead one to question the plausibility of Substance Dualism.

A similar challenge could be raised against Lewis's position on modality (see 1.2 above). It is easy to be suspicious of our having any knowledge about what goes on in the possible worlds that are not actual, since we have no perceptual access to them. So one might conclude that, according to Lewis's theory, we don't know such an obvious fact as, say, that it is possible that it is raining in Paris now. Maybe in our world and all those other worlds (that we are not part of) it is not raining in Paris now. Similar challenges have been raised against theories of causation that deny that causation is merely constant conjunction, theories of laws that deny that laws are nothing more than regularities, and accounts of identity or composition that take facts involving these concepts to be brute. Indeed, this sort of challenge can be raised against pretty much any view of a concept *F* that fails to make knowledge that there are *F*s easy as can be.

There are several reasons to be extremely cautious about raising this sort of skeptical challenge to a metaphysical theory.

One thing to keep in mind is that sometimes we don't know. There are a great many ways our world could be such that the people will not discover every fact. For example, suppose scientists want to know what happens on a certain date at a certain time as a result of a specific chancy astronomical process. They know that the result will be a quick flash of light, but they do not know what its intensity will be. They are paying close attention as the time approaches. When the time comes, the source supplying their instruments with electricity goes out, and they do not measure the intensity of the light. As a result, they never know its intensity. This 'skeptical' consequence is not the least bit worrisome; it accurately describes the situation these scientists are in. Ignorance is sometimes just what we should expect. Not one of us will ever know every truth there is to know.

Another point to keep in mind: epistemological questions of the kind we are considering have been known to badly befuddle metaphysicians. For example, George Berkeley ended up denying the existence of non-mental material objects. Berkeley was a Substance Monist, holding that everything is mental. He thought there were tables and chairs, but he didn't think they were material. Berkeley thought they were ideas. One reason that led him to this extreme metaphysical conclusion was a skeptical worry of the sort we are considering in this section. Concerns about the possibility that our sensory ideas might exist without there being any material bodies can make one wonder whether tables and chairs are really material bodies. If they were material, then it seems that we would not know that they exist, which we obviously do. Reasoning in this manner, Berkeley advanced a metaphysical position meant to give us suitable access to the external world.[15] For similar sorts of reasons, in the twentieth century, Phenomenalists[16] sought to paraphrase material-object sentences in a way that showed them to refer to nothing more than sensory states. Yet Phenomenalism and Berkeley's Idealism are dead ends; their defenders ran up against metaphysical conclusions every bit as absurd as what they saw as the looming skeptical conclusions about our knowledge of the external world. A tremendous majority of contemporary metaphysicians reasonably reject all variations of the thesis that tables and chairs and other objects are mind-dependent.

One final reason for caution about skeptical challenges to metaphysical theories: when considering any skeptical questions about metaphysical matters, we should also keep in mind that the history of philosophy is full of important and frustrating skeptical arguments that seem to show we don't know much of *anything*. Contemporary versions of the pertinent sort of skeptical concern tend to take the form of something like a relevant-alternatives attack. If minds are souls, then you can't tell that you are not talking to Madonna. If tables are (mind-independent) material objects, then you can't tell that you are not being deceived by an evil demon. Basically, what these philosophers are saying is that if the metaphysical theory is right, then there is a relevant alternative that we can't rule out, and this prevents us from having knowledge we ordinarily presume ourselves to have.

The danger of this kind of attack on a metaphysical theory is that relevant alternatives are ubiquitous. Suppose you are at the zoo in front of a cage labeled 'Zebra' and see, standing in front of you, a four-legged striped mammal that you take to be a zebra. A friend might give you some pause

---

[15] Berkeley, *A Treatise Concerning the Principles of Human Knowledge*, Part I, section 18.

[16] For example, Ayer, *The Foundations of Empirical Knowledge*; and C. I. Lewis, *An Analysis of Knowledge and Valuation*.

by claiming that you don't know that it is not a mule cleverly disguised to look like a zebra. Since a cleverly disguised mule would look just like the animal before you and the 'Zebra' sign would still be there and so on, it can seem that you do not know it is not a mule and so also that you don't know it is a zebra. That's really puzzling, because it sure seemed like you did know it was a zebra.[17] But notice that there is no substantive metaphysics at work here. No metaphysical theory is really needed to get this relevant-alternative challenge off the ground. All that is needed is a relevant alternative that is not easily ruled out by the putative knower. Thus we shouldn't simply assume that our ability to come up with skeptical alternatives should have any impact on how mentality, identity, causation, lawhood, or necessity should be explained. This manner of skeptical reasoning is as compelling about zebrahood as it is about key metaphysical concepts. If it works, it shows we don't know much of anything no matter what our metaphysics. Preoccupation with how-do-we-know questions within an introductory metaphysical investigation would be stultifying.

Obviously, skeptical worries should not be completely ignored. Some relevant alternatives seem more significant than others. For all we know, some skeptical hypotheses really can be used to challenge the truth of certain metaphysical views. Our point is just that there is a multifaceted, difficult epistemological issue here. We too think it would be a strange conclusion to come to that, say, we do not know there are material objects, or even, say, that you didn't know that was a zebra in the zebra exhibit that last time you went to the zoo. This epistemological issue should be and is the subject of much exciting philosophical research. Unfortunately, we are not in a position to take this issue on as well as everything else we hope to cover. So, we caution that you do not get too caught up with how-could-we-know questions as you encounter metaphysical accounts while reading our book – as we hope you are now eager to do.

[17] This example is from Dretske, "Epistemic Operators," pp. 1015–16.

2   Causation

2.1 A familiar, central, and tricky relation

At one time or another, most of us have had the experience of reaching for something too quickly. Let's say you go to grab a biscuit from across the dinner table and bump a glass with your elbow. Water from the glass spills. Not much could be more obvious, it seems, than that you bumped the glass and thereby *caused* the water to spill. To put this in a grand-sounding way, your bump of the glass stood in the relation of *causation* to the spill. That is what we are going to try to understand better in this chapter, that relation that holds between the bump and the spill in this mundane example. This is a terrific topic because causation is about as familiar, central, and tricky as metaphysical concepts come.

The spilled-water case should be enough to convince you that causation is a familiar concept. That it is a central concept is also straightforward: it is something we do whenever we affect what is around us. It is something we undergo whenever we are affected by what is around us. Molecular bonding, planetary rotation, human decisions, and life itself are all causal processes. Causation is part of scientific practice: at least typically, a scientific explanation of some event will include some mention of something that caused that event; you can't say why something happened without identifying what caused it to happen. Causation is part of philosophy too. It is so, in part, because philosophers try to improve our understanding of causation. Causation also plays a role in philosophy when the focus is on other matters. As we will see in Chapter 6, a key to the nature of mind is whether mental states can affect the material world. As we will see in Chapter 9, philosophers doing ontology wonder whether we should believe in abstract entities like Platonic universals if these entities do not participate in causal relations.

Why do we say that causation is tricky? As we are about to see, despite its familiarity and its centrality, there is a good deal of disagreement among metaphysicians about how to understand causation better. But causation's trickiness amounts to more than just that. (Disagreement is common in philosophy.) There is something about causation that makes theorizing about it especially challenging. Unlike many other areas of metaphysics, the current philosophical literature on causation is to a large degree not focused on which of two basic theories is correct. There is nothing corresponding to Dualism vs. Materialism (about the mind), Compatibilism vs. Incompatibilism (about freedom and Determinism), or The A Theory vs. The B Theory (about time). No, the study of causation has recently come to be better defined by a range of important examples. The interesting disagreements are more about what causes what in the examples – about where the causation lies – than they are about which theory gives the correct verdict about each example. In other words, we metaphysicians have been questioning what the correct verdicts are! Though we will sketch a handful of simplified but still representative accounts of causation, the primary goal of this chapter will be to present the important examples.

2.2 The relation and the relata

Before getting to the examples, there are two preliminary matters that need to be addressed. We need to restrict our attention to certain uses of the verb 'to cause'. Something also needs to be said about what causation relates.

No doubt you have seen or at least heard the US Surgeon General's warning, "Smoking causes lung cancer." That statement is not describing any particular smoking event. It does not mention any specific individual at any specific time or place doing any causing of anything. In this way, this claim is different from the claim that the bump of the glass caused the water to spill, which, in our opening example, was very much about what you did at a specific time and place. It may be helpful to think of the warning about smoking as describing a causal relation between two properties; maybe the Surgeon General is saying that the property of smoking causes the property of having cancer. Or, perhaps the warning needs to be understood as some kind of generalization about individual cases; maybe it is saying that everyone who smokes gets cancer. That is probably too strong, but maybe the Surgeon General is making a different kind of general remark, just saying that the number of cases where smoking causes cancer is high. Whatever is being said, this sort of causation – if that's what it is – is sometimes called *property-level* or *general-case* causation. It is *not* the focus of this chapter. Instead, we will look at examples of *single-case* causation, examples where both the cause and the effect are particulars – not properties.[1] The relevant causation sentences are ones that are nothing like generalizations.

Here is an assortment of relevant causation sentences that all seem plausible when taken to be about the spilled-water case:

(1) The bump caused the spill.
(2) You caused the spill.
(3) Your bumping the glass caused the spill.
(4) That you bumped the glass caused the spill.

Though these are all single-case causation sentences, they appear to refer to a variety of different kinds of causes. Sentence (1) refers to the bump, an *event*, as the cause. Sentence (2) says that you, a *person* or *agent*, caused the water to spill. Sentence (3) says that the cause was your bumping the glass; some philosophers will take that to be an event, others take it to be a *state of affairs*. In (4), the cause is that you bumped the glass, a *proposition* – more specifically, a *fact* (a true proposition). We won't bother, but we could have displayed an assortment of kinds of effects too.

The variety of causal relata has led to a remarkable number of philosophical reactions. Some metaphysicians have been inclined to think that there is more than one (single-case) causal relation. They think, for example, that *agent causation* is not *event causation* and that it is not *fact causation* either, that these three relations are distinct and call for different philosophical accounts. Others have thought that there is just one causal relation, but that it can relate many different kinds of particulars. Some try to paraphrase certain causal sentences in such a way that all causal sentences can be seen at a fundamental level to involve one relation that relates only one kind of thing. Many philosophers think that causation is most fundamentally a relation between events, but even they don't agree on what an event is! For example, some think events are unstructured individuals;[2]

---

[1] Chapter 9 takes a detailed look at properties and their relation to particulars.
[2] For example, Davidson, "Causal Relations" and "The Individuation of Events."

others think that all events are structured – that they all consist of an individual having a property at a time (e.g., you having the property of reaching at supper time).[3]

We will do our best not to get involved with these disputes about the causal relata. In presenting some theories of causation, we will take '*c* caused *e*' as our focus locution,[4] and try to minimize our assumptions about *c* and *e*. When we have to categorize *c* and *e*, we will tend to follow what we take to be the norm and call them events. We will do this just to regiment our own discussion. It is not meant to reflect any important assumptions of our discussion. With that in mind, we will also work diligently not to make any special assumptions about what events are. Pretty much, if not all, of what we will say about events could equally well be said in only slightly different terms about states of affairs or facts, whether events, states of affairs, or facts are structured or unstructured things. We will not have much to say in this chapter about sentences like (2) and the corresponding concept of *agent causation*. Agent causation will only come up again toward the end of Chapter 3.

2.3 Three theories of causation

It goes without saying that a cause causes an effect only if both the cause and the effect occur. So every theory of causation subscribes to *c* caused *e* only if *c* and *e* both take place. That causes and effects must take place in order to be causes and effects is about the only thing that is not controversial about causation. We won't explicitly put this necessary condition in our statement of the theories of causation.

---

[3] For example, Kim, "Events as Property Exemplifications."

[4] We will not resist using phrases of the form, 'caused *x* to *F*', which are a common and natural way of formulating causal claims. Also, we will not make a big deal about the difference between sentences that use 'caused' and those that instead use the phrase 'was a cause of'. Uttering Sentence (1) somehow makes the suggestion that the bump was the *only* cause of the spill, whereas saying, "The bump was a cause of the spill" seems to make the suggestion that there were other causes as well (cf., Unger, "The Uniqueness in Causation"). We suspect that this difference has more to do with the finer points of language usage than with the nature of causation. How could something have been *a cause of* something without also having *caused* that something? How could something have *caused* something without also having been *a cause of* that something?

One idea that has played a central role in the history of philosophy since David Hume is that causation is a matter of two things always being conjoined. Hume said, "We may define a cause to be an object, followed by another, and where all the objects similar to the first are followed by objects similar to the second."[5] Spelling out similarity in terms of sharing a property and putting this in terms of events c and e, we have our first theory for consideration:

Constant Conjunction
c causes[6] e if and only if there are properties F and G, such that c has F and e has G, and each event of kind F is followed by an event of kind G.

As illustration, consider Pompeii and Mt. Vesuvius. Before Pompeii was destroyed, an eruption began. The eruption had a certain complex property. The eruption was such and such distance from Pompeii, involved a certain massive amount of lava that was heading with a specific flow rate toward Pompeii. We would need to fill this in more, especially by mentioning certain features of Pompeii, like its expanse, but, once filled in enough, it would be plausible to think that whenever anything had that complex property, destruction of the nearby city would follow. So, according to Constant Conjunction, and plausibly enough, it is true that the eruption of Mt. Vesuvius caused the destruction of Pompeii.

It is doubtful that Hume or any other philosopher held anything quite as simplistic as Constant Conjunction as his or her official account of causation.[7] To see one reason why it is simplistic, note that it might be true just as a matter of pure coincidence that every coin that has ever been in a

---

[5] Hume, *An Inquiry Concerning Human Understanding*, p. 79, first published in 1748.

[6] The use of the present tense ('causes') here to describe causation between two (particular) events is grammatically odd, because it suggests that the relation expressed is constant or repeatable in some way. It would be more natural to use the past tense ('caused'), the present progressive tense ('is causing'), or the future tense ('will cause'). Since we do intend the account to apply to any pair of events – past, present, or future – and since it would be tedious to include all the tense variations, we have chosen to say 'causes'. If your grammar sensibilities are offended, we apologise. We will follow this same convention with all of the accounts of causation to be presented.

[7] Beauchamp and Rosenberg devote their book, *Hume and the Problem of Causation*, to spelling out the modifications needed to make a Constant-Conjunction account of causation much more tenable.

particular brand-new pair of pants has been a nickel. In fact, it may be that there was just one such coin and that is the only coin that will ever be in that pocket of those pants; the pants will be destroyed in a fire tonight. So, according to Constant Conjunction, that coin being in those pants caused it to be a nickel; anytime any event involving a coin being in that pocket occurs, it is followed by an event of a coin being a nickel. Of course, that is not at all a plausible consequence of Constant Conjunction. Any theory of causation that gives us a result like this needs to be reworked or dismissed. To avoid counterexamples of this sort, proponents of the idea that causation is Constant Conjunction will insist that the constant conjunction has to be of the right sort. Not just any true regularity connecting one kind of event with another can underwrite causal truths. Traditionally, proponents of this approach have argued that only laws of nature (or certain sorts of laws of nature) have that status.

One descendant of Constant Conjunction is an account defended by J. L. Mackie and also by Jonathan Bennett.[8] Greatly simplified, the idea is that what is important to causation is that the cause be an *ns condition* of the effect, that the cause occurring be a *necessary* part of a condition that together with the laws of nature is *sufficient* for the effect to occur.

NS Condition
   c causes *e* if and only if *c* is an ns condition for *e*.

Consider Mt. Vesuvius erupting and Pompeii being destroyed. Setting aside for the moment that the laws of nature of our universe may be indeterministic in important respects, it is plausible to think that there were conditions of our world at the time of the eruption that, in conjunction with the fact that Mt. Vesuvius erupted, together with the laws of nature, entail that Pompeii would be destroyed. What's more, without the fact that Mt. Vesuvius erupted, those conditions together with the laws of nature would not entail that Pompeii would be destroyed. The idea is that the eruption was a crucial part of a certain portion of a time-slice of our universe that under the governance of the laws of nature led ultimately to the destruction. With the eruption taking place, there was enough going on so that the destruction had to take place; without the eruption taking place, there wasn't.

---

[8] See Mackie, *The Cement of the Universe*; and Bennett, *Events and Their Names*.

In 1973, David Lewis made popular and sophisticated a different idea.[9] It is somewhat similar to NS Condition in that both ideas are based on the thought that the cause has to somehow be necessary for the effect. Suppose that Pedro is standing alone near an old abandoned house and whips a baseball at one of the windows. The window shatters. Evidently, the throw caused the window to shatter. But it also seems perfectly true that, if Pedro hadn't thrown the baseball, then the window wouldn't have shattered. Maybe causation between two events just amounts to it being the case that, if one event had not occurred, then the other would not have occurred.

Counterfactual Dependence
c causes *e* if and only if, if *c* weren't to occur, then *e* wouldn't occur.

Notice that the theory includes a counterfactual conditional, an 'if–then' sentence in the subjunctive mood.[10] It essentially says that there is causation between *c* and *e* if and only if *e* counterfactually depends on *c*. In a straightforward way, this theory avoids the problem offered above as trouble for Constant Conjunction. A more interesting relation is required to hold between the events than mere constant conjunction. It is not true that, if the coin weren't in those pants, then it wouldn't have been a nickel. Clearly, it still would have been a nickel; it just would have been a differently located nickel. Our other stand-by cases are readily handled too. For example, if the eruption of Mt. Vesuvius hadn't occurred, then neither would have the destruction of Pompeii. If the bump hadn't occurred, then neither would have the spill.

Many more accounts of causation have been offered. Indeed, there are so many theories and variations of theories dating back so far that there is no hope of covering all of them or even an important survey of them in a single chapter. The most important two classes of such theories to be set aside are the transference theories and the manipulability theories.[11]

---

[9] Lewis, "Causation."

[10] The subjunctive mood is important. Compare: 'If Oswald didn't shoot Kennedy, then someone else did', which is in the indicative mood and clearly true, with 'If Oswald hadn't shot Kennedy, then someone else would have', which is in the subjunctive mood and quite doubtful unless you have been convinced by some conspiracy theory about JFK's assassination.

[11] Recent work: Ehring defends a trope transference theory in *Causation and Persistence*. Menzies and Price defend a manipulability theory in "Causation as Secondary

Transference theories say that causation always involves the transfer of something (e.g., momentum) from one object to another. The main challenge for these theories is to say what is transferred from one thing to another in *all* cases of causation. Manipulability theories say that *c* causes *e* if and only if bringing about *c* would be an effective means for bringing about *e*. The main challenge here is whether these accounts can be non-circular or reductive in such a way as to be suitably illuminating, the worry being that bringing about and causing seem to be very similar concepts.

2.4 Three core issues

2.4.1 Lay of the land

In this section, we will introduce three core issues that all bring out some interesting features of causation and also raise at least preliminary trouble for either NS Condition or Counterfactual Dependence. (Constant Conjunction will also be discussed, but to a lesser degree.) Three more core issues will be introduced in 2.5.

2.4.2 Non-causal connections

We considered one case of a non-causal connection in 2.3, that of the nickel in the new pair of pants. It presented a serious problem for Constant Conjunction because being a coin in that pocket of those pants is constantly conjoined with being a nickel, though there is not a corresponding causal connection between the coin being in that pocket and that coin being a nickel.

A different kind of non-causal connection arises with *epiphenomena*. Let's start this example by making a certain simplifying assumption: that it is true and a law of nature that, whenever a properly functioning barometer's reading drops, a storm occurs shortly thereafter.[12] Then suppose a

---

Quality". In *Making Things Happen*, Woodward defends a non-reductive descendent of manipulability theories. He analyzes causation in terms of a causal notion of intervention.

[12] Even with the properly functioning clause, and even assuming it is true that, whenever a properly functioning barometer's reading drops, a storm occurs shortly thereafter,

storm is approaching your hometown, the atmospheric pressure drops dramatically, and your properly functioning barometer records the drop in pressure and displays the new reading. You predict there will be a storm. Your prediction is true; your hometown is deluged. In this example, there is a constant conjunction between changes in the barometric readings and storms. That obviously presents a problem for Constant Conjunction. It will have the consequence that the change in the barometric reading, what you used to predict the storm, caused the storm; and that's not correct. Barometers aren't weather-making machines! The theory needs to be revised or rejected.

This is a case of epiphenomena because the change in the barometric reading is a secondary phenomenon not involved in the processes producing the storm in your hometown. The difference between epiphenomena and causes is an important one. For example, in the study of disease, it is crucial for doctors to be able to distinguish the causes of the disease from its symptoms.

The change in the barometric reading together with the laws of nature entail that the storm will arrive. So, trivially, it is a necessary part of that sufficient condition for the effect. So, like Constant Conjunction, NS Condition has the unwanted consequence that the change in the reading caused the storm to arrive. For Counterfactual Dependence, everything depends on what would be the case if the reading hadn't dropped. If there had still been the actual drop in atmospheric pressure (it is just, say, that the properly functioning barometer would be malfunctioning), then the storm still would have occurred. So, Counterfactual Dependence would give the right answer: the change in reading did not cause the storm. But is that what would happen if the barometer hadn't shown a drop in pressure? Maybe, instead, in evaluating the key conditional, we should "backtrack" concluding that, if the reading hadn't dropped, then there wouldn't have been a drop in atmospheric pressure. The barometer would have kept working perfectly; it's just that there wouldn't have been a drop

---

this is probably not really a law of nature – the barometer could be functioning properly and be inside a decompression chamber when the reading drops without any storm following shortly thereafter. Philosophers have never objected to the barometer example on this score. The simplicity of the alignment of the causal connections indicates that corresponding laws are possible, and the possibility of the example is all that is important as regards testing metaphysical accounts of causation.

in pressure and so there also wouldn't have been a storm! On this way of evaluating the key counterfactual, it turns out true that the change in reading did cause the storm, and that's not correct. For this reason, defenders of counterfactual theories of causation often insist that the key conditional not be understood in such a backtracking manner.

A third kind of non-causal connection arises because of certain strong connections between events. When Socrates drank the hemlock and died in the Athenian prison, his wife, Xanthippe, became a widow.[13] Did Socrates' death cause Xanthippe to become a widow? It is clear that, had Socrates not died, Xanthippe would not have become a widow. It is also clear that Socrates dying is an ns condition of Xanthippe becoming a widow. So, Counterfactual Dependence and NS Condition both count Socrates' death as a cause of Xanthippe becoming a widow. Many philosophers find this conclusion unacceptable. The worry is that any relation holding between these two events is bound not to be of the tangible/physical sort one normally expects causation to be. The connection seems to be too much a conceptual matter. To drive home this point, sometimes it is argued that, since Xanthippe was not in the prison with Socrates, his death could not have caused her to become a widow. She became a widow the instant he died. Since there is no instantaneous causal action at a distance in a world like ours where no signals travel faster than light, his death didn't cause her widowhood.

This, our final example of a non-causal connection, is perplexing for a couple of reasons. For one, this may be a case where our simplifying approach to events becomes an issue. One might argue that Xanthippe becoming a widow is not an event in virtue of it not being suitably concrete or in virtue of it not being an intrinsic change in Xanthippe. For another reason, whether it is an event or, say, a state of affairs, it is odd to think that Xanthippe becoming a widow was *uncaused*. Yet if it were not uncaused, what else could have caused it other than Socrates' death? Can you think of a better candidate?

2.4.3 Simultaneous causation

There is an important part of Constant Conjunction that we have not said much about. It requires that the events of kind *F* are always *followed by* an

---

[13] Kim, "Noncausal Connections," pp. 41–2.

event of kind *G*. You were probably just assuming that causes always occur before their effects, and that this was an implicit part of NS Condition and Counterfactual Dependence too. Well, it is not. Bringing in time to help mark off which event is the effect and which event is the cause is actually a contentious part of Constant Conjunction.

Arguably, there are cases of causation between simultaneous events that would be ruled impossible by such a requirement. For example, suppose there is a perfectly rigid seesaw – when one end of the bar moves up or down, the other end moves in the opposite direction simultaneously. Suppose also that you push down on one side and the other side goes up. Then the one side going down caused the other side to go up. It is no objection to this example to point out that such a perfectly rigid seesaw is unrealistic. It may well be: that there is a perfectly rigid seesaw contradicts the law that no signals travel faster than the speed of light. What really matters though is that the case is possible, and it sure seems possible. Furthermore, denying that there is simultaneous causation in this simple case would be at odds with some of the good intuitions motivating the accounts set out in 2.3. For instance, consider Counterfactual Dependence. If the side you pushed hadn't gone down at the time it did, then the other side would not have gone up at exactly that same time. Regarding NS Condition, your pushing down on your end of the seesaw is an ns condition of the other side rising. Thus, by the lights of both Counterfactual Dependence and NS Condition, the causation is there.

This is not to say that Counterfactual Dependence and NS Condition are not threatened by this case of simultaneous causation. Though they do have the intuitive consequence that the side you pushed down on simultaneously caused the other side to rise, they say that the other side going up simultaneously caused your side to go down! That is the trouble for these two theories. They say that the seesaw case is a case of *mutual causation*. That doesn't seem right; in this case, *c* caused *e* but *e* didn't cause *c*.

2.4.4 Causes vs. background conditions

Nelson strikes a match at his neighborhood cookout in order to light the coals beneath his grill. It is a beautiful sunny day, there are no raindrops to worry about, not a bit of wind. Not surprisingly, the match lights. This story of Nelson and his match might seem boring. Indeed, it is; any ordinary case of causation would have sufficed to raise the present issue.

The issue is whether there is any important metaphysical difference between what are causes of an effect and what are sometimes thought of as mere background conditions. Most everyone will agree that Nelson striking the match caused it to light. Most everyone will also agree that it would be at least odd in typical conversations about the cookout to say, "The presence of oxygen caused the match to light." The tough question is: Did the presence of oxygen cause the match to light or was it only a background condition?

NS Condition and Counterfactual Dependence both imply that the presence of oxygen was a cause. That does seem at least a little worrisome; it really is odd to say that the presence of oxygen caused the match to light. But, fortunately for these theories, there is a plausible explanation of why it would be odd to say this even if the presence of oxygen was a cause. The explanation is based on the fact that participants in a typical conversation about the cookout will already take for granted that oxygen is required for a fire, and that it is usually odd to report what is already accepted as true. Yes, the presence of oxygen is an ns condition for the match lighting, and it is certainly true that, if oxygen hadn't been present, then the match wouldn't have lit. But it is just not so clear that the oxygen didn't cause the match to light.

The matter of background conditions gets more interesting when one realizes that these theories also count other things as causes that it would be odd even to describe as background conditions. (We will focus on Counterfactual Dependence, but all the same points could be made about NS Condition.) If the Big Bang had not occurred, then the match wouldn't have lit. If Nelson hadn't been born, the match wouldn't have lit. If the matchbook were disintegrated by a Martian ray gun, the match would not have lit. If you had swiped the match from Nelson, it would not have lit. So, according to Counterfactual Dependence, not only is the oxygen a cause – so is the Big Bang, Nelson's birth, that no ray guns from Mars blasted the matchbook, and that you didn't swipe the match. Was all that taken for granted in the conversation? If not, what explains the oddness of reporting these remarkable consequences of Counterfactual Dependence? It might be that these consequences of Counterfactual Dependence are false.

2.5 Three more core issues

2.5.1 You are here

Mostly to make sure that 2.4 isn't too long, we have saved three core matters for this fifth section. The cases to be discussed here also have a lot in common with each other, including that they all get a lot of attention in the recent metaphysical literature on causation.

2.5.2 Overdetermination

The standard story here is of a deserter sentenced to death. To keep it simple, we will suppose that the firing squad includes just two members, A and B, each of whom is a crack shot. The commanding officer gives the order to fire and the sharpshooters shoot their loaded rifles at exactly the same time. Side by side, the bullets from the two rifles simultaneously pierce the heart of the deserter, who dies soon thereafter from massive blood loss. Each shot was such that it would have caused the deserter to die if the other shot had never been fired. In some ways, this is a simple case. In other ways, it is not. It is certainly simple enough to describe the case as we just did. The hard part is coming to a reasonable conclusion about what the remaining causal truths are about this situation. We need to consider whether A's shot caused the deserter's death. We also need to consider whether B's shot did.

It is tempting to think that each of the shots caused the deserter to die. Given the circumstances at the time the triggers were pulled, given the laws governing how events take place in our example, each shot was an ns condition for the death. It is even part of the description of the example that either shot, had it been the only shot fired, would have caused the death. It would be strange if somehow the shots lacked that effect in virtue of the fact that they both occur. (Notice there is no significant interaction between the two shots.) These considerations, if telling, would stir up a whole lot of trouble for Counterfactual Dependence. On a perfectly natural way of evaluating the relevant counterfactual, it seems that, if A hadn't fired, then the deserter still would have died. So, according to Counterfactual Dependence, A's shot didn't cause the death. The same goes for B's shot. These consequences of Counterfactual Dependence contradict the tempting conclusion that each shot was a cause of the death.

But hold on. Don't dismiss Counterfactual Dependence too quickly! This is not a case where our intuitions are very clear or very strong. Maybe this theory has things right. Notice that A's shot didn't really make any difference regarding the deserter's death; the deserter would have died even if A had felt a last-second twinge of remorse and hadn't shot. The same point applies to B's shot. So maybe all that's true about the case is that the deserter died because *at least one* of the shots was fired. If that's the right description of the causation in this case, then Counterfactual Dependence seems to get things exactly right. NS Condition will agree that at least one shot being fired caused the death, but, as we have seen, it also holds the now not-so-obvious consequence that it is true that A's shot caused the death and that B's shot did as well. NS Condition and Counterfactual Dependence make conflicting judgments about our over-determination case, and yet both judgments have a certain amount of plausibility.

2.5.3 Preemption

Let's consider a case where there is more agreement among metaphys-icians about the causal facts. Two wires, one from Switch A and one from Switch B, lead through a junction box to a light bulb. Both switches are currently open, so no current reaches the junction box. The box is interest-ing because it only lets the current from one wire through at a time. More specifically, it will allow current to pass through from the first switch that is closed but not the second. If both switches are closed simultaneously and so the current from both switches reaches the junction box at the same time, only the current from Switch A passes through. Now what happens in the case of interest here is that both Switch A and Switch B are closed at the same time, the current from Switch A passes through the junction box, it gets to the light bulb, and the light bulb goes on. The current from Switch B stops once it gets to the junction box. What do you think the causal facts are about this hypothetical situation? Did the fact that Switch A was closed cause the light to go on? Did the fact that Switch B was closed cause the light bulb to go on?

This is what philosophers call a case of *preemption*. They call it that because there are two potential causes (in our case, the closing of Switch A and the closing of Switch B), but one of these events is preempted by the other from bringing about the effect. In some ways, preemption cases are like cases of overdetermination. For example, if either just Switch A or just Switch B hadn't been closed, the light bulb still would have gone on, just as if either just Sharpshooter A or just Sharpshooter B hadn't fired, then the deserter still would have died. So, as in the overdetermination case, neither of our two potential causes seems to make a difference with respect to the effect. In other ways, preemption cases are unlike cases of overdetermination. In typical overdetermination cases, there is a certain symmetry associated with the two potential causes that is not present in preemption cases. Sharpshooter A and Sharpshooter B have exactly the same claim to being causes of the deserter's death; not so for Switch A and Switch B. Regarding what causes what, Switch A seems to have a lot more going for it. The current makes it all the way from Switch A to the light bulb. No current makes it all the way from Switch B to the light bulb. It is for this reason that the widely accepted judgment on this preemption case is that Switch A caused the light bulb to go on and that Switch B did not.

Preemption cases have been a thorn in the side of a wide range of theories about causation. Counterfactual Dependence has the unintuitive consequence that closing Switch A did not cause the light bulb to go on; if Switch A hadn't been closed, then the light still would have gone on. The problem for NS Condition is different. It correctly counts that Switch A was closed as a cause of the light going on; the problem is that it also counts that Switch B was closed as a cause of the light going on. The closing of Switch B is an ns condition of the light going on.

The standard way for a theory of causation to try to sidestep problems with preemption is to make use of some intermediate chain of events running between the cause and the effect. Lewis's counterfactual account identified causation with the *ancestral* of Counterfactual Dependence. That is a fancy way of saying that an event could get counted as a cause either by having the effect, e, counterfactually depend on it *or* by being part of a chain of counterfactual dependencies. According to Lewis, it suffices for c to cause e that there be events, $e_1, e_2, \ldots, e_n$ such that e counterfactually depends on e_n, e_n causally depends on e_{n-1}, and so on back to e_1, which must counterfactually depend on c. One nice feature of this account is that it does not have the consequence that closing Switch A did not cause the light to go on; there is an intermediate chain of counterfactual dependencies corresponding to the current running through the wire from Switch A to the bulb. NS Condition can be revised in a slightly different fashion by requiring not just that c be an ns condition for e, but also that there be an event at each time between the occurrence of c and the occurrence of e such that c is an ns condition of it and it is an ns condition of e.[14] Since Switch B being closed is not an ns condition for any continuous event-chain that takes place between the current from Switch B reaching the junction box and the light going on, such a revision might allow NS Condition to avoid the implausible judgment that Switch B caused the light to go on.

The problem with any appeal to the intermediate chain of events is that the preempting could take place without any time left before the effect occurs. Such cases have been compellingly described by Jonathan Schaffer. Schaffer nicely labels these cases as cases of *trumping preemption*. Suppose a major and a sergeant at exactly the same time yell to the corporal, "Charge!" Orders from a major trump the orders from the sergeant because of the higher rank. When the corporal decides to charge, it is pretty clearly because the major ordered him to charge, not because the sergeant did. But notice that the decision to charge does not counterfactually depend on the major's order – if the major hadn't hollered, the corporal still would have decided to charge. Also notice that the sergeant's order is an ns condition of the charge. And it is at least not clear that there is a chain of intermediate events that will recover the correct judgments for either NS Condition or Counterfactual Dependence.

Here is another case of trumping preemption that's even more compelling. It shows that intermediate causal chains will not be of any help:

> Imagine that it is a law of magic that the first spell cast on a given day match the enchantment that midnight. Suppose that at noon Merlin casts a spell (the first of the day) to turn the prince into a frog, that at 6:00pm. Morgana casts a spell (the only other that day) to turn the prince into a frog, and that at midnight the prince becomes a frog.[15]

Lewis's appeal to an intermediate chain of events doesn't help. The sticking point is that there is no intermediate event between Merlin's spell and the enchantment – the spell acts directly. So the enchantment doesn't counterfactually depend on any intermediate event. While the appeal to temporally intermediate events spares NS Condition from saying that

[14] Bennett, *Events and Their Names*, p. 45.
[15] Schaffer, "Trumping Preemption," p. 165.

Morgana's spell caused the prince to turn into a frog, it also mistakenly rules that Merlin's spell was not a cause, either. There is no event temporally between Merlin's spell and the midnight enchantment for which Merlin's spell is an ns condition.

2.5.4 Transitivity

Some relations are transitive. Identity is transitive. If $a = b$ and $b = c$, then $a = c$. More generally, relation R is transitive if and only if, for all x, y, and z, if x stands in R to y and y stands in R to z, then x stands in R to z. Is causation transitive?

Lewis assumed that causation was transitive and held that counterfactual dependence was not. In fact, that's the justification he gives for not identifying causation with counterfactual dependence and instead identifying it with the ancestral of that relation. One can easily appreciate why Lewis took causation to be transitive: causation is making happen. If so, how can an event make another event happen and that second event make a third event happen and it not be true that the first event also made the third event happen? Indeed, in such a case, isn't it bound to be true that the first event made the third event happen by making the second event happen? At first glance anyway, transitivity seems to be an undeniable feature of the causal relation.

Here is a version of an example due to Hartry Field that at least appears to throw this common assumption for a loop.[16] Suppose Henry places a bomb outside Joe's door and lights the fuse. Once Henry leaves, Melissa happens to arrive at Joe's place. Seeing the bomb and being a friend of Joe's, she defuses the bomb, rendering it harmless. It seems that Henry placing the bomb in front of Joe's door caused Melissa to defuse it. It also seems that Melissa defusing the bomb caused Joe not to be killed. But is it true that Henry placing the bomb outside Joe's door caused Joe not to be killed? Well, if causation is transitive, that should be true, but it certainly seems to be at least a very, very odd thing to say.

It is interesting to contrast Lewis's approach with Counterfactual Dependence. Lewis invoked chains of counterfactual dependence with

---

[16] Reported in Hall, "Causation and the Price of Transitivity," p. 183, and in Maslen, "Causes, Contrasts, and the Nontransitivity of Causation," p. 350.

transitivity in mind and so his approach has the consequence that Henry placing the bomb outside Joe's door did cause Joe not to be killed. Is this a conclusion we should accept in order to preserve the transitivity of causation? Hard to say. In contrast, Counterfactual Dependence appears to have the consequence that causation is not transitive. According to this theory, Henry placing the bomb outside Joe's door did not cause Joe not to be killed, because it is not the case that, if Joe hadn't put the bomb outside of Henry's door, then Joe would have been killed. No consensus has emerged in the literature as to whether we should accept or deny the transitivity of causation.

2.6 Chancy causation

All the examples in the previous two sections could have taken place in a deterministic universe, a world where the state of the world at one time, together with the laws of nature, determine the state of the world at all other times. (See Chapter 3 for a more detailed discussion of Determinism.) The examples to be introduced in the present section will all be assumed to take place in an indeterministic world. All of these examples include an assignment of a less-than-unit chance to some event. Like the examples from 2.3 and 2.4, they all raise issues pertinent to understanding what causation is.

2.6.1 Is chancy causation possible?

The first of these examples was given by Fred Dretske and Aaron Snyder in order to show that there can be chancy causation:

> Box R contains a randomizing device; once activated it proceeds, in a perfectly random manner, to one of its one hundred different terminal states. Each of the terminal states may be supposed to be equally probable so that the probability of the box ending in state number 17 is 0.01. One can think of the device as embodying certain quantum mechanical processes – e.g. the emission of an electron (the momentum of which is appropriately confined by some slit) towards a screen which has one hundred different areas suitably marked off as terminal states. Attached to Box R is a loaded revolver which fires when (and only when) the terminal state happens to be number 17. We take this device and place it

next to a cat, point the revolver at the cat and activate the box. Things go badly for the cat; the improbable occurs and the cat is killed.[17]

As Dretske and Snyder go on to say about their case, it would be very natural to accuse them of killing the cat, of having caused the cat's death.[18] If this is correct, then it reveals something interesting and maybe even a little surprising about causation. Despite what our earlier examples might have suggested, causation doesn't have much at all to do with constant conjunction. The case is notable not just because there is no corresponding regularity and the cause isn't in any way sufficient for the effect. It is also notable because the cause didn't even make the effect likely; activating the box made the effect have a 0.01 chance of happening.

As should be pretty obvious, if activating the box caused the cat to die, NS Condition looks to be in serious trouble. There would be causation without anything even resembling Constant Conjunction. Even the complete state of the world at the time the contraption is set next to the cat fails to be sufficient for the cat's death. So, the activation and placement of the box can't be an ns condition of the death.

Counterfactual Dependence gives a different answer. Plausibly enough, if they had not activated the device, then the cat wouldn't have died. So despite being proposed with Determinism in mind, Counterfactual Dependence gives the result that there is causation in the Dretske–Snyder case. But Counterfactual Dependence gives questionable verdicts on other simple probabilistic cases. Suppose fair roulette wheels are genuinely indeterministic, that, even given the complete state of the world at the time the ball is released, the laws of nature do not determine whether the ball will settle on a red or a black space. Now consider an otherwise fair roulette wheel with a hidden switch that activates a series of magnets that attracts the metal ball to Red 32. The croupier drops the ball and hits the switch, and the ball eventually settles where it is supposed to. It seems that the croupier flipping the switch caused the ball to land in a red slot. But, notice, if the switch had not been flipped, then the ball might still have landed on red. So it would have been false that the ball wouldn't have

---

[17] Dretske and Snyder, "Causal Irregularity," pp. 69–70.

[18] We are assuming as Dretske and Snyder do that, in this thankfully hypothetical example, they are the miscreants who aim the revolver at the hapless cat.

landed on red. Counterfactual Dependence says that the croupier throwing the switch did not cause the ball to land on red.

Employing an idea of Lewis's,[19] a natural way to revise Counterfactual Dependence to avoid this consequence would be as follows:

Probabilistic Counterfactual Dependence
c causes e if and only if, if c weren't to occur, then the chance of e's occurring would be much less than it actually is.

On this theory, throwing the switch caused the ball to land on red, because, if the switch hadn't been thrown, the chance of the ball landing on red would have been much less than it actually was. An element of vagueness makes it difficult to know what this view says about the cat. If Dretske and Snyder's device hadn't been activated near the cat, the chance of the cat's death certainly would have been less than it actually was; it would have been something less than 0.01. But, even if it had been zero, it is not clear whether that is *much* less than it actually was. Is zero much less than 0.01?

There is another popular way of characterizing causation that allows for chancy causation. Instead of explaining causation in terms of counterfactuals about chance, the idea is to describe causation in terms of conditional probabilities. The basic idea is that causes raise the conditional probability of their effect, that the chance that e occurs should be greater given that c occurs than given that c doesn't occur.[20]

Probability Raising
c causes e if and only if the chance that e occurs given that c occurs is greater than the chance that e occurs given that c doesn't occur.

This basic idea looks promising given the two cases discussed in this subsection. Placing the contraption next to the cat certainly raises the probability that the cat will be killed (even though the probability that the cat is killed never gets above 0.01). By hitting the switch on the roulette table, the probability that the ball lands on red is raised from 0.50 all the way up to 1.00.

It is interesting that when Dretske and Snyder proposed their case, they were convinced that, though activating the device caused *the death of the cat,*

---

[19] See Postscript B to "Causation," in Lewis, *Philosophical Papers*, vol. II, pp. 175–184.

[20] Eells develops a sophisticated version of this approach in his *Probabilistic Causality*.

activating the device did not cause *the device to end up in state 17*. We can see why. It would be odd for a referee, say, to flip a fair coin, it land on heads, and then someone to claim that the ref caused the coin to land on heads! That does sound false; to say he caused it to land on heads suggests that the flip was fixed, that flipping the coin made it land on heads. Somehow when the indeterminacy is front and center in what we say, we are much more reluctant to take the chancy phenomena as caused. This observation opens the door for a response to Dretske and Snyder's case. It would be very odd to say that activating the device didn't cause it to end up in state 17, though it did cause the death of the cat. How could it cause the death of the cat except by having caused the device to be in state 17? Maybe we should have concluded that activating the box didn't cause the cat to die.

We leave this possibility as one for you to explore. For better or worse, it has been the popular judgment of the metaphysics community that there is chancy causation. We attribute that partly to the popularity of counterfactual approaches and their judgment in the Dretske–Snyder case. Another part of the motivation for this judgment stems from the thought that the actual world, our universe, may be indeterministic. If the lack of a deterministic connection from the present state of the world to any future states is enough to undermine any causal connection with any future states of the world, then denying the possibility of chancy causation may be tantamount to denying that there is any causation in our world. Given how central causation is to our conceptual framework, that would be tantamount to denying that there are any causal processes. That would mean that we would be in the absurd position of having to deny that there is any molecular bonding, planetary rotation, human decision and life. Just so, the more common reaction to the Dretske–Snyder case is to acknowledge the possibility of probabilistic causation.

2.6.2 Overlapping

Imagine that Merlin casts a spell with a .5 chance of turning the king and prince into frogs, that Morgana casts a spell with a (probabilistically independent) .5 chance of turning the prince and queen into frogs, and that the king and prince, but not the queen, then turn into frogs.[21]

---

[21] Schaffer, "Overlappings: Probability-Raising without Causation," p. 40.

This is labeled a case of overlapping because the effects intended by Morgana and Merlin overlap. The witch and the sorcerer are both trying to turn the prince into a frog. The overlap is partial, though. Through her single spell, Morgana wants to also turn the queen into a frog; while through his single spell, Merlin also means to turn the king into a frog. It is assumed that, when they work, spells work directly, not through any intermediate events.

The causal facts about this case are pretty straightforward. Since it was the king and the prince, not the queen and prince, that became amphibians, it was Merlin's spell that was effective; Merlin, not Morgana, caused the prince to be a frog. But these facts cut to the heart of the standard ways of dealing with chancy causation. If we consider the conditional probabilities, the probability of the prince turning into a frog given that Morgana casts her spell is greater than the conditional probability that the prince turns into a frog given that Morgana didn't cast her spell. Morgana's spell definitely raises the probability that the prince meets the amphibious fate. If we consider the counterfactuals, it is clear that if Morgana had not cast her spell, then the chance that the prince would become a frog would have been significantly less than it actually was. Probability Raising and Probabilistic Counterfactual Dependence seem bound to get the case wrong; they say Morgana's spell was causally effective.

2.6.3 Underdetermination

Underdetermination cases take matters one step further. Suppose Merlin and Morgana both cast spells with a 0.5 chance of turning the prince into a frog. Neither is concerned with anyone else. They are both just after the prince. Like the previous case, this example involves overlapping; it is just that now the overlap is complete. What happens is that the prince turns into a frog.[22]

Did Morgana turn the prince into a frog? Did Merlin? There seem to be at least two equally intuitive possibilities here that cannot be easily dismissed. The first is that Merlin did and that Morgana did not. The second is that Morgana did and Merlin did not. Nothing about the situation seems to say which is the case. The key causal facts in this case seem not

[22] Schaffer, "Overlappings: Probability-Raising without Causation," p. 45.

to be determined by the probabilities, nor by any facts about the putative causes or the effect, nor by any causal chains between them.[23] Since both possibilities seem equally good, for the moment, let's just suppose that it was Merlin who beat the 50:50 odds; it was his spell that worked. We'll also suppose that Morgana's didn't beat those odds; it lost out. As before, it turns out that Morgana casting her spell stands in probabilistic relations that often accompany a causal connection: her casting the spell raised the conditional probability of the prince turning into a frog, and, if she hadn't cast her spell, the probability of the prince turning into a frog would have been much less. Probability Raising and Probabilistic Counterfactual Dependence don't permit the result that only Merlin's spell worked, even though that seems to be a genuine possibility.

This case of underdetermination, a case of complete overlap, is potentially a serious challenge to the *possibility* of an account of causation. In the partial overlap case there was the fact that the king turned into the frog that made it clear that it was Merlin's spell, not Morgana's, that was effective. The presence of that fact gives some hope to those who want to provide an account of causation. There is at least a symptom indicating that there might be some underlying truthmaker for the causal facts. Lewis shows the following flicker of hope:

> We want to say that the raising that counts is the raising of the probability of the causal chain of events and absences whereby the effect was actually caused. Raising the probability of some unactualized alternative causal chain leading to the same effect doesn't count. But it would be circular to say it that way within an analysis of causation. I hope there is some non-circular way to say much the same thing, but I have none to offer.[24]

The complete overlap case appears to dash that hope. Nothing in the example suggests that there is any fact that might serve as a truthmaker for the claim that Merlin was the cause.

---

[23] We are setting aside the possibility that both spells worked. That seems fair since we could have built into the case that, in an appropriate number of cases when two spells are cast at exactly the same target, the target turns into a frog that is twice as green and twice as small as someone who is the victim of a one-spell transmogrification.

[24] David Lewis, "Causation as Influence," pp. 79–80.

There are different reactions one can have to this sort of underdetermination case. Most philosophers who have defended one of the standard accounts of causation will object that the example is somehow faulty. They hold that the thought that there could be a possible world where Merlin was the cause and a different possible world where Morgana was the cause plays on some sort of mistaken intuitions we have about causation. Schaffer agrees.[25] Others accept the example at face value, holding that causation is such a basic part of our conceptual framework that there is nothing interesting that can be said by way of a metaphysical account of causation. They take (single-case) causal facts to be fundamental facts. They believe in brute causation.[26] Despite how central causation is to our conceptual framework, others will resort to the idea that there really isn't any causation. In the underdetermination case, it seems as if there is nothing at all in the world that could make it true that only Merlin's spell was a cause or that only Morgana's spell was a cause. Some such *Anti-Realists*, the *Eliminativists* (e.g., Bertrand Russell in "On the Notion of Cause"), hold that causation sentences don't succeed in describing the world, and so also hold that, strictly speaking, nothing causes anything else. Others, the *Projectivists* (e.g., Simon Blackburn in "Hume and Thick Connexions" or Huw Price in "Causal Perspectivalism") will utter sentences like "The bump caused the spill," but are Anti-Realists in virtue of thinking that such utterances will project something about us rather than convey information about the way reality is independent of us.[27]

2.7 A concluding observation

The challenging examples for the assorted accounts of causation are many and varied. It would be easy to despair about the prospects for making any progress on the topic of causation, but don't. We think this is a really

---

[25] Schaffer, "Causation and Laws of Nature: Reductionism."

[26] See Carroll, "Anti-Reductionism," for the history of – and the motivation for – this anti-reductive stance on causation.

[27] The underdetermination cases are not the only arguments that make philosophers worry about the reality of causation. Some worry that the absence of the word 'causes' from the formulation of fundamental theories of physics is an indication that causation is merely a folk concept, maybe like the concept of a witch, that may get lots of use in ordinary conversation, but which has no application to the world since there are no witches. Our best physical theories include fundamental laws that

exciting time for metaphysicians. Philosophers are not doing drudge work; they are not digging in their heels trying to defend their favorite theory, holding whatever convenient position is necessary to do so. Rather they are, somewhat independently of specific theories, revisiting some fundamental issues in an open-minded and provocative manner. The questions are not: What's wrong with this theory? Is there any way of revising the theory to avoid the problem? Instead, the questions are: Is causation transitive? What causes what in cases of overdetermination? Is there a metaphysical difference between causes and background conditions? These are compelling issues; that they are being tackled augurs philosophical progress.

are equations relating various properties to other properties but without explicitly stating that there are any causal connections or even that there would be certain causal connections if certain conditions were to come to pass.

3   Freedom and Determinism

3.1 The Problem of Freedom and Determinism

Suppose that on your way home one day you discover someone else's wallet on the sidewalk. It's full of cash, credit cards, and so forth. But it also contains a driver's license, from which you can tell that the wallet belongs to a fellow who lives nearby, in a house that you'll pass on your way home. You deliberate about what to do. You could return the wallet to its owner with all of its contents intact, of course. Or you could return it after taking out some of the cash, or return it after taking out all of the cash, or just leave it where it is, or take out the cash and then leave it where it is. Suppose that while deliberating, you keep thinking about how you would really like to use the money to buy a bunch of new computer games. So in the end, even though you feel a little guilty about doing so, you decide to take all the cash and then leave the wallet where you found it. And that's what you do.

Now let's shift gears for a minute. We all know that the future is to some extent influenced by the past. For example, pink elephants don't just appear out of thin air. In order for a pink elephant to appear in a place, there has to be some sort of history leading up to that elephant being in that place. (Normally this would involve a series of events such as the elephant walking over to the location in question. Not to mention something that accounts for the elephant being pink.) So we know that the future is to some extent shaped by the past. But to what extent? Well, suppose it turns out that the future is *entirely fixed* by the past. That is, suppose it turns out that *every* event in the history of the world is completely determined by antecedent conditions. This supposition certainly seems like the kind of thing that might be true, and it also fits with the way we ordinarily think about events as always having causes.

Okay, now let's return to the example of you finding a wallet and keeping the money it contains. On our current supposition (that the future is entirely determined by the past), it turns out that, given the way things were way back when, it was guaranteed that you would find the wallet just as you did, go through the same thought processes that you in fact went through, and then decide and act as you did. In fact (given our current supposition) all of this was in some sense determined to happen long before you or any other humans walked the face of the earth.

One question that such a "deterministic" model raises is whether you were really acting freely when you took that money from the wallet. And in fact it is easy to appreciate the thought that you would *not* be acting freely when you took the money (or did anything else) in such a deterministic world. You would be more like a machine: a wind-up toy, or a robot, or a computer. Moreover, it seems to follow that you would not in that case be morally responsible for your action (any more than wind-up toys or computers are morally responsible for their actions).

But now consider the possibility that the world is not deterministic in the way mentioned above. And suppose that in fact there was some "randomness" in the causal history of your action of taking the money from the wallet. (For example, suppose that your deliberation process consisted of a series of neuron-firing events in your brain, and also that a certain crucial one of those events was not determined by everything that came before it, so that there was literally a fifty per cent chance that you would decide to take the money and a fifty per cent chance that you would decide to return the wallet intact.) Now it might be easier to see how you could be acting freely, in such an "indeterministic" universe. But it is still difficult to see how you could be *morally responsible* for your action in that case. After all, why should you be responsible for something that just happened randomly and was not, in any sense, up to you?

We seem to have a dilemma. On the one hand, if we say that your action was completely determined by the past, then it looks like we have to say that you are not acting freely and are not morally responsible for your action. But, on the other hand, if we say that there was some randomness in the causal history leading up to your action, then it appears that we have to say that your action is not really up to you and, hence, that you are not morally responsible for the action. Either way it seems difficult to give an account of your action according to which you are morally responsible for it. This is The Problem of Freedom and Determinism, which is the subject of the present chapter. We will begin our examination of this problem with a discussion of the notion of freedom.

3.2 Freedom

There are many different kinds of freedom. There is freedom to go and to do more or less as you please. (This is a kind of freedom that those in prison do not possess.) There is freedom from oppression by your government. There is freedom from financial worries. There is freedom from nagging by your parents. There is freedom to write and publish whatever you want.

Meanwhile, there is one particular kind of freedom that is especially relevant to the topic of freedom and Determinism: the kind of freedom that is required for moral responsibility. For even though moral responsibility requires none of the other kinds of freedom mentioned above, there is nevertheless *some* type of freedom that is a necessary condition for moral responsibility. After all, we don't take a person to be morally responsible for what they have done if we think that they were not acting freely in any way at all. (And this goes both for cases in which we think a person is morally responsible for performing an action that is morally wrong as well as cases in which we think a person is morally responsible for performing an action that is morally right.)

So there is a type of freedom that is relevant to moral responsibility – that is, a type of freedom that can be defined in terms of the role that it plays in our thinking about moral responsibility. For the purposes of this chapter, we will understand *moral freedom* to be the kind of freedom that is a necessary condition for moral responsibility. And for the remainder of the chapter, when we discuss freedom, it is this particular kind of freedom – moral freedom – that we will be talking about.

What can we say about this kind of freedom? Well, it is natural to think that people often are morally responsible for their actions. Which means that it is natural to think that people are at least sometimes free (in the sense required for moral responsibility). Here, then, is a very natural and intuitive thesis that most people would endorse.

Free Will
People sometimes act freely.

But as we will see, there are some philosophers who deny Free Will. And it is not just that these philosophers are being contrarians. Rather, they deny Free Will because there are seemingly powerful arguments for the conclusion that people never act freely. In order to appreciate those arguments, let us first consider the thesis known as Determinism.

3.3 Determinism

There are different forms of Determinism, but the intuitive idea behind all of them is that the past somehow determines what will happen in the future. For many years the main form that the determinist idea took in philosophical writings was in terms of causation, as in the following thesis.[1]

> *Universal Causation*
> Every event that occurs has a cause.[2]

Universal Causation is closely related to the following thesis, which has been endorsed by Leibniz and others.[3]

> *Sufficient Reason*
> There is a sufficient reason for everything that happens.

The relation between Universal Causation and Sufficient Reason, though close, is not identity. For the latter is an imprecise doctrine, insofar as it is not clear what should count as a "sufficient reason". Among the leading possibilities are (a) some kind of explanation (including a causal explanation), and (b) a reason in terms of the elusive in-virtue-of relation. In any case, since causes are naturally thought of as one species of sufficient reason, it makes sense to think of Universal Causation as a specific version of Sufficient Reason, which is the more general thesis.

---

[1] This thesis has been endorsed in one form or another by many philosophers. See, for example, Aristotle, *Physics*, Book II, chapter 4; and Kant, *Critique of Pure Reason*, B232–56. (All of the works of Aristotle noted in this chapter can be found in *The Basic Works of Aristotle*.)

[2] Some people who like Universal Causation, but who also think that there was a first event in the history of the universe, will want to amend the principle so that it says that every event that occurs, with the exception of the first event, has a cause.

[3] See, for example, Leibniz, *Philosophical Essays*, p. 31.

Meanwhile, in more recent times, the determinist idea has been understood in terms of laws of nature and *physically possible* futures. The concept of a law of nature is discussed at length in Chapter 4. But it is worth saying a bit more here about physical possibility and physical necessity. The *alethic modalities* are the notions of possibility and necessity that are connected with the laws of logic. (The word 'alethic' means having to do with truth.) When we talk of something being *logically possible* or *logically necessary*, we are talking about alethic modalities. The *nomic modalities*, on the other hand, are the notions of possibility and necessity that are connected with the laws of nature. ('Nomic' means having to do with laws.) To say that something is *physically possible* is to say that it is allowed by the laws of nature. So a physically possible future, relative to a certain time, is a way that things could continue from that time that is permitted by the laws of nature. (And a physically impossible future is one that is not permitted by the laws.) To say that something is *physically necessary*, however, is to say, roughly, that it is required by the laws of nature.[4,5]

In addition to the notion of physical necessity, our characterization of determinism in terms of laws of nature will depend on several key presuppositions. First, we will assume that it's possible for a proposition to "express" the state of the world at a particular time, and, in fact, that for every time, there is a proposition that expresses the state of the world at that time. In addition, our discussion will be much simpler if we agree to think of propositions as "tenseless" items that have fixed truth values (like the proposition that Juan is standing at noon on June 1, 2525), rather than thinking of propositions as "tensed" items that can change their truth values over time (like the proposition that it will be the case in 515 years that Juan is standing).[6] (It is also possible to formulate Determinism in a

---

[4] More precisely, to say that some event, *e*, is *physically necessary* as of time *t* is to say that conditions at *t* are such that *e* occurs in every physically possible future relative to *t*. In the text we sometimes speak of an event (or set of conditions) "making" another event physically necessary, which we take to be a shorter and simpler way of saying that, given that the first event occurs (or that the relevant conditions obtain), the second event is physically necessary at the time of that first event (or those conditions).

[5] Why "physical" possibility and necessity? Because the presumption is that all the laws of nature are reducible to the laws of physics. But "nomic" (or "lawful") possibility and necessity would work just as well, if we wanted to drop that presumption.

[6] For more on the issue of tensed vs. tenseless propositions, see Chapter 7.

way that is more friendly to the tensed way of thinking about propositions, but doing so would be a bit more complicated.)

The intuitive idea, then, is that at each instant, there is exactly one physically possible future. In other words, for any time, t, given the way the world is at t, and given the laws of nature, there is only one way that things could continue. Here is a way to formulate this thesis that is a variation on van Inwagen's formulation from page 65 of his *An Essay on Free Will*:

Determinism
For any propositions, p_1 and p_2, and times, t_1 and t_2, such that p_1 expresses the state of the world at t_1 and p_2 expresses the state of the world at t_2, the conjunction of p_1 with the laws of nature entails p_2.

This formulation has the consequence that the present always determines a unique future. But it also has the consequence that the present always determines a unique past. For there is nothing in the formulation requiring that time t_2 be *later than* time t_1. It could be earlier. This is a feature of van Inwagen's formulation as well, and it is a feature that he welcomes. Nevertheless, van Inwagen points out that it would be easy to reformulate Determinism so as to avoid the relevant commitment to "backwards determinism." We would just have to restrict the thesis in a way that requires that t_1 be earlier than t_2, as follows:

Future-Oriented Determinism
For any propositions, p_1 and p_2, and times, t_1 and t_2, such that t_1 is earlier than t_2, p_1 expresses the state of the world at t_1, and p_2 expresses the state of the world at t_2, the conjunction of p_1 with the laws of nature entails p_2.

It is important to appreciate how Determinism is different from Universal Causation. Determinism is formulated in terms of laws of nature (and hence in terms of physical necessity) rather than in terms of causation. This is important because it is at least arguably possible to have causation without having physical necessity. That is, a particular event can be caused without being made physically necessary. (For example, suppose there is a bomb with an indeterministic detonation device. It is a genuinely indeterministic matter, as far as the laws of nature are concerned, whether Tim pushing the button will result in the bomb being detonated; but his pushing the button ensures that there is, let's say, a "nomic" probability of 0.99 [on a scale from 0 to 1] that the bomb will detonate. Now suppose Tim pushes the button and the bomb ends up detonating. Then we will want to say that Tim pushing the button caused the explosion, but that the explosion was not made physically necessary by Tim pushing the button.) Meanwhile, you presumably cannot have physical necessity without having causation. In other words, if it is physically necessary that a particular event occurs, then that event must be caused. The upshot is that Determinism (as formulated here) captures a stronger version of the general idea that the past determines the future than is captured by Universal Causation.[7]

Here's an important question for students of The Problem of Freedom and Determinism: what status should we give to Determinism? Traditionally, many philosophers (including Leibniz and Kant) have thought that something like Determinism is an a priori, necessary truth. But nowadays most philosophers tend to think that if anything like Determinism is true, then it is contingently true, and also (relatedly) that whether Determinism is true is an empirical (rather than an a priori) matter. We tend to agree with most contemporary philosophers on these matters (that if determinism is true then it is contingently true, and that whether Determinism is true is an empirical matter), but we will not argue for these claims here. Instead, we now turn to a consideration of the popular view known as *Hard Determinism*.

3.4 Hard Determinism

Suppose that for whatever reason you think Determinism is true. Maybe you think (like Leibniz and Kant) that it's a conceptual truth. Or maybe you think it's just an empirical truth that is supported by our best evidence. Now consider some action of yours, and focus on the fact that (if Determinism is true) it was physically necessary a million years ago that you would perform that action.[8] It begins to look like you couldn't be responsible for that action, since, on our supposition, it was "predetermined" by past conditions and the laws of nature.

---

[7] For more on these issues, see 2.6 above.

[8] Recall that this is a somewhat loose way of saying that a million years ago, conditions were such that your eventual performance of the action in question was already required by the laws of nature.

Here is a traditional argument against moral responsibility that is meant to capture this intuitive idea.[9]

A Traditional Argument against Moral Responsibility
(1) Determinism is true.
(2) If Determinism is true, then every human action is "pre-determined" by conditions that obtained before the birth of its agent.
(3) If every human action is "pre-determined" by conditions that obtained before the birth of its agent, then no human ever acts freely.
(4) If no human ever acts freely, then humans are never morally responsible for their actions.

------

(5) Humans are never morally responsible for their actions.

We are currently supposing that Determinism is true. The rationale for premise (2) is that humans have been around for only about 100,000 years, but the universe is billions of years old, so that (if Determinism is true) every human action was made physically necessary by conditions that obtained before the birth of its agent. (The *agent* of an action is simply the one who performs that action.) The rationale for premise (3) is that an action that is made physically necessary by conditions that obtained before the birth of its agent is not under the control of its agent;[10] and if an action is not under the control of its agent, then it is not a free action. And the rationale for premise (4) is that, as we said above, the kind of freedom we are talking about here is a necessary condition for moral responsibility.

It might be thought that we can escape the conclusion of this argument by claiming that each person has an immaterial soul. But even if we do have immaterial souls, they must either be subject to deterministic laws of nature or else not. If they are, then the souls give us no way out of the above argument. Whereas if we have immaterial souls that are *not* subject to deterministic laws, then all the considerations raised below concerning Indeterminism will be relevant. So it appears that either way, the positing of immaterial souls will be immaterial to our discussion.

------

[9] See, for example, d'Holbach, "The Illusion of Free Will;" and Ree, "Determinism and the Illusion of Moral Responsibility." Not that anyone has ever presented the argument in exactly this form.

[10] Let's set aside the question of whether it's possible for a human to travel back in time to before he or she was born.

Returning to the above argument against moral responsibility: Hard Determinism is essentially the combination of Determinism with something like the reasoning contained in this argument. Here is an official statement of the view:

Hard Determinism
(i) Determinism is true. (ii) No human ever acts freely. (iii) Humans are never morally responsible for their actions.

Many find this position to be as inescapable as it is unpalatable. But as we will see, there are ways of at least trying to escape it.

3.5 Compatibilism

One way to avoid the conclusion of the above argument is to deny Determinism. Let's set that move aside for the moment. (We'll come back to it shortly.) What about premise (2)? Can it be rejected? Yes, but only if we insist either (i) that there are humans who have been around forever, or (ii) that there was a beginning of time and also that there are humans who have been around since that beginning. Each of these is a substantive and highly controversial empirical claim, however, and neither is the sort of claim on which one could comfortably pin one's hopes for freedom and responsibility.

What about rejecting premise (4)? Recall that the rationale for this premise was our stipulation that we are talking about the kind of freedom that is a necessary condition for moral responsibility. And this stipulation was based on the idea that we all share an intuition according to which there *is* a kind of freedom that is required for moral responsibility. Perhaps in a more in-depth discussion of these issues it would be worth questioning whether we all really do have such an intuition; but we will not do so here.

Let us then consider another way to avoid the conclusion: rejecting premise (3). Note that this premise is a conditional. To deny a conditional is to say that its consequent does not follow from its antecedent. So rejecting premise (3) involves saying that even if it's true that every human action ever performed is made physically necessary by conditions that obtained before the birth of its agent, it doesn't follow that we humans never act freely. For our purposes, this amounts to granting that every human action ever performed is made physically necessary by conditions that obtained before the birth of its agent, but nevertheless insisting that humans sometimes act freely. That is, rejecting premise (3) amounts to saying that someone can act freely even if their action was made physically necessary by conditions that obtained before they were born. Applied to the above example, in which you take the money from a wallet that you find on your way home, this strategy involves claiming both that your action was made physically necessary by conditions before you were born and also that you nevertheless acted freely.

The general idea that you can be free even if your actions are determined by conditions going on before you were born is known as *Compatibilism*.[11] Here is our official formulation of the view:

Compatibilism
Free Will is compatible with Determinism.

Typically, the Compatibilist will say that even if all our actions are determined from long ago, there is still an important distinction to be made between long-determined actions that are free and long-determined actions that are not free. And a favorite Compatibilist technique for motivating this distinction is to point out that, in the ordinary business of life (outside of "the philosophy room", that is), the factors that we attend to in judging whether an action is done freely have nothing to do with whether Determinism is true. Instead, the Compatibilist points out, we pay attention to whether the agent in question is unconstrained, and is able to move his or her body in normal ways, without being subject to strange powers like hypnosis or mind control.

Some examples that a Compatibilist might appeal to in motivating the claim that we typically draw a distinction between free actions and unfree actions without reference to Determinism are shown in Table 3.1.[12]

With respect to the first pair of examples, it's natural to say that the agent described in the left-hand column is acting freely while the one in the right-hand column is most definitely not acting freely. But notice that

---

[11] Examples of Compatibilists include Aristotle (see his *Physics*, Book II, chapter 4); Hume (*Inquiry Concerning Human Understanding*, Section VIII); Hobart ("Free Will as Involving Determinism and Inconceivable without It"); Stace ("The Problem of Free Will"); and Lewis ("Are We Free to Break the Laws?").

[12] Stace uses a similar table of examples in "The Problem of Free Will."

Table 3.1 *A Compatibilist table of free and unfree actions*

Actions that would ordinarily be considered free	*Actions that would ordinarily be considered unfree*
A man walks down the street, stops at an intersection where he encounters a "Don't Walk" sign, notices a button for getting the "Walk" sign to light up, deliberates about what to do, consciously decides to push the button, and then voluntarily pushes the button.	A man's body is tightly bound in such a way that his captors can control his bodily movements. His captors force him, against his will, to move toward the button for a "Walk" sign. Then they force him, still against his will, to move in such a way that his finger pushes the button.
A woman in a restaurant peruses the menu, deliberates in the normal way, and then orders Chicken Parmesan, because it's her favorite dish.	A woman in a restaurant has been hypnotized so that if she hears the words "Afghanistan banana stand," she will automatically say "Chicken Parmesan." When it's her turn to order, her companion says "Afghanistan banana stand," and so the woman utters the words "Chicken Parmesan."
A man walks, of his own volition, into the back room of a bar. He thoughtfully picks up a gun he finds there. When he notices his sworn enemy bound helplessly to a chair, he says with a sneer, "At long last, here is my chance to kill you." Then he shoots his enemy.	A man has had a brain-control device implanted in his head by Martians, who are able to force him to do and say whatever they want. The Martians force the man to walk into the back room of a bar, pick up a gun, and shoot an innocent victim, despite the fact that shooting anyone goes completely against this man's character.
A woman is talking to her best friend. She wants to show her friend the latest family snapshots, which are in her wallet. So she hands over the wallet with a big smile.	A woman is held up at gunpoint. She hates to do so, because it contains not just cash and credit cards but also her cherished family photos, but reluctantly she hands over her wallet.

there is nothing in our description of these two examples about whether Determinism is true. Nor is there anything in the descriptions about whether either man's action is determined by conditions that obtained before he was born. And similar things are true with respect to our other pairs of examples.[13] The Compatibilist will typically take this to be strong evidence showing that whether we consider some action to be free has everything to do with the satisfying of various conditions – including, perhaps, the absence of external constraints, mind-control devices, and coercive threats, together with a proper fit between what the agent wants to do and what he or she actually does – none of which has anything to do with the truth or falsity of Determinism. And the Compatibilist will further take this as evidence that freedom is compatible both with an action being pre-determined in the relevant way, and also with the truth of Determinism.

In what follows we will consider three representative versions of Compatibilism, beginning with one that we will call *Hobartian Compatibilism*.[14] To appreciate the basic idea behind Hobartian Compatibilism, let's suppose that when you took that money from that wallet, these two things were true of you: (i) if you had wanted to return the wallet instead of taking the money, then you would have decided to return the wallet (in short, your decision was based on your desires); and (ii) if you had decided to return the wallet, then you would have returned the wallet (in short, your action was based on your decision). On these suppositions, according to this Compatibilist way of thinking, you were acting freely when you took the money.

More generally, the Compatibilist who takes this line will focus on whether an action satisfies the following two conditions:

The Desire Condition
If the agent had desired to act differently, then he or she would have decided to act differently.

---

[13] With the possible exception of the last pair. For some Compatibilists have argued that coerced actions like the woman handing over her wallet in the last example are in fact free actions. See, for example, Markosian, "A Compatibilist Version of the Theory of Agent Causation."

[14] This view is defended in Hobart, "Free Will as Involving Determinism and Inconceivable without It."

The Decision Condition
If the agent had decided to act differently, then he or she would have acted differently.

And such a Compatibilist will say that free actions are those actions that satisfy these two conditions. Here is our official formulation of this view.

Hobartian Compatibilism
An action is free if and only if it satisfies both The Desire Condition and The Decision Condition.

In addition to endorsing the above claim, Hobartian Compatibilists will typically also hold both (i) that we humans often perform free actions, and (ii) that we humans are in general morally responsible for our free actions. For there would be little satisfaction in saying that the conditions for an action being free are consistent with Determinism, but that in fact our actions never satisfy those conditions. Nor would it be very satisfying to say that we act freely but are for some other reason not responsible for our actions.[15]

Other Compatibilists prefer to focus on the question of whether the agent in question is, at the time of acting, under any unusual constraints, such as those present in the examples on the right-hand side of our table above.[16] Here is a definition that will help us to formulate this version of Compatibilism:

Action *A* is *unconstrained* =df at the time of *A*, the behavior of *A*'s agent is not inhibited in any unusual way (by, for example, metal bars, or a straitjacket, or strings, or wires, or hypnosis).[17]

And here is our official formulation of the view:

Stacean Compatibilism
An action is free if and only if it is unconstrained.

---

[15] Similar remarks apply to other forms of Compatibilism, including Stacean Compatibilism and Combo Compatibilism (see below).

[16] Stace, in "The Problem of Free Will," is an example of such a Compatibilist.

[17] Throughout this text we use the expression '= df' as an abbreviation for 'means, by definition'.

Of course, it is possible to combine the ideas behind both Hobartian and Stacean Compatibilism into a single view. Doing so will give us the following:

Combo Compatibilism
An action is free if and only if (i) it satisfies both The Desire Condition and The Decision Condition, and (ii) it is unconstrained.

So much for our representative versions of Compatibilism. We now turn to its rival, Incompatibilism.

3.6 Incompatibilism

Most people will find it easy enough to appreciate the intuition that our actions cannot be free if they are made physically necessary by events going on before our births. Here is a way to articulate this intuition.

Incompatibilism
The Free Will Principle is incompatible with Determinism.

Incompatibilism is closely related to Hard Determinism, but the two views are nevertheless distinct. For one thing, Hard Determinism has (what is arguably) an empirical component – the claim that Determinism is true – that Incompatibilism lacks. And for another thing, Incompatibilism, in virtue of claiming that freedom is *incompatible* with Determinism, makes a modal claim that is not, technically, a part of Hard Determinism. Still, the two views are closely related, in the sense that most Hard Determinists endorse tenets (ii) and (iii) of their view (the claims that humans are neither free nor morally responsible for their actions) precisely because they think that Determinism is true *and also believe Incompatibilism*. (For this reason, Incompatibilism can be seen as the philosophical engine that drives Hard Determinism.) In any case, it is worth emphasizing that Incompatibilism, unlike Hard Determinism, is not (even arguably) susceptible to empirical refutation.

There have been a number of important arguments for Incompatibilism over the years, but the most important one in recent philosophical literature is one that has been developed and defended by Peter van Inwagen, and that he calls "The Consequence Argument." Here is an informal characterization of the argument that appears in several places in van Inwagen's *An Essay on Free Will*.[18]

---

[18] See, for example, van Inwagen, *An Essay on Free Will*, pp. v, 16, 56, and 222.

If determinism is true, then our acts are the consequences of the laws of nature and events in the remote past. But it is not up to us what went on before we were born, and neither is it up to us what the laws of nature are. Therefore, the consequences of these things (including our present acts) are not up to us.

As we will see, there are at least two main ways of developing this line of thought, giving us two distinct versions of The Consequence Argument.[19] One way of capturing the reasoning suggested in the above passage involves appealing to something like the following two principles (in which 'S' is a variable ranging over agents, 'A' is a variable ranging over actions, and 'p' and 'q' are variables ranging over propositions).[20]

The Transfer Principle for Inability
For any agent, S, and propositions, p and q, if p is true and S is not able to change the fact that p is true, and if q is a consequence of p and S is not able to change the fact that q is a consequence of p, then q is true and S is not able to change the fact that q is true.

Alternative Possibilities
S does A freely only if S could have done something other than A.

The version of The Consequence Argument that is based on these two principles looks like this.

The "Ability" Version of The Consequence Argument
(1) If Determinism is true then our actions are the consequences of the laws of nature and events in the remote past.
(2) We're not able to change the laws of nature.
(3) We're not able to change events in the remote past.
(4) If our actions are the consequences of the laws of nature and events in the remote past, if we're not able to change the laws of nature, and if we're also not able to change events in the remote past, then we're never able to do anything other than what we in fact do.

[19] In *An Essay on Free Will*, van Inwagen develops three different, detailed versions of The Consequence Argument. Neither of the two arguments presented below is meant to be identical to any of van Inwagen's three detailed versions. Rather, the two arguments presented here are meant to represent two fairly intuitive ways of capturing the general idea behind all three of van Inwagen's versions.

[20] Variations on Alternative Possibilities have been much discussed in the literature ever since the publication of Harry Frankfurt's "Alternate Possibilities and Moral Responsibility" (in which he discusses [and rejects] a version of that principle

(5) If we're never able to do anything other than what we in fact do, then we never act freely.

_____

(6) If Determinism is true, then we never act freely.

Premise (1) of this argument merely mentions an indisputable consequence of Determinism (given the assumption that the universe is old enough for there to be a remote past, that is). The rationale for premise (2) is that we are powerless when it comes to changing anything about laws of nature; and the rationale for premise (3) is, similarly, that there is nothing any of us can do to change the past. Meanwhile, the rationale for premise (4) is The Transfer Principle for Inability (the idea being that our powerlessness to alter the laws and the past events "transfers" to the actions that are entailed by them, rendering us equally powerless to avoid those actions); and the rationale for premise (5) is Alternative Possibilities.

There are two main Compatibilist objections that can be raised against this argument. The first involves attacking premise (4) and The Transfer Principle for Inability. Here is the idea. Suppose a Compatibilist grants the antecedent of premise (4); that is, suppose he or she grants (i) that our actions are the consequences of the laws of nature and events in the remote past, (ii) that we're not able to change the laws of nature, and (iii) that we're also not able to change events in the remote past. But suppose our Compatibilist still wants to deny the consequent of premise (4). In other words, suppose he or she wants to insist that we _are_ sometimes able to do things other than what we in fact do. Then what our Compatibilist will need is a plausible account of ability according to which one can be _able_ to do a thing even though it is a deterministic matter that one will _not_ do that thing. And it turns out that it is not difficult to find such an account of ability. Here is one.[21]

> _The Conditional Analysis of Ability_
> _S_ is _able_ to do _A_ =df if _S_ were to try to do _A_ then _S_ would succeed at doing _A_.

according to which the ability to do otherwise is a necessary condition for moral responsibility).

[21] This account of ability is discussed by John Martin Fischer in the Introduction to his _Moral Responsibility_. (Fischer does not defend The Conditional Analysis of Ability, and in fact that account faces some potentially serious difficulties, which we will here overlook. The point for present purposes is merely that there are more or less

For example, this analysis yields the result that in our earlier case, in which you found a wallet but did not return it to its owner, you were nevertheless able to return the wallet, since it is true that if you had tried to return the wallet, then you would have succeeded. Moreover, this result is consistent with it having been a deterministic matter all along that you were not going to return the wallet.

Notice that our Compatibilist can make this move without having to say either that we are able to change the laws of nature or that we are able to change the past. The Compatibilist who endorses something like The Conditional Analysis of Ability need not (and in fact should not) say that if you had tried to change the laws of nature (or the past) then you would have succeeded. All our Compatibilist is committed to is the claim that if you had tried to return the wallet then you would have succeeded at doing that.

Perhaps the Incompatibilist will press our Compatibilist at this point by asking what would have happened if you had tried to return the wallet (and succeeded at doing so). Wouldn't that have resulted in a change in either the laws of nature or else the past (given what the Compatibilist is granting about how the past and the laws entail that you will not return the wallet)?

If the Incompatibilist does ask such a thing, then our Compatibilist ought to reply that you trying to return the wallet (and succeeding at doing so) would not have resulted in you changing either the laws or the past. For although (given what the Compatibilist is granting) the nearest possible worlds in which you try to return the wallet are worlds with different laws or different pasts (or both) from the actual laws and past, it is still not the case in any of those possible worlds that you *change* the laws or the past.[22]

We will leave it to the reader to decide whether he or she accepts our imagined Compatibilist's objection to premise (4) of The 'Ability' Version of The Consequence Argument, and we will turn now to the second main objection to that argument available to the Compatibilist, which involves attacking premise (5). Recall the premise and the principle on which it was based.

plausible accounts of ability according to which a person can be able to do a thing even though it is a deterministic matter that he or she will not do that thing.)

[22] For an example of this approach see Lewis, "Are We Free to Break the Laws?" For more on the idea that the semantics for counterfactual conditionals involve reference to possible worlds, see 4.2.

(5) If we're never able to do anything other than what we in fact do, then
     we never act freely.

Alternative Possibilities
S does *A* freely only if *S* could have done something other than *A*.

Harry Frankfurt and others have argued that the principle and the
premise of the argument are both false.[23] And they have based their case
on examples like the following.

A Frankfurt-style Example
Franny and Zoe are partners in crime. Franny is worried that Zoe will
back out of their assassination plot at the last minute, so she resolves
to use her extraordinary powers (of hypnosis or direct-nervous-system
control or whatever) if necessary to ensure that Zoe will go through with
the plan no matter what. When the time comes, Zoe ends up choosing to
go ahead with the assassination, so that Franny does not have to use her
extraordinary powers after all.

The idea is that Zoe is morally responsible for what she does in this case,
even though it is also true that she could not have done otherwise. And
the further idea is that this shows that the ability to do otherwise is not a
necessary condition for moral responsibility (and hence not a necessary condition for freedom) after all. Such claims by Compatibilists have sparked a
great deal of discussion about whether these putative counterexamples to
Alternative Possibilities are genuine counterexamples to that principle.

We turn now to a second version of The Consequence Argument that is
designed to get around the Frankfurt-style objection to premise (5) of the
above version. This second version of the argument involves appealing to
something like the following two principles.[24]

The Transfer Principle for Lack of Control
For any agent, *S*, and propositions, *p* and *q*, if *p* is true and *S* has no control
over whether *p* is true, and if *q* is a consequence of *p* and *S* has no control
over that, then *q* is true and *S* has no control over whether *q* is true.

The Necessity of Control for Freedom
S does *A* freely only if *S* has some control over *A*.

---

[23] See, for example, Frankfurt, "Alternate Possibilities and Moral Responsibility."
[24] The Transfer Principle for Lack of Control is closely related to the inference rule that
van Inwagen calls "Rule (β)". See van Inwagen, *An Essay on Free Will*, p. 94.

Consideration of these two principles leads to the following version of The Consequence Argument.

The "Control" Version of The Consequence Argument

(1) If Determinism is true then our actions are the consequences of the laws of nature and events in the remote past.

(2) We have no control over the laws of nature.

(3) We have no control over events in the remote past.

(4) If our actions are the consequences of the laws of nature and events in the remote past, if we have no control over the laws of nature, and if we also have no control over events in the remote past, then we have no control over our actions.

(5) If we have no control over our actions, then we never act freely.

_____

(6) If Determinism is true, then we never act freely.

The rationales for the first three premises are the same as before. Meanwhile, the rationale for premise (4) is The Transfer Principle for Lack of Control. The idea is that our powerlessness to exert any control over the laws or the past "transfers" to the actions that are entailed by them, rendering us equally powerless to exert any control over those actions.[25] And the rationale for premise (5) is The Necessity of Control for Freedom. (For surely having some control over our actions is a necessary condition for freedom.)

We saw above that one possible objection to The "Ability" Version of The Consequence Argument involved appealing to Frankfurt-style examples as a reason for rejecting the fifth premise of the argument and denying the principle – Alternative Possibilities – on which that premise was based. But it does not appear that anything like this kind of move will work in the present case. For it is one thing to say that Zoe is responsible for her action (and hence is acting freely), even though she could not have done otherwise; but it would be quite a different matter to say that Zoe is responsible for her action (and hence is acting freely), *even though she had no control*

_____

[25] The Transfer Principle for Lack of Control also supports the following, slightly weaker claim: if our actions are the consequences of the laws of nature and events in the remote past, *if we have no control over whether that is so*, if we have no control over the laws of nature, and if we also have no control over events in the remote past, then we have no control over our actions. This claim is slightly weaker than premise (4) of the argument because its antecedent is slightly stronger than the antecedent of that premise. And the slightly weaker claim would serve just as well in the argument.

whatsoever over her action. For even in a Frankfurt case, the agent (who is after all not actually affected by the villain-in-waiting) seems to have a great deal of control over her action. In fact, that's exactly why we want to say that Zoe, in the above example, is responsible for her action!

To put the point a slightly different way: even if Frankfurt-style examples are indeed counterexamples to Alternative Possibilities, they do not seem to pose any threat to The Necessity of Control for Freedom. So the first thing to notice about The "Control" Version of The Consequence Argument is that, even taking into account the possibility of Frankfurt-style examples, there does not seem to be a plausible objection to premise (5).

What about rejecting premise (4)? Recall that that premise is a conditional.

(4) If our actions are the consequences of the laws of nature and events in the remote past, if we have no control over the laws of nature, and if we also have no control over events in the remote past, then we have no control over our actions.

To reject the premise, then, one must say each of the following three things: (i) our actions are the consequences of the laws of nature and events in the remote past; (ii) we have no control over either the laws of nature or events in the remote past; and (iii) we nevertheless do have some control over our actions. And to make all three of these claims, one must deny The Transfer Principle for Lack of Control.

The Compatibilist who denies this principle will typically say something like the following. "In order for you to have control over an action you per- form, your action must satisfy various conditions, such as being caused by volitions within you and not being subject to any unusual constraints. But when these conditions are properly spelled out, it becomes clear that their satisfaction is consistent with your action being a consequence of things (like the laws of nature and past events) that are not under your control."

3.7 Simple Indeterminism

So far we have focused on what Incompatibilists think free actions can- not be like. (They cannot be completely determined by laws of nature and events in the remote past.) But the Incompatibilist also needs a positive account of free actions. For it is not enough just to say that if the world is indeterministic, then we are free. If Determinism is the threat to freedom that the Incompatibilist thinks it is, then the mere existence of one or two undetermined events in some remote corner of the universe will not be sufficient to make us free. What is needed by Incompatibilists is an account of exactly how indeterministic events play a role in the actions of ours that are performed freely. Not only that: they also need a plausible account of when we are and when we are not morally responsible for our actions.

A natural starting point in the search for such an account is to say that it is precisely at the moment of acting that the indeterminism must "kick in" in order for an agent to be free and morally responsible. In order to capture this idea more precisely, the following definition will come in handy:

> Event E is *undetermined* =df it is not the case that there is some time, t, such that (i) t is earlier than the time of E and (ii) the conjunction of any proposition expressing the state of the world at t with the laws of nature entails that E will occur.

Here is a view that captures the idea that our free actions must be undetermined in this way:

> *Simple Indeterminism*
> (i) There are some undetermined actions. (ii) An action is free if and only if it is undetermined. (iii) Agents are in general morally responsible for their own undetermined actions.[26]

Although Simple Indeterminism is a natural way to try to capture the basic Incompatibilist intuition, it is open to what seems like a pretty devastating objection. Suppose you buy an ice cream cone; but as soon as the cone is handed to you, your body suddenly moves in an indeterministic way, and the result is that (very much to your alarm and chagrin) you throw the cone – ice cream and all – right back at your friendly server.

---

[26] Why the words 'in general' in the third tenet? Mainly because acting freely and being morally responsible for your actions are not the same thing. Freedom is a necessary condition for moral responsibility, but it is surely not a sufficient condition. Other conditions that must also be satisfied in order for an agent to be morally responsible for an action no doubt include such things as being conscious, having a sense of oneself as an agent, possessing moral concepts, and having the ability to form intentions.

According to Simple Indeterminism, you are acting freely in this example, since your action is undetermined, and you are also morally responsible for your action.[27] But it doesn't seem like you really are morally responsible for what you do in this case. After all, you did not try to throw the ice cream back at the server; you did not know that you were going to do that; and you did not even want to do that.

Here is a principle to bolster the claim that you are not morally responsible for your action in this case:

Pure Chance
If an event is undetermined, then no one is responsible for that event.

The main idea behind Pure Chance is that when an event is undetermined, its occurrence is like a cosmic roll of the dice. If the universe's history were rewound to a time just before that event and then allowed to unfold again, with the same laws of nature and the same past, the undetermined event might happen again, and it might not. And the factor that would determine whether the event in question happened again, during the replay, would be pure chance. In particular, no action by any agent would be responsible for things going one way rather than another.[28]

Notice that it won't do at this point for the Simple Indeterminist to say that in the ice cream example you are not morally responsible because you neither tried nor wanted to do what you in fact did. For one thing, we often take people to be morally responsible for accidentally behaving in certain ways (as when someone carelessly causes a car accident, for example), even though we know that the agents in question neither intend nor want to do the things they do. And for another thing, there is simply no getting around the fact that Simple Indeterminism, given the way it is stated, is committed to you being responsible for your action in the ice cream case.

---

[27] Assuming the story is told in a suitable way, that is, so that whatever other conditions besides freedom are required for moral responsibility are also satisfied.

[28] Perhaps it will be thought that a case like the following is a counterexample to Pure Chance: Tim pushes a button to make it an indeterministic but very, very probable matter that a certain bomb will go off, and the bomb then detonates. According to the principle, Tim is not responsible for the explosion, but it seems like he really is. A defender of Pure Chance can plausibly reply to this objection, however, by insisting that what Tim is responsible for is pushing the button, which (given the circumstances) is a very bad thing to do, regardless of whether the bomb goes off or not.

For the view says nothing about either trying or wanting to perform the action that you end up performing.

There is nevertheless a possible reply to this objection to Simple Indeterminism. Maybe the Simple Indeterminist can say that Pure Chance is false. Maybe you are morally responsible for throwing your ice cream after all. Maybe (the Simple Indeterminist can say) you should not have put yourself in a situation in which it was physically possible (even if tremendously unlikely) that you would throw your ice cream like that; and maybe, since you did put yourself in such a situation, you are morally responsible for what ended up happening.

Unfortunately for the Simple Indeterminist, however, there is a powerful counter to this reply to the objection. According to Simple Indeterminism, you are acting freely, and hence can be morally responsible, only in cases in which the actions you perform are not made physically necessary beforehand. So, according to Simple Indeterminism, if you had managed to make it physically necessary that you would receive your ice cream nicely (without throwing it back, but with a polite "Thank you!"), then you would not have been doing so freely, and would then not have been morally responsible (and hence would not have deserved any credit) for doing so. In other words, Simple Indeterminism requires that when you act freely (and are morally responsible for your actions), you act in an indeterministic way. So it would be contrary to the entire program of the Simple Indeterminist to say that you ought not to put yourself in situations in which your behavior will be undetermined. That would be tantamount to saying that you ought not to behave in such a way that you will be morally responsible for your behavior.

3.8 Volitional Indeterminism

Perhaps we went wrong in placing the indeterminism in the causal history of a free action right at the moment of action. Perhaps what the Incompatibilist Indeterminist needs to say is that free actions are the results of real decisions by their agents, but decisions that are themselves undetermined. Here is a new definition that will be useful in capturing such a view:

A is a *volition* =df A is a mental act of choosing or willing.

And here is one way to formulate the view:

Volitional Indeterminism
(i) Some actions are caused by undetermined volitions within their agents.
(ii) An action is free if and only if either (a) it is itself an undetermined volition, or (b) it is caused by an undetermined volition within its agent.
(iii) Agents are in general morally responsible for their own undetermined volitions, and for actions they perform that are caused by such volitions.

It should be clear that Volitional Indeterminism is an improvement over Simple Indeterminism, since it yields what seems to be the correct result in the above ice-cream case (namely, that you are not morally responsible for spontaneously throwing your ice cream).

But Volitional Indeterminism is nevertheless open to objection. Here is another example. You again buy an ice-cream cone; but this time, as soon as the cone is handed to you, your mind suddenly behaves in an indeterministic way: for no reason at all, and despite the fact that doing so goes completely against your character, you suddenly decide to throw the ice-cream cone right back at your friendly server. As soon as this undetermined decision is made, you regret it, and immediately change your mind – you realize that you do not want to throw your ice-cream cone (not at the vendor or anywhere else). But it is too late: your undetermined volition has already resulted in a signal being sent to the relevant muscles, and before you can get another message back out to your arm and hand, the ice cream (cone and all) is flying toward your startled server.

Now, according to Volitional Indeterminism, you are acting freely in this case, and are morally responsible for your action. But there are good reasons to think that you are not in fact morally responsible for throwing your ice-cream even in this example. The main problem is that it just seems like a random act on your part, since it resulted from a random volition within you. But in order to make the problem more specific, consider the following two principles, one old and one new:

Pure Chance
If an event is undetermined, then no one is responsible for that event.

The Transfer Principle for Non-Responsibility
If S is not responsible for e_1, and e_1 makes e_2 physically necessary, then S is not responsible for e_2.

Each of these principles is independently plausible. But together they entail that you are not responsible for throwing your ice cream in our latest example. The reason for this is that, according to Pure Chance, you are not responsible for your undetermined volition to throw the ice cream; and given that you are not responsible for that volition, it follows from The Transfer Principle for Non-Responsibility that you are also not responsible for the resulting action.

3.9 Libertarian Agent Causation

Views that combine Incompatibilism with the claim that we (sometimes) do in fact act freely are often referred to in the literature on freedom and Determinism as *libertarian* views. (But this kind of "libertarianism" should not be confused with the political variety.) One kind of libertarian view is represented by Simple Indeterminism and Volitional Indeterminism. The view that we will call *Libertarian Agent Causation*, and which is the main topic of this section, represents an alternative type of libertarian view.

First, a word about the motivation for this new type of libertarian view. Once we focus on Pure Chance and The Transfer Principle for Non-Responsibility, we can see that there is going to be a challenge for any libertarian view of responsibility. For it appears that, wherever you put the indeterminism that is required for freedom on a libertarian view, you will have the same problem that arises in our second ice-cream case, on account of the combination of Pure Chance and The Transfer Principle for Non-Responsibility. Thus we have what might be called *The Libertarian's Dilemma*: the problem of trying to find a way to accommodate the Incompatibilist intuition (according to which we cannot be free if our actions are determined by conditions outside of us) while at the same time avoiding the element of luck and concomitant lack of responsibility that seem to come with positing some indeterminism in the history of an action. In response to this problem, some philosophers have resorted to views that appeal to the notion of "agent causation."

Here is the basic idea behind Libertarian Agent Causation. In many philosophical discussions of the concept of causation, it is presupposed that the causal relata (the things that get caused and the things that do the causing) are always events.[29] This tradition is sufficiently well established

[29] Or states of affairs. In this chapter, as in Chapter 2, we will (somewhat misleadingly, but for the sake of simplicity) write as if the view that the causal relata are events

that it's fair to say that any departure from it counts as a radical way of thinking.[30] Nevertheless, ever since Aristotle there have been some philosophers who are willing to be radical in this way. According to such philosophers, events may be the only things that can be *caused*, but they are not the only things that can be *causes*. For agents, too, according to this line of thought, can also be causes. The idea is that when you move your hand, for example, an event in your brain sends a signal to your muscles telling them to move in the relevant way; and this brain event is not caused by any other events; but the brain event nevertheless *is* caused; for it is caused by something that is not an event – namely, you. Because the relevant brain event is not caused by any other events, proponents of this view feel that they are safe from the traditional Incompatibilist arguments against freedom. And because the brain event in question is caused by you, proponents of the view feel that they have an easy answer to the question of why you should be responsible for the action that ensues.

There are two important presuppositions of Libertarian Agent Causation. First, the view presupposes that some events are like the brain event described in the previous paragraph: they occur in the brains of human agents; they are not caused by any previous events (and, hence, they are not made physically necessary by previous events); and they result in actions performed by the agents in whom they occur. (Note that this first presupposition is one that Libertarian Agent Causation shares with the previous Libertarian view we considered, Volitional Indeterminism.)

The second important presupposition of Libertarian Agent Causation is that agents are in a special category among things, insofar as they have genuine causal powers.[31] In particular, the view presupposes that it is

and the view that the causal relata are states of affairs amount to the same thing. For more on the question of what are the causal relata, see Chapter 2.

[30] Not that we don't have ways of talking that make it *appear* as if things other than events can be causes and effects. ("The rock caused the window to break." "Sarah caused a commotion." "The hurricane caused this mess.") According to the traditional way of thinking about causation, however, all such talk, when properly analyzed, turns out to be talk about causation between events. ("The rock hitting the window caused the window to break." "Sarah's entrance caused a commotion." "The hurricane caused all of these things to come to be arranged in this messy way.")

[31] Here is the sense in which the causal powers of agents are said to be genuine. A rock can "cause" a window to break by being caught up in an event – the throwing of the rock through the window – that causes the window to break; and an agent can do that, too. But in such cases, neither the rock nor the agent is really causing the

possible for an agent to cause an event that is not caused by any other events. Here is an example from Aristotle (by way of Roderick Chisholm) to illustrate the assumption behind the view.[32] Suppose a man is holding a wooden staff, which he uses to move a stone on the ground. Then, according to the proponent of Libertarian Agent Causation, the situation can be illustrated by the diagram below, in which the arrows represent causation.

agent
↓

brain event → muscles contract → hand moves → staff moves → stone moves

In the example, we are to suppose, the brain event is not made physically necessary (and moreover is not caused) by any previous events. (This feature of the case is represented in the diagram by the fact that there is no arrow going from any other event to the brain event.) But the brain event is nevertheless caused; for it is caused by the agent (as indicated by the arrow pointing from the agent to the brain event). The situation is often characterized by proponents of the idea of agent causation as one in which the agent initiates a causal chain. Sometimes the agent is said to be a "prime mover unmoved," meaning one who causes without being caused to do so.[33]

Here, then, are a definition and an official statement of the view.

Action A is *externally caused* =df A is caused by some event(s) outside of A's agent.

Libertarian Agent Causation
(i) There are some actions that are not externally caused but that are caused by their agents. (ii) An action is free if and only if (a) it is not externally caused and (b) it is caused by its own agent. (iii) Agents are in general morally responsible for their actions when those actions are (a) not externally caused and (b) caused by their agents.

window to break (for it is the relevant event that is doing the causing). Meanwhile, an agent can also do something that a rock cannot do, and that is to be a real cause of the breaking of a window (as, for example, when the agent throws him or herself through the window).

[32] See Aristotle, *Physics*, Book II, chapter 4; and Chisholm, "Human Freedom and the Self."
[33] See, for example, Aristotle, *Physics*, Book II, chapter 4; and Chisholm, "Human Freedom and the Self."

In the example captured by the above diagram, the movement of the agent's hand satisfies both conditions for freedom in tenet (ii) of Libertarian Agent Causation. For it is not externally caused, despite the fact that it is caused by some other events (namely, the relevant brain event and the sending of the signal from the brain to the muscles). In other words, there is no event outside of the agent that causes the movement of the hand. And the movement of the hand is caused, indirectly, by its agent, since the agent causes the brain event, which causes the movement of the hand.

Note that the view gets the intuitive result in this case: the agent is acting freely and is morally responsible. More generally, note that if we grant the two presuppositions of Libertarian Agent Causation – (i) that there are action-causing events in human brains that are not themselves caused by any other events, and (ii) that these non-event-caused but action-causing events are caused by the relevant agents – then Libertarian Agent Causation is no doubt a very attractive theory. If there really were an event in your brain, for example, that was not caused by any other events, that was somehow directly caused by you, and that caused you to act in a certain way, then it would certainly be plausible to say that you were acting freely and were morally responsible for your action.

But those are all big ifs, which raise important questions about the theory, beginning with the questions raised by the first presupposition of the view. Not surprisingly, then, the first objection that is likely to be raised against Libertarian Agent Causation is that it is based on false presuppositions. Whether there are any events in human brains that are not caused by other events and, if so, whether such brain events are themselves the causes of actions by their agents are empirical questions that we will not attempt to answer. Instead, we will merely note for the record that one possible line of objection to Libertarian Agent Causation would be to attack the empirical presuppositions behind the theory.

A second objection that has been raised against Libertarian Agent Causation is what we will call The Mystery Objection. Even if it turns out that the answers to the relevant empirical questions are favorable to Libertarian Agent Causation, there is still a further, more purely metaphysical, and potentially more difficult problem facing the view: many people think that the whole idea of agent causation is incoherent. That is, many people believe, on philosophical grounds, that it does not make sense to say that an agent can be the cause of an event. One way to put the objection is in the form of a question: we know what it means to say that one event causes another event, but what could it possibly mean to say that an agent causes an event?

It turns out that at least some proponents of Libertarian Agent Causation think that they have an excellent answer to this question, which goes roughly as follows. It's true that the idea of agent causation is a little bit mysterious, and also that we are unable to give a satisfactory analysis of the notion of agent causation. But that is because the idea of causation in general, including the idea of event causation, is something of a mystery. As we noted in Chapter 2, finding the correct analysis of the concept of causation is currently an unsolved problem in philosophy. So our inability to give a satisfactory analysis of agent causation is not a difficulty peculiar to Libertarian Agent Causation. It is, instead, a more general problem facing everyone who believes in causation in general (and that includes virtually everyone).[34]

In fact, some proponents of this reply to the objection think that they also have an even stronger reply available. It goes like this. It is not merely that our concept of agent causation is *no more mysterious* than our concept of event causation. It is actually *less mysterious*. For the concept of agent causation is the basis for our idea of causation in general. Here's why. Very young infants have no fancy concepts like the idea of causation. But early on (we can suppose) they do notice with some interest that there are these little hand-shaped things that sometimes wave around in their field of vision. And a little bit later they notice with even greater interest that they themselves are able to control the movements of these hands. That is, they notice that they are able to make them move this way or that way. And so they come to have the idea that they can cause certain things to happen. In other words, they come to have the idea of agent causation.

Later on, they observe patterns in the events outside of their crib. For example, they notice that when one rolling ball hits another ball, the second ball rolls away. And they then apply the idea of causation that they themselves got from observing to the events involving the balls. And in this way they come to have the idea of event causation. Thus (according

---

[34] This response to The Mystery Objection (or something very close to it) is offered by Thomas Reid and Roderick Chisholm. See Reid, *Essays on the Active Powers of Man*, Essay IV, chapter 4; and Chisholm, "Human Freedom and the Self."

to the proponent of Libertarian Agent Causation who takes this line) we actually have a firmer grasp on the notion of agent causation than we do on the notion of event causation, and this is precisely because we, being agents and not events, experience the phenomenon of agent causation firsthand.[35]

There is a third likely objection to Libertarian Agent Causation. Suppose we grant the empirical presuppositions of Libertarian Agent Causation, and suppose we also grant that there is no problem in principle with the notion of an event being caused by an agent. Then there is still an important objection that can be raised against Libertarian Agent Causation: it is not that the idea of agent causation is incoherent, but, rather, that there simply is no such thing as agent causation. This objection may or may not be combined with a specific analysis of the general concept of causation. If it is so combined, the claim would be both that that analysis of causation is the correct one, and also that it follows from that analysis that there is no causation by agents. But either way, the objection is based on the assertion that there simply is no such thing as agent causation, together with some justification for this assertion. Many philosophers will no doubt want to offer as the requisite justification an argument that appeals to some principle of theoretical parsimony. Event causation (according to this argument) is sufficient to do all the causal work that is needed in our theorizing about the natural world; so there is simply no need to posit the existence of any further kind of causation.

For most of its career, the critics of Libertarian Agent Causation have been content to raise one or several of the above objections to the view. But recently a new objection has been raised.[36] Suppose we are perfectly willing to make the radical supposition that there is such a thing as agent causation. Now consider what appears to be a paradigm case of a free action involving agent causation: Yasmine asks Imran to pass her the salt, and Imran politely does so. If there is such a phenomenon as agent causation, then this will surely be an example in which the agent – Imran – causes his own action. (Provided the details of the story are filled out in the natural way: no strange wires hooked up to Imran's brain; no weird

---

[35] For something like this reply on behalf of Libertarian Agent Causation, see (again) Reid, *Essays on the Active Powers of Man*, Essay IV, chapter 4; and Chisholm, "Human Freedom and the Self."

[36] See Markosian, "A Compatibilist Version of the Theory of Agent Causation."

forces operating on him; Imran hears Yasmine's request, considers it for a moment or two, and then voluntarily decides to comply; and so on.) But it also seems clear that in this case there is an event outside of the agent – namely, Yasmine's asking Imran to pass the salt – that also causes the relevant action. After all, Imran never would have thought to pass the salt to Yasmine at that moment if Yasmine had not asked. And, in general, whatever theory of causation between events one accepts, one is going to want to say that in this case the request to pass the salt causes the passing of the salt.

This suggests that there is a problem with the crucial second tenet of Libertarian Agent Causation: (ii) an action is free if and only if (a) it is not externally caused and (b) it is caused by its own agent. And the problem is that the first condition that Libertarian Agent Causation places on an action being free – that it not be externally caused – is too strict. For we do not want to say that many ordinary actions that are caused by their agents and that seem perfectly free (like Imran passing the salt when asked in our example) are in fact not free.

Notice, by the way, that this will be a general problem for any Libertarian theory according to which an action is free only if it is not caused by any event outside of its agent. For the Libertarian (assuming he or she is not a Simple Indeterminist) is going to specify some condition – in addition to being not externally caused – that must be satisfied in order for any action to be free. This condition will be designed to get around the difficulty with Simple Indeterminism. But then, if the extra condition is at all plausible, it is going to make the requirement that the action not be externally caused seem like a mistake, because of cases like the "pass the salt" example.

3.10 Compatibilist Agent Causation

In response to this problem, there are various ways that one could relax that first condition placed by Libertarian Agent Causation on an action being free, and we do not have the space here to consider more than the most extreme example of such a way.[37] But maybe the most sensible move

---

[37] For a more thorough discussion of ways to relax the condition that Libertarian Agent Causation places on an action being free, see Markosian, "A Compatibilist Version of the Theory of Agent Causation."

in response to this issue for someone who believes in agent causation is to remove the first condition (requiring that the action not be externally caused) altogether, and simply say that any action that is caused by its agent is free, regardless of whether that action is also caused (or made physically necessary or whatever) by events outside of that agent.

Doing so will result in the following view of freedom and responsibility:

Compatibilist Agent Causation
(i) There are some agent-caused actions. (ii) An action is free if and only if it is an agent-caused action. (iii) Agents are in general morally responsible for their own agent-caused actions.

This view will admittedly be unusual among agent causation theories, insofar as it is a version of Compatibilism. For according to Compatibilist Agent Causation, an agent can act freely even in a completely deterministic world. (Provided that there can be agent causation in such a world, that is.) Thus, according to Compatibilist Agent Causation, The Free Will Principle and Determinism could both be true. And so Compatibilist Agent Causation, unlike other views that posit agent causation, is a wholly Compatibilist theory. But for precisely that reason, many proponents of traditional agent causation theories (like Libertarian Agent Causation) will find Compatibilist Agent Causation to be unacceptable.

Here is the kind of case that critics of Compatibilist Agent Causation would take to pose a serious problem for the view. Suppose Martians kidnap a man and reconfigure his brain to make it physically necessary that the next day he will cause himself to commit a certain crime (one that he would not ordinarily have committed), and suppose that the man then goes on to cause himself to commit the crime in question. According to Compatibilist Agent Causation, this man is acting freely (and is morally responsible for his action), since his action is caused by him (in addition to being caused by the Martians, of course). But many people find this result to be counterintuitive.[38]

Meanwhile, Compatibilist Agent Causation is also subject to the second objection to Libertarian Agent Causation considered above (that the

---

[38] For more discussion of this kind of objection to Compatibilist Agent Causation, see Markosian, "A Compatibilist Version of the Theory of Agent Causation."

idea of agent causation is mysterious), as well as the third objection (that, mysterious or not, agent causation is simply not a phenomenon that really occurs).

On the plus side, however, it should be noted that Compatibilist Agent Causation has several potential advantages over Libertarian Agent Causation. One such advantage is that it is not susceptible to the "pass the salt" objection discussed above. Compatibilist Agent Causation is consistent with the intuitive claim that an agent who caused his or her own action would be acting freely, even if his/her action were also caused by a polite request from someone else. A second potential advantage of Compatibilist Agent Causation over its Libertarian rival is that it does not share Libertarian Agent Causation's empirical presupposition that there are events in human brains that are not caused by other events but that are themselves the causes of actions by their agents.

3.11 No easy answers

It is tempting to think of The Problem of Freedom and Determinism as beginning with the observation that our acting freely is inconsistent with the truth of Determinism, and ultimately ending either with the discovery that Determinism is true (so that we are not free) or else the discovery that Determinism is false (so that we are free after all). But if you take away only one thing from this chapter it should be that this temptation must be resisted. For (as we have tried to show) even if you reject Determinism, it is still hard to give a plausible and satisfying account of freedom and responsibility. Moreover (as we have also tried to show), the fundamental issue to be addressed by anyone confronting The Problem of Freedom and Determinism is the debate between Compatibilists and Incompatibilists. And here it is important to recognize that Compatibilists and Incompatibilists alike have interesting arguments that must be answered regardless of whether or not it turns out that Determinism is true.

The good news for students of The Problem of Freedom and Determinism is that you do not have to attempt to settle the question of whether Determinism is true. So you don't need to rush out and get advanced degrees in both theoretical and experimental physics. (But feel free.) The bad news for students of The Problem of Freedom and Determinism is that you do need to answer some questions that are more purely philosoph-ical, and in some ways even harder, than any empirical questions about the truth of Determinism. We have in mind questions such as the follow-ing. Is freedom compatible with Determinism? If the answer is Yes, then what is wrong with the various arguments for Incompatibilism? Also, if freedom is compatible with Determinism, then what are the correct accounts of freedom and responsibility? In particular, how is it possible for an action to be free if it is made physically necessary by conditions that obtained long before the birth of its agent? And how can an agent be morally responsible for such an action? If, on the other hand, freedom is not compatible with Determinism, then what is wrong with the various arguments for Compatibilism? Also, given that freedom is not compatible with Determinism, what are the correct accounts of freedom and respon-sibility? In particular, how is it possible for an agent to be morally respon-sible for an action that is the result of some indeterministic event? Or is it instead that freedom is incompatible with Determinism and also true that we are never free (and hence never morally responsible)? Finally, if the lat-ter is the case, then what are we to make of our everyday talk about agents (sometimes) acting freely and being morally responsible for their actions?

4 Laws of nature

4.1 Law or accident?

In 1766, a mathematics professor, Titius, described the distances of the planetary orbits from the Sun as falling into a simple pattern. If the distance between the Sun and Saturn's orbit is divided into 100 equal units, then Mercury's orbit is 4 of those units from the Sun, Venus 4 + 3, Earth 4 + 6, and Mars 4 + 12. As far as Titius knew, there was a gap at 4 + 24 units, but Jupiter is at 4 + 48 and Saturn, of course, is at 4 + 96 units. This numerical progression doesn't reflect the distances perfectly. Its accuracy depends on such things as what point of the planet's orbit (closest, farthest, or average distance from the Sun) is chosen. Nevertheless, it is easy enough for us to appreciate why Titius was impressed by the pattern.

A controversy emerged. An astronomer, Bode, promoted the principle. His position was strengthened by the discovery of Uranus at approximately 4 + 192 units and the discovery of the asteroid Ceres (taken to be a minor planet) at 4 + 24 units. Critics of the principle included Gauss, Delambre, and Laplace. Delambre and Laplace are reported to have called it a "mere game with numbers."[1]

What exactly was at issue? On one reasonable understanding of this episode in the history of astronomy, these scientists disagreed about whether Titius had discovered a *law of nature*. Science includes many principles that were at least once thought to be laws. Famous examples include Newton's law of gravitation, his three laws of motion, the ideal gas laws, Einstein's principle that no signals travel faster than light, Mendel's laws, the economic laws of supply and demand, and more. In essence, the controversy was whether Titius's principle was on a par with these scientific

[1] For further discussion, see Jaki, "The Early History of the Titius–Bode Law."

propositions. Does the principle reflect something fundamental about how the universe works? Or does it describe an accident of nature, just saying something about how the orbits of the planets happen to be spaced?

Laws of nature are not just important to scientists. They are also a matter of great interest to us metaphysicians. We aren't so much concerned with discovering laws. We are not in the business of figuring out *what the laws are*. We leave that to the scientists. Metaphysicians care about *what it is to be a law*, about *lawhood*, about whatever it is that is the essential difference between something being a law and something not being a law. That's exactly what this fourth chapter is about.

We have already encountered some good reasons for undertaking this investigation. Lawhood is pretty clearly a part of our scientific conceptual framework. So it is the job of philosophers of science, if not also us metaphysicians, to understand lawhood better. But, in earlier chapters, we have come across some reasons why metaphysicians in particular definitely should engage with this concept. As we saw in Chapter 3, lawhood is critical to the standard formulation of Determinism; Determinism holds if the state of the universe at any one time together with the *laws of nature* determine what the state of the universe will be at all other times. As a result, lawhood is also central to the philosophical puzzles that arise about freedom and responsibility. In Chapter 2, we saw that lawhood is thought by some to be a key element of plausible accounts of causation; for example, according to NS Condition, a cause occurring must be a necessary part of a condition that together with the *laws of nature* is sufficient for the effect to occur. Let's see what we can find out about what it is to be a law.

4.2 Starting points

We begin this investigation by highlighting some plausible assumptions that have greatly shaped current discussions of laws of nature.

In our daily inquiries, we take ourselves to be seeking, and sometimes finding, truth. It would be surprising if scientists – our most revered investigators – sought less. So to the extent that laws are one object of scientific discovery, it is natural to think that *all laws are true*. This connection between lawhood and truth is reflected in the historical episode described at the start of this chapter. Despite its accuracy about Ceres and the seven major planets nearest to the Sun, the numerical progression proposed by

Titius clearly is not in line with the orbital distances of Neptune and Pluto. Titius's principle (in its 1766 formulation and some other formulations) was jettisoned after Neptune was discovered in 1846. Astronomers judged it not to be a law. Why? Obviously, this judgment was made because, in order for something to be a law of nature, it must be true. The determination of Neptune's orbital distance from the Sun showed Titius's principle to be false, and so not a law of nature.

The assumption that all laws are true can lead to some confusion. Strictly speaking, many propositions that are called 'laws' are not really laws. For example, though it is false, Titius's principle is commonly known as Bode's law or the Titius–Bode law. While a good approximation, Newton's law of gravity is false and so not really a law. Why are these principles still called 'laws'? This may be because the propositions were given *names* including the word 'law' when they were believed to be laws, or because of a tendency to use the word 'law' to describe any general proposition or any proposition at one time taken to be a law by scientists. One should be wary of this confusion because, for expository reasons, we will frequently rely on simple and familiar generalizations from the history of science (or on even simpler, wholly fictitious examples) that are no longer (or perhaps never were) believed to be true.

Something else important is suggested by the examples of laws of nature provided so far: *that all laws are generalizations.* They all make a claim to the effect that all things or events have a certain property, usually a certain conditional property. For example, that no signals travel faster than light says about every individual thing in our universe that if it is a signal then it is traveling at a speed less than or equal to the speed of light. The Titius–Bode law says about every individual thing that if it is a planet orbiting the Sun then its orbital distance from the Sun falls in the progression described above. Note that we are reluctant to accept anything but general propositions as laws. For instance, it would be strange to think that some singular fact (e.g., that the Earth has mass 5.98×10^{24} kilograms) could be a law of nature, no matter how interesting or scientifically important it might be.

As was the case with the idea that truth is a necessary condition of lawhood, we should be careful about the assumption that generality is one too. In taking laws to be generalizations, we are not thereby denying that laws sometimes refer to specific objects, times, or places. (Generalizations referring to specific material objects will be discussed in 4.3.) Nor do we thereby deny either that there might be certain probabilistic laws or even what philosophers sometimes call *ceteris paribus laws*. The probabilistic generalizations that all uranium atoms have a half-life of 1,500 years or that all silver atoms exposed to a non-homogeneous magnetic field have a fifty per cent chance of having spin up are perfectly good candidates to be laws of nature. They are generalizations despite including an element of probability. Similarly, if it is true that, ceteris paribus (i.e., other things being equal), price is inversely proportional to supply, we do not intend anything we have said to disqualify this (hedged) generalization from being a law.

Suppose that it's a law that all copper expands when heated. Then consider any bit of copper b that, in fact, is not heated. Even if particular circumstances had been different, even if b were heated, the laws governing our world surely would be unchanged. Thus, we naturally accept the counterfactual conditional that, if b were (still) copper and heated, then b would expand. It is very natural to think that *all laws of nature support counterfactual conditionals*; they are somehow or other part of what makes a wide range of counterfactuals true.

Most have correctly recognized that lawhood is somehow conceptually entwined with the counterfactual conditional. Indeed, it is the account of counterfactuals in terms of lawhood championed by Roderick Chisholm[2] and Nelson Goodman[3] that provoked much of the recent philosophical interest in laws of nature. Very roughly, their account maintains that, if P were the case, then Q would be the case if and only if there is a valid argument of the form:

$$L_1, ..., L_r$$
$$P, I_1, ..., I_k$$
$$\overline{}$$
$$Q$$

where $L_1 - L_r$ are laws, and $I_1 - I_k$ are non-laws *cotenable* with P. Since 'cotenable' is a technical term, this account needs to be supplemented with some characterization of cotenability. Even so, it is clear how the account was intended to apply to cases like our case of b, that unheated bit of copper. Since the law that all copper expands when heated together with

[2] Chisholm, "The Contrary-to-Fact Conditional" and "Law Statements and Counterfactual Inference."

[3] Goodman, "The Problem of Counterfactual Conditionals."

the conjunction that b is heated and b is copper entails that b expands, there is the true counterfactual conditional that, if b were heated, it would expand.

David Lewis defended a different account in his book *Counterfactuals*. Like his approach to (metaphysical) necessity, it invokes possible worlds. He argued that what determines whether Q would be the case if P were the case has to do with what other 'nearby' possible worlds are like. Very roughly, what it depends on is whether Q is true in worlds that are otherwise most similar to the actual world but in which P is true. So to determine whether, if P were true, then Q would be true, ask yourself what the nearest P-is-true worlds are. Then check to see if, in those worlds, Q is also true. Laws of nature are important to Lewis's account because one factor identified by Lewis as very important to whether a world is similar to our world is whether the worlds are in agreement on their laws. So since it is true that in the worlds most similar to ours where b is copper and b is heated that all copper expands when heated, it is also true in those worlds that b expands. Thus, if b were copper and b were heated, then b would expand.

Metaphysicians have generally held that *some* (metaphysically) contingent propositions could be laws of nature. For example, any possible world that as a matter of law obeys the general principles of Newtonian physics is a world in which Newton's first law of motion – the generalization that all inertial bodies have no acceleration – is true. A possible world containing accelerating inertial bodies is a world in which Newton's first law is false. Two reasons can be given for believing that it is possible for a contingent proposition to be a law of nature. The first reason is the plausibility of judgments of possibility engendered by examples like the one just given regarding an inertial body with no acceleration. Just as there is a possible world in which it is raining in Paris now, there are possible worlds with accelerating inertial bodies. The second reason is that there are laws of nature that can only be discovered in an a posteriori manner. If necessity is always associated with laws of nature, then it is not clear why scientists cannot always get by with a priori methods.

Philosophers known as *Necessitarians* hold that *no* laws of nature are contingent.[4] They often argue that their position is a consequence of the

---

[4] See, for example, Shoemaker, "Causal and Metaphysical Necessity."

correct theory of the individuation of properties. Roughly, they maintain that no basic physical property would be the property it is unless it had the causal powers it does, and hence obeyed the laws that it does. For example, Alexander Bird has argued that charge has as part of its essence the power to repel like-charged particles.[5] So the generalization that any charged particle repels any like-charged particle is necessarily true. Intuitively, it also seems like a law. The Necessitarians argue that our intuitive judgments that a law of one possible world could be false in another are tainted by misleading considerations about what is conceivable or can be imagined. They also often cite Saul Kripke's arguments – see Chapter 1 – meant to reveal certain a posteriori necessary truths in order to argue that the a posteriori nature of some laws does not prevent their lawhood from requiring a metaphysically necessary connection between properties. As Necessitarians see it, it is also a virtue of their position that they can explain why laws are counterfactual-supporting; they support counterfactuals in the same way that other necessary truths do.

The primary worry for Necessitarians concerns their ability to sustain their dismissals of the traditional reasons for thinking that some laws are contingent. The problem is that they too make distinctions between necessary truths and contingent ones, and even seem to rely on considerations of conceivability to do so.[6] Prima facie, there is nothing especially suspicious about the judgment that it is possible that an object travels faster than light. How is it any worse than the judgment that it is possible that it is raining in Paris?

Is it true, perhaps even necessarily true, that *all* laws are contingent? This is neither a terribly important nor a terribly interesting issue. The point that isolates the Necessitarians is whether a contingent proposition could be a law. Contingent laws are one thing that makes the problem of laws challenging. They have an especially interesting modal character, involving a contingent modality not identifiable with anything like metaphysical necessity. Many metaphysicians adopt the position that all laws are contingent. Mathematical principles, like one stating the commutative property of addition, are thought to be properly disqualified from being laws of nature because they are necessarily true. There are some minor

---

[5] Bird, *Nature's Metaphysics*.
[6] Compare Sidelle, "On the Metaphysical Contingency of Laws of Nature," p. 311.

considerations weighing against the position that all laws are contingent. Necessary truths certainly cannot be disqualified for being too accidental. It is also natural to think that all deductive consequences of laws are themselves laws, though the deductive consequences of any proposition include all logical truths. For convenience, we will adopt the position that *all laws are contingent*. Even if it is not quite correct, assuming that all laws are contingent has the virtue of focusing our discussion on the most puzzling and interesting group of laws.

It seems that sometimes we make reasonable inferences even though our premises don't guarantee the truth of our conclusion. For example, we sometimes examine a sample of things with some common property *F*, notice that these things also all have some other property *G*, then conclude that all *F*s are *G*s. This manner of reasoning is sometimes known as *enumerative induction*. One of the great philosophical examples of the twentieth century was designed to show that, even if we were to set aside the most straightforward skeptical worries about inductive reasoning, providing a plausible theory of what counts as good inductive reasoning would still be a formidable task. Goodman argued that, even if one is willing to admit that good reasoning need not be valid reasoning – that good reasoning need not guarantee the truth of the conclusion – there is something else to worry about: enumerative induction doesn't work with some concepts.[7]

Goodman's classic example is the concept *grue*. 'Grue' is a word Goodman made up and introduced via a stipulative definition. In close analogy with Goodman, we'll say:

> *x* is grue = df *x* is green and first observed before the year 2050 or blue otherwise.

So, for example, that emerald you are holding in your hand (lucky you) is grue, because it is green and at least you have observed it before 2050. A blue sapphire lodged deep beneath the surface of the Earth that will never be dug up and never examined before 2050? Well, that's grue also. An emerald next to it that also will never be dug up or observed is not grue; it is not first examined before 2050 and it is green. Goodman argued that the generalization that all emeralds are grue is not confirmable by a less-than-complete enumerative induction: if a person were to examine a sample of

---

[7] From "The New Riddle of Induction," first published in 1954 in Goodman's *Fact, Fiction, and Forecast*, pp. 72–5.

grue emeralds, the examination would not be reason to conclude that all emeralds are grue. Your examination right now, before 2050, of that sample of emeralds in front of you, all of which are green, and so all of which are grue, does not give you reason to think that all emeralds are grue. For that generalization implies that emeralds not first examined before 2050 are blue! Introducing a bit of Goodman's terminology, the concept of being grue is not *projectible* with respect to the concept of being an emerald. Enumerative induction doesn't work with all concepts.

What does any of this have to do with laws of nature? Well, many philosophers have thought that it is a necessary condition of lawhood that the concepts included in the law be projectible. It certainly would be bizarre for a scientist to conclude that all emeralds are grue and insofar as scientists are thought to be looking for laws and sometimes confirming them, you can see why someone might expect laws to include only projectible concepts. We will go along with taking projectibility to be a necessary condition of lawhood. We will assume that *all laws are confirmable by induction*. But, even so, in 4.4, we will consider some of the roadblocks to using the notion of projectibility to say anything more about what it is to be a law.

To summarize, in this second section of Chapter 4, we have identified five standard assumptions about laws of nature:

All laws are true.
All laws are generalizations.
All laws support counterfactuals.
All laws are contingent.
All laws are confirmable by induction.

These are assumptions that we adopt also. Still, we have not yet said anything about how these assumptions have been – or should be – used to give an account of what it is to be a law. This is the topic for the remainder of this chapter.

4.3 Regularity accounts

Many philosophers adopt a framework that takes lawhood to be the conjunction of truth and *lawlikeness*. That is, many philosophers accept

Regularity
P is a law if and only if P is true and P is lawlike.

'Lawlike' is introduced as a placeholder. It simply stands for that property other than truth that a proposition must satisfy in order to be a law. Within this framework, what is needed to give an account of lawhood is an account of lawlikeness.

We stipulate *regularity accounts* to be versions of Regularity that hold that lawlikeness is an essential feature of every lawlike proposition. So, by definition, according to all regularity accounts, no matter how lawlikeness is spelled out according to the account, if a proposition is lawlike in one possible world, it is also lawlike in all possible worlds. Our reason for making this stipulation is twofold. First, it does reflect an element of many early attempts to give an account of lawhood. For example, it was – and still often is – thought important that, in addition to being true, a law must (i) be contingent and (ii) have a certain logical structure, and these two features are usually thought to be essential features of propositions that have them. Second, the stipulation lets us draw a fairly precise line between regularity accounts and other accounts of lawhood. This will allow us to present a criticism that challenges all regularity accounts at once. As we will see soon, the assumption that lawlikeness is an essential feature of a proposition is problematic for certain subtle, but significant reasons.

We begin by focusing on a simplistic version of Regularity that makes lawlikeness a matter of being contingent and general: P is lawlike if and only if P is a contingent generalization. This account does make some true pronouncements. For example, it says that it is a law that no signals travel faster than light. Still, the proposal faces at least three serious sorts of problems. A careful look at these problems will give us a better appreciation of how daunting the challenge is to understand better what it is to be a law of nature.

First, there are many contingently true *restricted* generalizations that are not laws. These generalizations are restricted in virtue of referring to particular material objects. Examples include the propositions that all rocks in this box contain iron, that all the screws in Smith's car are rusty, and that all the apples in the refrigerator are yellow. Though these might all be true, none of them is a law. Even assuming they are all true, they seem much too accidental. A piece of pure quartz in the box, a stainless steel screw in Smith's car, a Ruby Red in the refrigerator – these are all things that readily could have been in place and each one, *had* it been in place, *would* have made the corresponding generalization false. So, there doesn't seem to be the appropriate support of counterfactuals needed for these generalizations to be laws. It does not help to add a necessary condition to Regularity requiring that laws not be restricted. The problem with such a necessary condition is that there are generalizations that could express laws that are restricted. Galileo's law of free fall is the generalization that, *on Earth*, free-falling bodies accelerate at a rate of 9.8 meters per second squared. This generalization refers to Earth and yet it could be a law. The Titius–Bode law refers to the Sun but it was not for this reason that doubts were raised about its lawhood. Michael Tooley has presented an especially nice example of how our world might have included a restricted law:

> Suppose, for example, the world were as follows: All the fruit in Smith's garden at any time are apples. When one attempts to take an orange into the garden, it turns into an elephant. Bananas so treated become apples as they cross the boundary, while pears are resisted by a force that cannot be overcome. Cherry trees planted in the garden bear apples, or they bear nothing at all. If all these things were true, there would be a very strong case for its being a law that all the fruit in Smith's garden are apples.[8]

Though hypothetical, this example is sufficient to show that restricted contingent generalizations can be laws.

Second, there are many contingently true generalizations that are not about anything in our universe: all unicorns are slow, all plaid pandas weigh five kilograms or less, and so on. These are usually called *vacuously true generalizations*. They have the form that all Fs are Gs and what makes them vacuously true is that there are no Fs. It may seem a little odd to even count these generalizations as true, but they are true. The easiest way to see this is to recognize the equivalence between generalizations of the form 'all Fs are Gs' and generalizations of the form 'No F is not G.' For example, the proposition that all signals travel at speeds less than or equal to the speed of light is equivalent to the proposition that no signals travel faster than light. Similarly, that all plaid pandas weigh less than or equal to five kilograms is equivalent to the proposition that no plaid pandas weigh more than five kilograms. Notice that there is nothing odd about taking this latter proposition to be true. It is just so much common sense. The problem vacuously true generalizations present for

---

[8] Tooley, "The Nature of Laws," pp. 120–1.

Regularity is that, though true, they need not be laws. Regularity counts them as laws, but really they are sometimes too accidental. Think about some corresponding counterfactuals. Even if there were a plaid panda, there is no reason to think that it would weigh no more than five kilograms. If there were a unicorn, there is no guarantee that it would be slow. Furthermore, there is no quick fix to this problem. Demanding that a law of nature not be vacuously true would not solve anything. There are vacuously true generalizations that are not accidentally true, even some that scientists have accepted as laws. Newton's first law of motion is a good example. It is a law that all inertial bodies have no acceleration even though there are no inertial bodies – in our universe every body has some force exerted on it.

Though a lot of energy has been expended trying to answer the problem of vacuously true generalizations and the problem of restricted generalizations, there is a third problem for Regularity that is more vexing: there are contingently true generalizations that fail to be laws that make no mention of any particular material object and that are also not vacuously true. Consider the unrestricted and non-vacuous generalization that all gold spheres are less than a mile in diameter. There have never been any gold spheres greater than a mile in diameter, and in all likelihood there never will be. Nevertheless, even assuming there never will be gold spheres that big, this is still not a law. Again, it is just too accidental. If we were curious and persistent (and wealthy!) enough, we could just gather that much gold together and create a one-mile-in-diameter gold sphere.

Another counterexample, one similar to the gold spheres case, derives from a famous example proposed by Karl Popper.[9] Moas are an extinct species of New Zealand birds. We can suppose that the longest-lived moa – let's call her Marge – just missed living fifty years, dying on the day before her fiftieth birthday. There was nothing about the genetic structure of moas that prevented any of them from living longer than fifty years. Their early deaths were quite accidental, the longer-lived ones – including Marge – dying as a result of a virus. Coming from India, this virus was blown into New Zealand by a certain wind. In absence of this wind, the virus would never have gotten there. Then the generalization that all moas die before

---

[9] Popper, *The Logic of Scientific Discovery*, pp. 427–8, first published in German in 1934. See also Armstrong, *What Is a Law of Nature?*, p. 18.

age fifty apparently is not a law. Since it is a true, contingent generalization, Regularity has the mistaken consequence that it is. Once again we encounter problems involving implications about counterfactuals. If it were a law that all moas die before age fifty, then it should be true that, if Marge were a moa and had not contracted the virus, then Marge would have died before age fifty. But that counterfactual is false. If Marge were a moa and had not contracted the virus, then she would probably have lived at least one more day.

The perplexing nature of these last two counterexamples to Regularity is clearly revealed when the gold sphere generalization is paired with a remarkably similar generalization about uranium spheres:

> All gold spheres are less than a mile in diameter.
> All uranium spheres are less than a mile in diameter.

Though the former is not a law, the latter arguably is. The latter is not nearly so accidental as the former, since uranium's critical mass is such as to guarantee that such a large sphere will never exist.[10] What makes the difference? What makes the former an accidental generalization and the latter a law?

We can turn this sort of puzzle into an objection against *all* regularity accounts. Consider again the generalization that all gold spheres are less than a mile in diameter. That generalization, though it is not a law, could be a law. For example, "if gold were unstable in such a way that there was no chance whatever that a large amount of gold could last long enough to be formed into a one-mile sphere,"[11] then it might well be a law that all gold spheres are less than a mile in diameter. In such possible worlds, the generalization is a law, and hence it is also lawlike. But, in the actual world, the generalization is true, and not a law. So, in our world, it is not lawlike. Thus a single proposition is lawlike in one possible world and not lawlike in another. Any essential feature of a proposition must be exhibited by the proposition in all possible worlds. Hence, lawlikeness must not be an essential property of propositions. Since, by definition, all regularity accounts take lawlikeness to be an essential feature of propositions, all such accounts fail.[12]

---

[10] Van Fraassen, *Laws and Symmetry*, p. 27.

[11] Postscript C to "A Subjectivist Guide to Objective Chance," in Lewis, *Philosophical Papers*, vol. II, p. 123.

[12] Compare Tooley, *Causation*, p. 52.

Despite the limitations of regularity accounts and (hopefully) because we have sketched what those limitations are, we suspect that you may already have a better idea of what lawhood is. What seems to be missing from regularity accounts is some kind of requirement ensuring that laws not be accidentally true, something to ensure that they would remain true under a range of counterfactual possibilities. This is precisely the sort of thing that seems to have bothered Delambre and Laplace when they accused Titius's principle of being a mere game with numbers. With only a handful of known planets in our solar system at the time, it was hardly surprising that someone could cook up a neat progression that picked out the orbital distances reasonably well, and the critics seemed well aware that there was more to being a law than just getting the distances right. They knew it was important that the progression hold up even if certain possibilities came to pass (e.g., if there were other planets). Understandably, they just didn't see any good reason to think that it would.

What if we were to try to revise the regularity account to reflect these plausible thoughts about the importance of being non-accidental? Consider:

Counterfactual
P is a law if and only if P is a contingently true generalization that would hold over a range of counterfactual possibilities.

Setting aside natural concerns about what exactly the range of possibilities is, Counterfactual holds some promise. For example, since the restricted generalization that all the screws in Smith's car are rusty would not be true if there were a stainless steel screw holding the radiator to the chassis, this account might appropriately disqualify this restricted generalization from being a law. Similarly, since the generalization that all plaid pandas weigh five kilograms would not be true if some poor adult panda had its fur dyed plaid, this vacuously true generalization is also correctly disqualified by the account. In contrast, we would fully expect a law like Newton's first law of motion to hold up under these and many other counterfactual possibilities. Whether the Titius–Bode law was really a law would have turned on whether it would maintain its plausibility under various counterfactual possibilities.

Nevertheless, most philosophers would be disappointed if this was all that could be said about lawhood. The leading philosophical accounts of counterfactuals invoke lawhood and so there is a significant threat of circularity here. The fear is that we would have explained lawhood in terms of counterfactuals and then turned around and explained the counterfactuals in terms of lawhood – not a satisfying state of affairs for a responsible philosopher looking for illumination about both counterfactuals and laws. At its root, the problem is that laws and counterfactuals are too similar for an account of lawhood in terms of counterfactuals to be very informative. What philosophers have wanted (and what some would say they really *need*) is an account of lawhood that doesn't appeal to counterfactuals or any other concepts that are too similar to lawhood. These concepts are sometimes called *nomic concepts* and are thought to include the concepts of causation, explanation, chance, and dispositions as well as counterfactuals. Philosophers have wanted to give a thoroughly nonnomic account of what it is to be a law.

4.4 Goodman, Lewis, and Armstrong

4.4.1 Introduction

There are three popular ways that metaphysicians have tried to give an account of lawhood without invoking any nomic terms. The first is an approach championed by Goodman that puts the connections between laws and induction front and center. The second is an approach advocated by Lewis. The third is an approach advocated by David Armstrong. In this section, we will consider some attractive features of these philosophical routes to understanding lawhood. In 4.5, we will discuss some *nonsupervenience* examples that will reveal some potential weaknesses.

4.4.2 Goodman on laws

Goodman thought that the difference between laws of nature and accidental truths was linked inextricably with the problem of induction. He said:

> Only a statement that is lawlike – regardless of its truth or falsity or its scientific importance – is capable of receiving confirmation from an instance of it; accidental statements are not.[13]

[13] Goodman, *Fact, Fiction, and Forecast*, p. 73.

So, in addition to thinking that projectibility was a necessary condition of being a law, Goodman thought that being projectible was sufficient for being lawlike. His claim appears to be that, if a generalization is accidentally true (and so not lawlike), then an instance of the generalization cannot confirm – *can be no evidence* – that the generalization is true. The idea is that the generalizations that are not lawlike are bound to be too accidental for one instance to indicate their truth. They might still be true, but just one instance doesn't decide their truth. Finding one rusty screw in Smith's car shouldn't lead us to believe that all the screws in Smith's car are rusty.

Despite the importance of Goodman's example of grue to the prospects of providing a theory of induction, there are serious concerns whether he has correctly identified how the issues about projectibility hook up with lawlikeness. Suppose that we throw a brand-new die twice and then destroy it. Also suppose that we are interested in whether it will come up six both times it is tossed. We throw it the first time and it does land on six. Notice that this single instance has increased dramatically the probability that this die will land on six on every toss. Before the first toss that probability was $\frac{1}{36}$, or about per cent. Now that the first toss has landed as a six that probability has gone up to $\frac{1}{6}$ or about seventeen per cent. Our observation of one instance of the generalization that this die will always land on six has provided evidence for this generalization. A variation of this case makes more trouble. Suppose we know that the die will only be tossed *once* before it is destroyed and then see it land on six. The probability that the die will always land on six increases from about seventeen per cent to 100 per cent!

It is standard to respond to such examples by suggesting that what does require lawlikeness is confirmation of the generalization's *unexamined* instances. If this is correct, what matters in our first example is whether the first toss increases the probability that the second toss will land on six. And, of course, it does not. The probability of the second toss landing on six is $\frac{1}{6}$ before the first toss is made, and this probability is still $\frac{1}{6}$ after the first toss is made. In our second example, it is also true (trivially so) that the probability of the generalization holding for unexamined instances is not raised; there are no unexamined instances. In our second example, there has been an exhaustive examination of the instances.

Unfortunately, there are other problems. Some of these may seem trivial, but we should always remember that philosophers like to get at the strict and literal truth, and these other problems at least strongly indicate that followers of Goodman really have their work cut out for them. The biggest problem is that background beliefs can really mess things up. We have already seen evidence of this in the earlier examples where our prior knowledge that the die would only be tossed just once (or just twice) played a major role. The role of background beliefs, however, could have been more dramatic. Suppose you know that Sam always sorts his coins by what pocket they are in and that he has lots of coins in every pocket. Sam shows you one of the coins from his left front pants pocket and you see that it is a nickel. Evidently, this instance of the generalization that all the coins in Sam's left front pocket are nickels has confirmed this generalization. Given your background knowledge, you seem perfectly justified in believing that this generalization is true, even though it is not lawlike.

We will remain agnostic about whether there is some confirmability condition that is a sufficient condition of lawlikeness. In fact, we will have little more to say about Goodman's approach to lawhood, limiting most of our attention to the two most popular approaches: Lewis's approach and Armstrong's approach. We will continue to assume that the concepts included in laws are projectible; all this will amount to is that we will develop our examples using concepts that seem quite natural and scientifically appropriate, ones that seem like they should be perfectly projectible ones. There is still a lot to discuss, even setting this interesting and difficult issue about the relationship between laws and inductive reasoning off to one side.

4.4.3 Lewis on laws

A *deductive system* is a set of axioms, really just any set of propositions. The logical consequences of the axioms are known as the theorems of the system. Deductive systems may have many different properties. Truth (all true axioms) is one straightforward one. Simplicity and strength are other examples, though they are not nearly so straightforward. Strength has to do with something like how interesting or applicable the theorems of the system are. Simplicity has to do with things like how many axioms there are and how complicated they are. Strength and simplicity compete. It is easy to make a system stronger by sacrificing simplicity: include all the truths as axioms. It is easy to make a system simple by sacrificing strength: have just the axiom that 2 + 2 = 4.

According to Lewis, the laws of nature are the contingent generalizations that belong to all the suitably ideal deductive systems.[14]

Systems
P is a law of nature if and only if P is contingent and P appears as a theorem or axiom in every true deductive system with a best combination of simplicity and strength.

So, for example, the thought is that it is a law that all uranium spheres are less than a mile in diameter because it is, arguably, part of the best deductive systems; quantum theory is an excellent theory of our universe and is arguably part of all the best systems, and it is plausible to think that quantum theory plus truths describing the nature of uranium would logically entail that there are no uranium spheres of that size. It is doubtful that the generalization that all gold spheres are less than a mile in diameter would be part of the best systems. It could be added as an axiom to any system, but not without sacrificing something in terms of simplicity.

Systems is appealing. For one thing, it appears prepared to deal with the challenge posed by vacuous laws. With Systems, there is no exclusion of vacuously true generalizations from the realm of laws, and yet only those vacuously true generalizations that belong to the best systems qualify. For another thing, Systems appears prepared to deal with restricted generalizations. The best systems could include some particular fact, say, about the mass of Earth, and so it could turn out that the theorems of all the best systems include a generalization like Galileo's free-fall law; yet the best systems are not likely to include some particular facts about, say, Smith's car. Furthermore, it is reasonable to think that one goal of scientific theorizing is the formulation of true theories that are well balanced in terms of their simplicity and strength. So Systems in addition to all its other attractions seems to underwrite the truism that an aim of science is the discovery of laws of nature.

One last aspect of Systems that is appealing to many (though not all) is that it is in keeping with broadly *Humean* constraints on an account of lawhood. Hume was the great denier of necessary connections. If e caused f, then, for Hume, there is not any kind of necessitation in nature that is

---

[14] See Lewis, *Counterfactuals*, pp. 72–7, "New Work for a Theory of Universals," pp. 365–8, and Postscript C to "A Subjectivist Guide to Objective Chance," in *Philosophical Papers*, vol. II, pp. 121–31.

the causation. For Hume, if they were anything at all, causal connections had to be nothing more than constructs out of other simpler concepts given to us directly in perceptual sensations. Contemporary Humeans like Lewis believe something similar about lawful connections. If there is some kind of law about signals and a maximum velocity, then there is not any kind of lawful connection or relation in nature linking signal-hood with that velocity. For Humeans, signalhood doesn't necessitate any-thing in any interesting sense. Regularity, the account from 4.3, is a good example of a Humean account. If it were correct, then lawhood would be a construct out of truth and a couple of arguably logical features: contin-gency and generality. Systems is another Humean approach; lawhood is just a construct of certain deductive relationships and certain theoretical considerations about simplicity, strength, and best balance. If Systems is correct, then there don't have to be any mysterious necessitation relations in nature in order for there to be laws of nature. Indeed, Systems is the centerpiece of Lewis's defense of *Humean Supervenience*, "the doctrine that all there is in the world is a vast mosaic of local matters of particular fact, just one little thing and then another."[15]

Other features of Systems have made philosophers wary.[16] Some argue that this approach will have the untoward consequence that laws are inappropriately mind-dependent in virtue of the account's appeal to the concepts of simplicity, strength, and best balance, concepts whose applica-tion seems to depend on cognitive abilities, interests, and purposes. The appeal to simplicity raises further questions stemming from the apparent need for a regimented language to permit reasonable comparisons of the systems. Interestingly, sometimes the view is abandoned because it satis-fies the broadly Humean constraints on an account of laws of nature; some argue that which generalizations are laws is not determined by local mat-ters of particular fact. We will consider an argument to this effect in 4.5.

4.4.4 Armstrong on laws

The main rival to Systems appeals to a special universal[17] to distinguish laws from non-laws.

---

[15] From the Introduction to Lewis, *Philosophical Papers*, vol. II, p. ix.

[16] See, especially, Armstrong, *What Is a Law of Nature?*, pp. 66–73; van Fraassen, *Laws and Symmetry*, pp. 40–64; Carroll, "The Humean Tradition," pp. 197–206.

[17] Universals are discussed at length in Chapter 9.

Universals
It is a law that *F*s are *G*s if and only if *F*-ness stands in relation N to *G*-ness.[18]

This is the view of Armstrong. 'N' is intended to be the name for a law-making universal. Armstrong sometimes says that *F*-ness *necessitates* *G*-ness. As does Systems, this framework appears to hold promise. Maybe the difference between the uranium spheres generalization and the gold spheres generalization is that being uranium does necessitate being less than a mile in diameter, but being gold does not. It could be that being a screw in Smith's car does not stand in N to being rusty though being a free-falling body does stand in this relation to a 9.8 meters-per-second squared acceleration. Being inertial may necessitate zero acceleration, but being a unicorn may not necessitate being slow. Some universalists also think that the framework supports the idea that laws can play a special explanatory role in inductive inferences, since on this view laws aren't mere regularities.

Armstrong's account is intended as an account of lawhood that does not use any nomic terms. 'N' is a name, not an abbreviation for some nomic phrase like 'causally necessitates'. 'N' is meant to refer directly to a certain entity in the world. What is somewhat remarkable is how diametrically opposed Universals is to Systems in this regard, despite the fact that both accounts seek a non-nomic characterization of what it is to be a law. For Armstrong, a contingent necessitation relation, a necessary connection in nature, is exactly what makes the difference between a law and an accident. In virtue of its appeal to this lawmaking universal, Universals is decidedly not a Humean account of lawhood.

The trouble for Universals is that more has to be said about what N is. This is the problem Bas van Fraassen calls *The Identification Problem*. He couples this with a second problem, what he calls *The Inference Problem*.[19] The essence of this pair of problems was captured early on by Lewis:

> Whatever N may be, I cannot see how it could be absolutely impossible to have N(F,G) and Fa without Ga. (Unless N just is constant conjunction, or constant conjunction plus something else, in which case Armstrong's theory turns into a form of the regularity theory he rejects.) The mystery

[18] Armstrong, *What Is a Law of Nature?*, p. 85.
[19] Van Fraassen, *Laws and Symmetry*, p. 96.

is somewhat hidden by Armstrong's terminology. He uses 'necessitates' as a name for the lawmaking universal N; and who would be surprised to hear that if F 'necessitates' G and a has F, then a must have G? But I say that N deserves the name of 'necessitation' only if, somehow, it really can enter into the requisite necessary connections. It can't enter into them just by bearing a name, any more than one can have mighty biceps just by being called 'Armstrong.'[20]

Basically, there needs to be a specification of what the lawmaking relation is (The Identification Problem). Then there needs to be a determination of whether it is suited to the task (The Inference Problem): Does N holding between *F* and *G* entail that *F*s are *G*s? Does its holding support corresponding counterfactuals? Do laws really turn out to be contingent and to have a role in inductive inference?

4.5 Laws and supervenience

Rather than trying to detail all the critical issues that divide the proponents of Systems and Universals, we will do better to focus our attention on one crucial issue. The issue concerns supervenience. It concerns whether Humean considerations determine what the laws are. There are some important examples that *appear* to show that they do not. The examples affect philosophers in remarkably different ways. Some take the examples at face value and are moved to *abandon* Humean accounts of lawhood in favor of Universals or some other non-Humean account. For others, the examples lead them to *strengthen* their commitment to Systems or some other Humean proposal.

Tooley asks us to suppose that there are ten different kinds of fundamental particle.[21] With this supposition, it turns out that there are fifty-five possible kinds of two-particle interaction. Suppose also that fifty-four of these kinds of interaction have been studied and fifty-four corresponding laws have been proposed and thoroughly tested. What has not been studied at all is any interactions between the last two kinds of particle, which Tooley arbitrarily labels as 'X' and 'Y' particles. There have been plenty of the first fifty-four kinds of interaction, but not a single interaction of the

---

[20] Lewis, "New Work for a Theory of Universals," p. 366.
[21] Tooley, "The Nature of Laws," p. 669.

fifty-fifth kind; X and Y particles have never crossed paths. Furthermore, these X–Y interactions will never be studied because conditions are such that these two kinds of particles never will interact.

One thing that is ingenious about this example is that, at least at first glance, it seems that there could well be a law about X–Y interactions. After all, in the example, scientists have already discovered laws for all of the other fifty-four kinds of interactions. Indeed, it is even true that nine of these laws are about X particles and that nine are about Y particles. So, there is some reason to think that there is also a law about what happens when X and Y particles get together, despite the fact that they never will. Another thing that is ingenious about Tooley's example is that it seems that many, many different X–Y interaction laws are perfectly consistent with all the events that might take place during the complete history of this universe – past, present, and future. Even given the complete history of this universe, the complete actual sequence of events and any other considerations a Humean might think important, there could be a law that, when X particles and Y particles interact, they are destroyed. But, then again, even given the complete history of this universe, and adding in whatever other Humean considerations you like, there could be a law that, when X particles and Y particles interact, they bond.

This non-supervenience suggested by Tooley's example is not unique to his example. If the complete history of his ten-particle world doesn't determine whether it is lawfully or accidentally true that X–Y interactions lead to bonding, then maybe other histories leave the status of their laws unfixed too. Consider the possibility that there is a single material object traveling through otherwise empty space at a constant velocity of, say, one meter per second. It seems that this might just be a very barren Newtonian universe in which it is true that all bodies have a velocity of one meter per second, but where that is *not* a law of nature; it just so happens that there is nothing to alter the object's motion. But one has to admit that it might also be the case that this world is not Newtonian and that it *is* a law that all bodies travel at one meter per second; it could be that this generalization is no coincidence and would have held true even if there were other bodies slamming into the moving object. Furthermore, we should consider our own situation. Maybe lawful underdetermination is *actual*. It can seem that our complete history is consistent with it being a law that all gold spheres are less than a mile in diameter. Even though we will never gather that much gold, maybe it is true that, if we were to, then the gold would start to decay or explode or disappear. Similarly, it can seem that our complete history is consistent with it being a remarkable accident that no signal travels faster than light. Maybe we will just never be smart enough to generate the conditions under which a signal would travel much, much faster than light. Prima facie, this is perfectly consistent with the goings-on in our world. The lawfulness of our laws seems like something the actual course of events doesn't determine.

Tooley takes his example to make a case against Humean attempts to solve the problem of laws. (He favors a non-Humean approach similar to Universals.) One can begin to see why he thinks that by considering what Regularity (4.3) says about his ten-particle world:

> When X and Y particles interact, they are destroyed.
> When X and Y particles interact, they bond.

Regularity says about Tooley's example that both of these X–Y generalizations are laws. But that is impossible because destruction and bonding are incompatible. It cannot be true that, if there were an X–Y interaction, then both destruction and bonding would occur. This problem for the regularity account is a consequence of the fact that the considerations appealed to in that account do not differentiate between these two generalizations. Because the two X–Y generalizations are both true contingent generalizations, they both get counted as laws. The trouble does not stop there for Humeans; Systems does not appear to be in much better shape than Regularity. For not only do the two key X–Y generalizations not differ regarding their logical form, their contingency, or their truth, neither do they differ regarding their simplicity or their strength. Evidently, either they would both belong to all the best systems or neither would. It seems to be quite unreasonable to expect that all the best systems would include one of these generalizations and not the other.

In contrast, Universals seems to be in better shape. In virtue of its appeal to facts about universals, it opens up the possibility that there is something that grounds the lawhood of exactly one of the generalizations. For all that has been said, it might be the case that being an X–Y interaction necessitates destruction though being an X–Y interaction does not necessitate bonding. It could also go the other way: being an X–Y interaction might necessitate that bonding occur but not necessitate that destruction occur. Indeed, that is what Tooley thinks ultimately determines what the laws really are in his example. The other non-supervenience examples are dealt with in the same way. Wondering what determines whether it is a law in the single-body example that all bodies have a velocity of one meter per second? For Tooley, it just depends on what a law making relation relates. Why is it not a law in our world that all gold spheres are less than a mile in diameter? According to Tooley, it is because being a gold sphere doesn't stand in a law making relation to being less than a mile in diameter.

Many philosophers are not prepared to draw the conclusions drawn by Tooley. Even though Armstrong is quite prepared to believe in universals and in their importance to metaphysics, he is troubled by the idea that there could be an uninstantiated universal (e.g., being an X–Y interaction), which is floating about free of any physical objects and yet is managing to necessitate another universal. Other philosophers see Tooley's example as highlighting The Identification Problem. It is awfully convenient that his universals line up as they do in the Plato's Heaven of his ten-particle universe, doling out lawfulness to exactly the one X–Y generalization that really is the law. Why should we believe that these universals do line up so nicely? What do we know about this necessitation relation? What relation is it? In this spirit, Marc Lange is with Tooley in denying Humean Supervenience but is not drawn to appeal to universals. Lange rejects all attempts to say what it is to be a law that do not appeal to nomic concepts. His *Laws and Lawmakers* explains what it is to be a law in terms of a counterfactual notion of stability.

You may have noticed a similarity between Tooley's non-supervenience example and the underdetermination case from 2.6.3. In both examples, there are facts of the matter that seem not to be fixed by the more basic facts of the case. Here, the issue is about which X–Y generalization (if either) is a law of nature. In Chapter 2, the matter is whether it was Morgana or Merlin that turned the prince into a frog. The similarity is no surprise. Determination is just the inverse of supervenience: P determines Q if and only if Q supervenes on P. Just so, Tooley-style non-supervenience cases often generate the same kind of philosophical anxiety about lawhood that the underdetermination case does about causation. The fallout is a range of *Anti-Realisms* about laws similar to the Anti-Realist stance some take about causation. *Eliminativists* hold that there are no laws. For example, van

Fraassen develops this view at length in his *Laws and Symmetry*. He finds
support for this in the problems facing certain accounts of lawhood and
in the perceived failure of philosophers to describe an adequate epistemology that permits rational belief in laws. Other philosophers are *Projectivists*;
though they will use sentences like 'It is a law that no signals travel faster
than light,' they are Anti-Realists in virtue of thinking that such sentences
are not (purely) fact stating.[22] Whether this Einsteinian generalization is a
law is not a fact about the universe; it is not something out there waiting
to be discovered. Rather lawhood sentences project a certain attitude (in
addition to belief) about the pertinent regularity.

The challenge for any Anti-Realism is to minimize the havoc lawless
or causationless reality would play with our folk and scientific practices.
Regarding science, the examples of laws listed at the start of this chapter
attest to 'law' having a visible role that scientists seem prepared to take as
fact-stating. Regarding our folk practices, though 'law' is not often part of
run-of-the-mill conversations, an Anti-Realism about lawhood would still
have wide-ranging consequences. This is due to lawhood's ties to other
concepts, especially the other nomic ones, and especially counterfactuals. Would an ordinary match in normal conditions light if struck? It
seems it would, but only because we take nature to be lawful. We think
this counterfactual is true because we believe there are laws. Were there
no laws, it would not be the case that, if the match were struck, it would
light. And, though some have questioned whether causation has a role
to play in the physical theory,[23] it is perfectly obvious that causation is
central to our folk and scientific practices. Human decisions, molecular
bonding, even growing older are causal processes. Scientific explanations
of particular events are causal explanations. Suffice to say that the bulk
of our concepts are loaded with causal commitments. Those who dare to
deny the reality of either laws or causation have a lot of explaining to do.

---

[22] For example, Ward, "Humeanism without Humean Supervenience: A Projectivist
   Account of Laws and Possibilities."
[23] For example, Russell, "On the Notion of Cause."

5   Personal identity

5.1 Introduction

Suppose you have always wanted to travel to Paris but could never afford the trip from New York. And suppose that now a new company, 15-Minute Travel, is offering to send you with their super-high-tech "transporter" machine. Here's how the transporter machine works. You step into a fancy-looking booth in New York and, once you are ready to go, you press a green button marked "Paris". You are then scanned by a device that records the exact position, nature, and velocity of every subatomic particle in your body. This information – your "personal blueprint" – is then recorded on a zirconium microchip. At the same time, your body is disassembled, and the resulting subatomic particles are rearranged, so that they make up a small quantity of "transport dust" – a dense but compact and virtually undamagable ashlike substance. Next, the transport dust and the zirconium chip are safely sealed inside a small cylinder, like the canisters used by drive-through banks, and the cylinder then travels through a special underground tube, powered by electromagnetic technology, at speeds exceeding 10,000 miles per hour. The cylinder arrives at the company's terminal in Paris in less than fifteen minutes and, once it is safely ensconced in a booth just like the one in New York, the transport dust is rearranged, in precise accordance with your personal blueprint. You then emerge from the booth in Paris, feeling as if the whole experience has taken no time at all.

Or anyway, the company insists that the person who will emerge from the booth in Paris will be you. And why not? That person will be completely indiscernible from you in every way, even on a subatomic level. What's more, the person who will emerge from the booth in Paris will be composed of your particles, will have all of your memories and other psychological properties, and will in fact take himself or herself to be you.

Not only that, but it turns out that the price for this fabulous service is an amazingly low $2.99 (or $4.99 for the round trip). And the best part, according to the company's brochure, is that you will emerge from the booth in Paris feeling fresh as a daisy, with absolutely no wear and tear as a result of travel. It will be as if you were simply on "pause" for fifteen minutes while the rest of the world aged a tiny bit and you relocated to Paris. Oh, and one other thing: you will be permitted to bring along up to 150 pounds of luggage at no additional charge.

Suppose further that 15-Minute Travel has many impressive testimonials. Millions of customers have used the service so far, and no one is even the tiniest bit dissatisfied with the results. Everyone who comes out of one of the company's booths swears that he or she survived the trip without any trouble at all, and that it was an utterly painless process. In fact, they all say that transporter travel is the only way to go, and they cannot believe that they ever used to travel by any other method. Even the families of all the customers are delighted with the way 15-Minute Travel's transporter machine enabled their loved ones to travel conveniently and inexpensively.

This example raises several important questions. Here are two of them:

> (Q1) If 15-Minute Travel's transporter machine were actual, would it be a good idea to pay the money, step into the booth, and push the button?

> (Q2) If the machine were real, and if you did step into the booth in New York and push the button, would it be you who came out of the booth in Paris?

In a random sampling of ordinary people, both Nahid and Zane Markosian said "Yes" to both Q1 and Q2. The transporter machine, in their view, would be a handy and inexpensive way to travel to Paris. Others, however, said "No" to both of these questions. The transporter machine, according to these people, merely presents us with an interesting way to go out of existence. For when you get disassembled, according to this other school of thought, that's it: you go out of existence, and the lookalike who emerges from the booth in Paris claiming to be you is a brand-new person who *appears* to be you but is in fact not the real thing.

Here is another example. Suppose an eccentric billionaire has a photo of a ten-year-old boy named Will Martinez that he was friends with fifty years ago. Suppose the two families have long since moved apart, and lost touch with one another. But now suppose the billionaire wants to find his childhood friend and award him a million-dollar grant, with no strings attached. So he (the billionaire) places an ad in the paper, and as a result, hundreds of people line up outside his office, claiming to be the very same Will Martinez that the billionaire was friends with so many years ago.

This example raises some more questions. The main one is: Which candidate is the real Will Martinez? But there are two closely related questions here that it is better to keep separate:

(Q3) How could the billionaire determine which candidate is the real Will Martinez? That is, what test could the billionaire use to pick the right one?

(Q4) What actually makes it true of the right candidate that he is the right one? That is, in virtue of what is it the case that *this one*, and not any of the others, is the right candidate?

Questions like Q1–Q4 would be easier to answer if we had a better understanding of what it takes for a person to persist through time, and what it takes for someone now to be the same person as someone from an earlier time. The Problem of Personal Identity can be understood as the problem of coming up with a metaphysical theory that provides answers to these and related questions. But as we will see, it can be difficult to characterize the problem in a more precise way.

5.2 Characterizing The Problem of Personal Identity

Here is one way of characterizing our problem:

The Traditional Characterization of The Problem of Personal Identity
The problem of personal identity is the problem raised by the following question: *If* x *is a person at* t_1 *and* y *is a person at* t_2, *then under what circumstances is* y *the same person as* x?

The question mentioned in The Traditional Characterization is certainly an intuitively appealing way of getting at the question behind such puzzles as those raised by our transporter and billionaire cases above. But there is a potential problem. Some philosophers have doubts about whether 'x is the same person as y' expresses a real relation. There's the property of being a person, these philosophers say, and there's the relation of classical identity, which sometimes relates things that have that property. But there is no special relation, according to such skeptics, that it makes sense to call the *same person* relation.

Such skeptics will in general have a problem with "concept-relative identity" or "sortal identity". They will doubt that there is such a relation as the *same-car* relation, or the *same-human* relation, or the *same-planet* relation. They will in general insist that, where φ is some sortal predicate, the best we can mean by saying "x is the same φ as y" is that x and y are both φs and x is identical to y.

Partly as a result of such worries, some philosophers prefer alternative ways of characterizing our problem about personal identity.[1] For such philosophers, the problem of personal identity is best thought of in this way. Human people like you typically persist through time. It therefore makes sense to ask about the persistence conditions for such people. (The persistence conditions for a type of object are the conditions under which an object of that type will continue to exist over time.) One way to ask about the persistence conditions for human people is to ask the question mentioned in the following characterization of the problem of personal identity.

> *The "Classical-Identity" Characterization of The Problem of Personal Identity*
> The problem of personal identity is the problem raised by the following question: *If* x *is a person at* t$_1$ *and* y *is a thing that exists at* t$_2$, *then under what circumstances is* y *identical to* x?

Here is one reason why this is a good way of characterizing the problem of personal identity: there are no suspect properties or relations mentioned in the question being asked; for no one doubts that there is such a property as being a person, or that there is such a relation as identity.

One minor worry that is likely to arise in connection with The "Classical-Identity" Characterization of The Problem of Personal Identity concerns the lack of any requirement that y should be a person at the later time. After all, one might think, isn't it supposed to be the problem of *personal*

---

[1] Olson is such a philosopher. See *The Human Animal*, Chapter 2.

identity? But there is a possible way to assuage this worry. The problem could be characterized as follows:

> *A Variation on The "Classical-Identity" Characterization of The Problem of Personal Identity*
> The problem of personal identity is the problem raised by the following question: *If* x *is a person at* t_1 *and* y *is a person at* t_2*, then under what circumstances is* y *identical to* x*?*

Still, there may be further problems. To begin with, consider the following example.[2] Suppose a man lives a long life and then dies. Suppose his body is then preserved as a mummy for several hundred years, before it is rearranged in various ways and (somewhat miraculously) reanimated by a very powerful being with a strange agenda. But suppose that the resulting person is a woman, who has no memories of the life of the earlier man, and who has a personality that is completely different from his.

Some of us will want to say that in this case there is a single thing in the story that is a man at the beginning, a mummy in the middle, and a woman at the end. But some of us will also want to say that the woman in question is not the same person as the man. (Partly because of the long period when the mummy was not alive, partly because of the woman's lack of any memories of the man's experiences, and partly because of the personality differences.) Unfortunately, however, The "Classical-Identity" Characterization of our problem (as well as the above variation on that characterization) will not permit us to say both of these things, and will in fact entail that any theory of personal identity according to which there is a single thing in the story, but the woman is not the same person as the man, is automatically false.

That is one objection that can be raised against the two classical-identity characterizations of our problem. There is another objection, which has to do with the notion of a "substance concept." The substance concept of an object is, roughly, the answer that it would be most informative to give in response to the question "What is it?" as applied to that object. More precisely, the substance concept of an object is the property, among

---

[2] The example, and some of the points below, are borrowed from Markosian, "Identifying the Problem of Personal Identity."

the many properties possessed by that object, that determines the object's persistence conditions.

Here is the alleged problem. The questions raised by The "Classical-Identity" Characterization of The Problem of Personal Identity and the above variation on that characterization are fine questions to ask, provided that we want to say that *person* is our substance concept. But they are not the most perspicuous questions to ask if we want to allow that that *person* may not be our substance concept. (For in that case, they amount to asking: *What are the persistence conditions for the things that may be, but need not be, human people?*) And many philosophers want to say something like the following: (i) *physical object* is our substance concept, so that our persistence conditions are whatever are the persistence conditions for physical objects; (ii) it makes sense to talk about whether *x* is the same person as *y*; and (iii) such talk is not merely about the identity relation holding between an *x* and a *y* in cases in which *x* is a person. Such philosophers, then, will have to look elsewhere for an acceptable characterization of the problem of personal identity.

One natural place to look is toward the view known as Four-Dimensionalism, according to which each physical object that persists through time does so in virtue of having different temporal parts at the different moments at which it is present.[3] If we assume that Four-Dimensionalism is the correct account of persistence, then we should say that each person is a fusion of many different temporal parts. A temporal part of a person is also known as a *person-stage*. A Four-Dimensionalist will understand 'person *x* at t_1' and 'person *y* at t_2' to refer to two different person-stages; and if they happen to be stages of the same person, then the Four-Dimensionalist will say that the two stages stand in the *different stages of a single person* relation. For the Four-Dimensionalist, then, our problem can be characterized as follows:

> *The Four-Dimensionalist Characterization of the Problem of Personal Identity*
> The problem of personal identity is the problem raised by the following question: *If* x *is a person-stage at* t_1 *and* y *is a person-stage at* t_2*, then under what circumstances are* x *and* y *related by the* different stages of a single person *relation?*

---

[3] For more on Four-Dimensionalism, see Chapter 7 below.

Notice that the Four-Dimensionalist has given us a way of making sense of talk about a *same person* relation: it is the *different stages of a single person* relation which appears to be unproblematic. But notice also that the relation the Four-Dimensionalist has given us to focus on is, strictly speaking, a relation between person-stages rather than a relation between people.

In any case, on the Four-Dimensionalist approach, what is wanted for the purposes of dealing with the transporter case is a theory about the circumstances under which the person-stage who pushes the green button in the booth in New York and the person-stage who emerges from the booth in Paris are stages of a single person. And what is wanted in the Will Martinez case is a theory about what would make it true that the ten-year-old Will Martinez person-stage and a particular one of the many candidate person-stages lined up outside the billionaire's office are stages of a single person.

In light of all of this, it seems clear that The Four-Dimensionalist Characterization is a great way to characterize our problem, provided Four-Dimensionalism is the right view of persistence. So Four-Dimensionalists should be perfectly well satisfied with The Four-Dimensionalist Characterization of the Problem of Personal Identity. But Three-Dimensionalists (who reject the ontology of temporal parts) should not be.[4]

Given how satisfying The Four-Dimensionalist Characterization is for the Four-Dimensionalist, it is worth exploring whether there is a way to make sense of talk of a *same person* (or *same car*, and so on) relation in a way that is based on Four-Dimensionalist thinking about such matters, but that does not presuppose an ontology of temporal parts. And we think, in fact, that there is. We think that some sense can be made of the ideas of *same person*, *same car*, *same storm*, and so forth, and also that there is something to the traditional philosopher's project of attempting to give, at least for some sortal predicates, persistence conditions for things falling under those sortals.

In order to do so, the Three-Dimensionalist needs only to make a small number of independently plausible background assumptions. One of these is that there are such things as properties and relations. Another is that properties and relations are sometimes instantiated (as when, for example, a particular leaf is green at noon on July 31, 1993). The third

---

[4] For more on Three-Dimensionalism, see Chapter 7 below.

main background assumption is that these instantiations typically persist over some period of time (as when the leaf being green begins in May and lasts until sometime in October). And the final background assumption is that these persisting instantiations – these episodes of properties and relations – are like events insofar as they, unlike physical objects, persist over time in virtue of having different temporal parts. (We take it that this is perfectly consistent with the Three-Dimensionalist's central claim, namely, that it is not the case that *physical objects* persist in virtue of having different temporal parts at different times.)

Given these background assumptions, it makes sense to ask, of a particular object having a certain property at a given time and, say, the same object having the same property at a different time, whether these two instantiations of the relevant property are parts of a single episode of that property. Is Ned's shirt being blue at noon today part of the same episode of blueness as his shirt being blue at noon two weeks ago, or was the shirt perhaps dyed red for some of the intervening time? Or, considering the case involving the mummy discussed above, is this woman being a person at this later time a part of the same episode of personhood as that man being a person at the earlier time? (According to what we were suggesting in our previous discussion of the case, the most plausible answer to this question, given the details of the case, is No, despite the fact that there is a single thing involved in the case, which is a man and a person at the earlier time and a woman and a person at the later time.)

This line of thought suggests that the following may be a good way to characterize our problem of personal identity:

> *The Episodic Characterization of The Problem of Personal Identity*
> The problem of personal identity is the problem raised by the following question: *If x is a person at t_1 and y is a person at t_2, then under what circumstances are x's instantiation of personhood at t_1 and y's instantiation of personhood at t_2 parts of a single episode of personhood?*

The Episodic Characterization has at least three points in its favor. The first is that it allows us to make sense of talk of a *same person* relation (as well as a *same φ* relation, for many other instances of φ). The second is that it does not confuse classical identity with any other relation. And the third is that it is consistent with both The Four-Dimensionalist view of persistence and The Three-Dimensionalist view of persistence.

The main disadvantage of The Episodic Characterization is that it comes with certain Platonistic presuppositions about properties, instantiations of properties, and episodes. Those with nominalistic leanings will of course find these commitments objectionable, and may wonder whether there is any way of tweaking the view so as to retain its advantages without the controversial presuppositions. But those who do not mind the Platonistic presuppositions should find The Episodic Characterization a very attractive way of framing the problem of personal identity.

We have seen that there are various ways of characterizing the problem of personal identity, with each characterization focusing on a specific question. But is one characterization the best? Is one of the relevant questions more important, or clearer, or more closely connected with what philosophers should have in mind when they talk about personal identity? Perhaps. But we think that there is no need to decide which of the relevant questions we should take to be the focus of the problem of personal identity. For surely each one of the five questions in question is interesting in its own right. Each one is such that any reasonable philosopher would love to have a good answer to it. And each one has something to do with the general idea of personal identity. So we say, let all of these five questions be considered relevant to The Problem of Personal Identity. As we will understand it, then, The Problem of Personal Identity is the problem raised by the various questions mentioned in all of the above characterizations of the problem.[5] And as we will understand the problem, any self-respecting theory of personal identity should provide answers to at least some of the above five questions.

5.3 Physical approaches to personal identity

Take an easy case. Suppose that in addition to the photo of the ten-year-old Will Martinez, we have (somewhat surprisingly) a long, unbroken sequence of video footage that clearly shows, near its beginning, young Will playing with the future billionaire, and that stays focused on Will for

---

[5] One caveat: the Three-Dimensionalist should leave the Four-Dimensionalist Characterization off the list.

fifty years, taking us (the viewers) right up to a live shot of the sixty-year-old Will as he sits among the candidates waiting outside the billionaire's office. (Suppose we're able to fast-forward the videotape in order to start from the beginning and catch up to the live shot in a matter of several days.) Such a videotape would certainly establish that the relevant sixty-year-old candidate is the real Will Martinez.

But why, exactly? Well, because the videotape would allow us to track the real Will Martinez through (virtually) every moment from the time he was a ten-year-old until the present. There he is, on the videotape, from one moment to the next. One moral we might draw from this example is that the correct theory of personal identity will be in terms of the kind of spatio-temporal continuity that is captured by our videotape. If we draw this moral from the example, then we will probably find something like the following theory of personal identity to be plausible. (Note: we formulate The Spatio-Temporal Theory as an answer to the question posed in The Traditional Characterization of the Problem of Personal Identity, but we trust that it will be clear to readers how the theory could be formulated in response to the other characterizations of that problem. Similar remarks apply to the other theories of personal identity considered below.)

The Spatio-Temporal Continuity Theory of Personal Identity
If x is a person at t_1 and y is a person at t_2, then y is the same person as x iff there is the right kind of spatio-temporal continuity between x and y.

On the other hand, we might draw a different moral from the videotape example. We might think that what makes it easy to know who the real Will Martinez is at the end of the videotape story is the fact that we have been tracking this one particular human body for the entire period since he was a ten-year-old. If we take this moral from the example, then we will likely be attracted to the following theory of personal identity:

The Same-Body Theory of Personal Identity
If x is a person at t_1 and y is a person at t_2, then y is the same person as x iff x and y have the same body.[6]

There are, however, powerful objections to both The Spatio-Temporal Continuity Theory and The Same-Body Theory. Here is one. Suppose that

[6] For a discussion of a view like The Same-Body Theory, see Thomson, "People and Their Bodies."

some evil but powerful and incredibly advanced brain scientists kidnap the two authors of this book, surgically remove John's brain from his body, do the same thing to Ned, and then successfully implant John's brain into Ned's body and Ned's brain into John's body. The result of these nefarious actions is a person who looks just like John but thinks just like Ned, and another person who looks just like Ned but thinks just like John. And it appears that both The Spatio-Temporal Continuity Theory and The Same-Body Theory yield the result that the person who looks like John after the brain-swapping *is* John, and the one who looks like Ned *is* Ned.[7]

Meanwhile, we take it that most people will say the opposite. Most people, we take it, will say that in this example, John's identity goes with John's brain, and similarly with Ned's identity. (After all, John's family, after getting over the initial shock, will welcome the character with Ned's body and John's brain into their home more readily than they will welcome the character with Ned's brain and John's body.) In fact, most people will want to describe the case as more of a *body-transplant* case than a *brain-transplant* case.

If this is right, then it will behoove us to consider the following theory of personal identity:

The Same-Brain Theory of Personal Identity
If x is a person at t_1 and y is a person at t_2, then y is the same person as x iff x and y have the same brain.

The Same-Brain Theory does seem to get better results in cases like the body transplant than either The Spatio-Temporal Continuity Theory or The Same-Body Theory. That is certainly good news. But there are two objections to all three of these physical theories of personal identity. First, recall the continuous videotape connecting the ten-year-old Will Martinez with one of the grown-up candidates. But now suppose that when we slow down the videotape, we can see a ten-second period in which the twenty-five-year-old Will pauses and his eyes roll up into his head. And suppose that after this eye-rolling episode we seem to observe a person with a completely different personality, who apparently has no memories of any

---

[7] There is room for the proponent of The Spatio-Temporal Continuity Theory to insist that when "the right kind of spatio-temporal continuity between x and y" is properly understood, his or her theory will give the intuitively correct result in the brain-transplant case.

experiences from before the eye-rolling episode. And suppose, moreover, we learn that the same nefarious brain scientists from our earlier example have, using subtle laser technology, dramatically reconfigured the brain of the man we are watching during that ten-second, eye-rolling episode. Then it will be plausible to say that what we have in this case is spatio-temporal continuity, sameness of body, and sameness of brain, but without personal identity. And if this is right, then we have here a counterexample to all three of the physical theories above.[8]

Here is another possible counterexample. Suppose it turns out that people do in fact have souls. And suppose we learn that at a certain point in the Will Martinez videotape, the body we are watching suddenly has its soul snatched away. Perhaps there was, as in the previous example, a tell-tale eye-rolling episode; and perhaps we somehow learn, through a very reliable source, that that was the moment when young Will's soul was snatched away from his body. Moreover, suppose further that the body in question – young Will's body – immediately gets a new soul, with a completely different personality, and with no memories of any of Will's experiences. Then it would be tempting (again) to say that what we have in this case is spatio-temporal continuity, sameness of body, and sameness of brain. But surely we should not say, in the imagined circumstance, that the person who results from the soul-replacement is the same person as the young Will. In other words, it seems clear that in this case we have spatio-temporal continuity, sameness of body, and sameness of brain, but without personal identity.

This last example suggests that we might want to try formulating a theory of personal identity based on the assumption that we human people do in fact have non-physical souls.

---

[8] This claim needs to be qualified. The eye-rolling case may not be a counterexample to either The Same-Body Theory, The Spatio-Temporal Theory, or The Same-Brain Theory, if those theories are understood as attempts to answer the questions raised by the "Classical-Identity" characterizations of our problem. For understood in that way, the relevant theories merely say that the pre-eye-roll Will is (classically) identical to the post-eye-roll Will, and that claim need not conflict with the intuition that pre-eye-roll Will and post-eye-roll Will are not *the same person*.

5.4 Soulful approaches to personal identity

If you are a Dualist or an Idealist, or, more generally, if you believe in souls, then a certain picture of personal identity is likely to appeal to you. On this picture, what a younger version of you and an older version of you have in common is your soul. The reason that the person reading this book today is the same person your mother gave birth to some years ago is that you have the same soul as that newborn baby.

Here is a natural way to capture this idea:

The Same-Soul Theory of Personal Identity
If x is a person at t_1 and y is a person at t_2, then y is the same person as x iff x and y have the same soul.

Of course, one objection to The Same-Soul Theory that many people will have is that it is based on a mistake. For many people reject the thesis that there are souls. But we take it that, at least among people who are leaning toward belief in a soul (i.e., among those who are leaning toward some form of Dualism or Idealism), The Same-Soul Theory has a great deal of initial plausibility. It turns out, however, that, even granting for the sake of argument that we all have souls, there are still some surprisingly persuasive objections to the view.

One such objection is raised by John Locke in his influential *An Essay Concerning Human Understanding*.[9] Here is a variation on Locke's objection. Suppose it turns out that you happen to have a soul that has been recycled: your soul – the very one that currently animates your body – was previously connected with a man named Nestor who was present at the siege of Troy. Then according to The Same-Soul Theory, you and Nestor will be the same person. But suppose that (as is no doubt the case) you have absolutely no memory of the siege of Troy, or any of Nestor's experiences. In fact, suppose you don't have even the slightest inkling of your soul ever having been associated with another body in a previous life. Then the verdict yielded by The Same-Soul Theory, that you are the same person as Nestor, seems wrong. For it is natural to think that, even in these circumstances, you are not Nestor.

---

[9] See Book II, chapter XXVII.

To make the problem seem especially acute, focus on the very plausible claim that questions of personal identity have a great deal to do with moral responsibility. And suppose that Nestor committed some horrific acts during his lifetime. Are you the person who committed those acts? Are you morally responsible for them? (There are of course ways for the proponent of The Same-Soul Theory to avoid the consequence that, in the imagined scenario, you are responsible for Nestor's misdeeds. But they may involve saying controversial things about personal responsibility.)

Here is one last objection to The Same-Soul Theory.[10] Suppose it turns out that you are sharing your soul with a man on the other side of the world, in such a way that when you are awake, he is asleep, and when he is awake, you are asleep. (Perhaps it is a man who gets an unusual amount of sleep.) That is, your soul actually leaves your body when you sleep and migrates over to this other body on the other side of the planet. But suppose that you never have any memories of his actions, nor does he have any memories of yours. And suppose that you and this man with whom you are sharing a soul have personalities that are polar opposites of one another: you are kind, intelligent, curious, and caring, while he is unkind, stupid, incurious, and uncaring. On The Same-Soul Theory, you and the man with whom you share a soul are the same person. So on that view, you spend a good deal of time each night on the other side of the world, having experiences and performing actions that you never recall when you are over here. This too will seem to many people like a bad consequence of The Same-Soul Theory.

Some proponents of The Same-Soul Theory might be motivated by these last two objections to modify the theory. The idea would be to get around the above objections by making the possession of memories of one's soul's previous experiences an additional necessary condition for personal identity. Here is one way such a theory could go:

The Same-Soul plus Memories Theory of Personal Identity
If x is a person at t_1 and y is a person at t_2, then y is the same person as x iff (i) x and y have the same soul, and (ii) y has memories at t_2 of some of x's experiences at t_1.

It's clear that Materialists, who do not believe in souls, will have to find an alternative to the same-soul approach. And the objections involving

---

[10] This one is also based on an objection raised by Locke in the same chapter.

the recycling and sharing of souls seem to point toward some kind of psychological criterion for personal identity. Additional pressure to move in the direction of a psychological criterion for personal identity comes from one of the objections raised above to the various physical approaches to personal identity, namely, the one that involved a human being whose brain is radically rearranged in such a way that he suddenly gets a completely new and utterly different personality. So it is in that direction that we now turn.

5.5 Psychological approaches to personal identity

There are several different ways to incorporate psychological criteria into a theory of personal identity. One natural way is to make the having of memories a necessary and sufficient condition for personal identity, in the manner of The Same-Soul plus Memories Theory, but to do away with the same-soul requirement. Here is a formulation of such a view:

> *The Simple Memory Theory of Personal Identity*
> If x is a person at t_1 and y is a person at t_2, then y is the same person as x iff y has memories at t_2 of some of x's experiences at t_1.

There is an obvious problem with The Simple Memory Theory. Most of us do not have perfect memories. We have forgotten whole days, complete weeks, or even entire months of our own lives. For example, it is quite likely that there is some past time, t, such that you were a person at t, but you have no memories now of your experiences at t. Still, we all think that you are the same person as the person who had the relevant experiences at t. We think that there is one person – you – who both had the experiences then and fails to remember them now.

Just as the problem is obvious, so is the basic idea behind the solution. What is needed, in order to preserve the spirit of The Simple Memory Theory, is to relax the memory requirement just a little bit. We should not require, in order for y (who is a person at t_2) to be the same person as x (who is a person at t_1), that y have memories at t_2 of x's experiences at t_1. Instead, we should allow, for example, that there be some person, z, and some in-between time, t, such that z has memories at t of x's experiences at t_1, and y has memories at t_2 of z's experiences at t. More generally, we should allow for a series of such times and people and memories that connect x at t_1, on one end of the series, with y at t_2, on the other end. Let's say that if there is such a series connecting x at t_1 with y at t_2 then x and y are *memory-connected*. Then we can formulate the relevant theory of personal identity as follows:

> *The Memory-Connected Theory of Personal Identity*
> If x is a person at t_1 and y is a person at t_2, then y is the same person as x iff x and y are *memory-connected*.

The Memory-Connected Theory yields plausible results in a wide variety of cases. But the theory is likely to face several objections. One objection challenges the claim that being memory-connected is necessary for personal identity. Imagine a case involving a man who suffers total amnesia, perhaps as a result of a head injury. He regains consciousness, and has the same personality as before, but is unable to remember anything about his previous life. He can't even remember his family. Still, his loved ones crowd into his hospital room, eager to see him, and they subsequently devote hours, days, and even months to helping him with his recovery. As they do so they are completely convinced that the man they are now dealing with is the same person they knew before the injury. Is it possible for them to be right about this? Not according to The Memory-Connected Theory.

Or take a less exotic case. Suppose you go out drinking one night, have a few too many, and then have a few more. Suppose you then do some very embarrassing and inappropriate things that you would normally never do. And, finally, suppose that in the morning (and ever after) you have absolutely no memories at all of your drunken, embarrassing behavior. Then according to The Memory-Connected Theory, it was not you who did those things; and so, presumably, you (the later you, that is) are not morally responsible for the drunken actions that you cannot remember. To many of us this seems like the wrong result: surely it is not that easy to get out of being morally responsible for wrongful actions.[11]

Another objection to The Memory-Connected Theory begins with the drawing of a distinction between apparent memories and genuine

---

[11] We are overlooking several interesting ways for the proponent of The Memory-Connected Theory to respond to this objection while still sticking to the essential idea behind that theory. We encourage the reader to explore such ways on his or her own.

memories. Apparent memories are memories held by people who may or may not have actually had the experiences "remembered," whereas genuine memories are strictly the real deal.

Given this distinction, we can ask the proponent of The Memory-Connected Theory whether apparent memories are sufficient for personal identity, or whether, instead, what are required are genuine memories. If the answer given is that apparent memories suffice, then there seem to be various counterexamples to the theory. For example, suppose that some evil brain scientists scramble the brains of two people, Simon and Paula, with the result that the one who now looks like Simon retains his personality but now has all of Paula's memories, and vice versa. Surely we do not want to say that after the brain-scrambling, the person who now has Simon's memories and Paula's personality (and body) is the same person as the one who was Simon before the scrambling. (We may in fact want to say that neither Simon nor Paula has survived the scrambling, but in any case the verdict forced on us by The Memory-Connected Theory, namely, that the person who now looks like Simon is in fact Paula, seems pretty clearly wrong.)

On the other hand, if the proponent of The Memory-Connected Theory says that the kind of memories required for personal identity are genuine memories, then we can ask him or her what determines whether a particular memory is genuine as opposed to merely apparent. And it seems like the most straightforward answer would be that genuine memories are memories such that the person having the memory is the same person as the one who had the remembered experience. But if the Memory-Connected Theorist gives this answer, then his or her theory has become blatantly circular.

In light of this, it seems to us that the only viable (read: non-circular) version of The Memory-Connected Theory will be one that makes apparent memories sufficient for personal identity. But then, as noted above, there will be various potential counterexamples. Our view is that all of these considerations show that proponents of taking a psychological approach to personal identity should eschew any theory that uses memories as the sole factor in determining personal identity, and should instead appeal to some additional psychological (or even physical) criteria. For example, it might be thought that what is required for personal identity is not just memory-connectedness but also similarity in personality and general flow of consciousness.

In order to appreciate the plausibility of this idea, consider the following example. Suppose that yet another company, 1-Second Travel, is offering even faster trips to Paris, with a new and improved transporter machine. Here's how 1-Second Travel's transporter machine works. You step into a booth similar to 15-Minute Travel's booths, and your body is scanned and blueprinted in the same way. But then your body is instantaneously converted from matter into energy, and that energy is then beamed, at speeds approaching the speed of light, to the destination location, where it is then instantaneously converted back into matter, according to the blueprint. 1-Second Travel's brochure boasts that they will get you to Paris much faster than 15-Minute Travel can; and not only that, but their service is considerably cheaper, at 99 cents each way (or $1.49 for the round trip). Finally, suppose that, as with 15-Minute Travel, 1-Second Travel has millions of satisfied customers who swear by the company's results.

If your intuition is that 15-Minute Travel is offering a good deal, then you should be even more excited about 1-Second Travel. For with 1-Second, there is a much shorter loss of consciousness (but still some physical continuity). Not to mention what you will save in time and money.

You might worry about that one-second gap in your conscious life that will occur if you choose 1-Second Travel. (If so, you were probably never tempted by 15-Minute Travel in the first place, since their system involves a full fifteen-minute loss of consciousness.) But 1-Second Travel helpfully points out that in every person's life, including people who never partake of 1-Second Travel's services, there are countless gaps in consciousness. After all, people normally sleep at night, with long periods of non-consciousness. And some people even get knocked unconscious, or go into comas, and so forth. In most of those cases, the gap is way more extreme than in the case of 1-Second Travel's transporter machine. Not only that, but it's safe to say that all of those naturally occurring gaps in consciousness result in much more psychologically significant breaks than those produced by 1-Second's machine. (For when one regains consciousness after a deep sleep, or being knocked out, or being in a coma, one is almost never in a conscious state that is anything close to the state one was in right before losing consciousness.)

Consideration of 1-Second Travel raises some questions similar to ones we have already considered. For example: if 1-Second Travel's transporter machine were real, would it be a good idea to sign up for their service?

And: if you did use their service, would it be you who stepped out of the machine in Paris?

But notice that there will be the right kind of psychological continuity between you in New York and the person who will emerge from the booth in Paris. So if you like the psychological approach to personal identity, then you should presumably think that 1-Second Travel's service is a good way to get to Paris. And in that case, you should think that having your body disassembled and converted to energy is consistent with your continuing to exist later on. (This is an important point that we will return to below.)

Meanwhile, here is yet another example. Suppose that a still newer company, Instantaneous Travel, is offering even faster trips to Paris, with its own new and improved transporter machine. Here's how the Instantaneous Travel transporter machine works. You step into a booth similar to 1-Second Travel's booths, and your body is scanned and blueprinted in the same way. But then, at exactly the same instant, two things happen: (1) in New York, your body is entirely disassembled, so that in the place where your body was, there is only a loose pile of "particle dust"; and (2) in Paris, some handy particles are rearranged according to your blueprint so that they compose a particle-for-particle duplicate of you at the exact moment of your disassembly in New York.[12] Moreover, suppose that Instantaneous Travel is even less expensive than 1-Second Travel, charging a mere 39 cents each way. Not only that, but Instantaneous boasts that theirs is the only service available featuring complete psychological continuity without any temporal gaps, so that, on their plan, you never have to worry about going out of existence for even a fraction of a second. Finally, suppose that, as with 15-Minute Travel and 1-Second Travel, Instantaneous Travel has millions of satisfied customers who swear by the company's results.

---

[12] Some readers will wonder how the assembly in Paris can be simultaneous with the disassembly in New York, given the universal speed limit (namely, the speed of light), which applies to any method of transmitting information. Three possible answers: (i) Instantaneous Travel has developed sophisticated software that allows them to predict, based on your blueprint at the time of the scanning, and with unfailing accuracy, exactly how your every particle will be arranged a second later, at the time of the simultaneous disassembly (in New York) and reassembly (in Paris); (ii) the example concerns a universe very much like ours, but with slightly different laws of nature that do allow for the instantaneous transmission of information; or (iii) Instantaneous Travel actually offers merely near-instantaneous travel.

Some familiar questions arise concerning this new technology. First: if Instantaneous Travel's transporter machine were real, would it be a good idea to sign up for their service? Second: if you did use their service, would it be you who stepped out of the machine in Paris?

Notice, again, that there will be the right kind of psychological continuity between you in New York and the person who shows up in Paris. In fact, as Instantaneous advertises, the psychological continuity is even better in their case than it is in the case of 1-Second Travel, since there will be no temporal gap at all between your conscious life in New York and the conscious life of the person in Paris. So if you like the psychological approach, then you should actually prefer Instantaneous Travel's method over 1-Second Travel's.

The downside to Instantaneous Travel's program, of course, is that there is no physical continuity at all between the person who steps into the booth in New York and the one who emerges in Paris. This makes consideration of the different services offered by Instantaneous Travel and 1-Second Travel an especially good test case for determining whether one's intuitions support a purely physical criterion for personal identity, a purely psychological criterion, or some combination of the two.

The Psychological Continuity Theory is based on the intuition that Instantaneous Travel is a good way to go. Let us understand psychological continuity between x at t_1 and y at t_2 as involving some combination of memory-connectedness, personality-connectedness (which will be like memory-connectedness, but incorporating more of the features that go toward determining someone's personality), and general flow of consciousness (pretending we have some idea what that means) between x at t_1 and y at t_2. Then The Psychological Continuity Theory can be formulated as follows:

The Psychological Continuity Theory of Personal Identity
If x is a person at t_1 and y is a person at t_2, then y is the same person as x iff there is the right kind of psychological continuity between x at t_1 and y at t_2.[13]

(We leave unspecified the details concerning what exactly the notion of psychological continuity amounts to, but we take it that the central

---

[13] For defenses of views like The Psychological Continuity Theory, see, for example, Lewis, "Survival and Identity"; and Parfit, *Reasons and Persons*.

idea is clear enough without further elucidation.) If you like psychological approaches to personal identity in general, then The Psychological Continuity Theory is probably appealing to you. But there may be problems with the theory. For example, suppose you push the green button in the booth in New York and disappear, according to plan. And suppose that, also according to plan, someone who looks just like you appears in the booth in Paris at exactly the same instant. So far, so good. But now suppose that there is a glitch in the system, with the result that at the same instant that you disappear in New York and your look-alike appears in Paris, another look-alike pops into an Instantaneous Travel booth in Rio de Janeiro (which, as it happens, is another destination you have always wanted to visit).

Now a question arises: which one is you? On the one hand, the Rio and Paris look-alikes are both psychologically continuous with the original you in New York; so according to The Psychological Continuity Theory, each one is you. But on the other hand, it's natural to think that you can't be in two places at the same time; so there is a strong reason not to say that the two look-alikes in Rio and Paris are both you. (Moreover, the Paris and Rio look-alikes are clearly not identical to each other, which means that, by the transitivity of identity, they cannot both be identical to the original you.)

It's obvious that something has to give here, but it's not obvious what. Perhaps the proponent of The Psychological Continuity Theory can put enough weight on the notion of *the right kind of psychological continuity* to solve this problem, without in the end offering a circular theory. Or perhaps there are other ways of modifying the theory to deal with this kind of example.

In the next section we will encounter another objection to The Psychological Continuity Theory, which some philosophers take to be the most serious objection facing that theory. But first we will examine one of the main rivals of the psychological approach to personal identity.

5.6 Biological approaches to personal identity

Just as proponents of the psychological approach claim that psychological factors are essential to personal identity, so proponents of the biological approach claim that biological factors are the key. The main example of this approach is The Same-Life Theory of Personal Identity, which is developed and defended (under a different name) by Eric Olson in his book, *The Human Animal*. The basic idea behind this theory is that you will persist for as long as your life continues, and no longer, and that in order for a person to be the same person as some earlier person, the later person must be the same organism as the earlier one. There are three crucial presuppositions behind this view: (i) that there are such events as lives, (ii) that a life can persist over a longish period of time, and (iii) that we can talk sensibly about a particular life that's going on at one time being *the same life* as a certain life that was going on at an earlier time.

Here is a way of formulating this view.[14]

The Same-Life Theory of Personal Identity
If x is a person at t_1 and y is a person at t_2, then y is the same person as x iff x's life at t_1 and y's life at t_2 are the same life.

We'll be able to understand this view better if we examine some of its consequences, and we can do that by looking at the results yielded by The Same-Life Theory for some of the different puzzle cases we have considered so far. Let's begin with the original transporter case, involving the services offered by 15-Minute Travel. Here the main question facing the proponent of The Same-Life Theory is whether to say that a human life is the kind of event that can be temporally gappy, and can jump across an ocean. If the proponent of The Same-Life Theory says that a human life cannot do these things, then he or she must say that your life ends when you are disassembled in New York, and that a new life begins when the transport dust is assembled according to your blueprint in Paris. If this is what he or she says, then he or she should also say that the person who comes out of the booth in Paris is not you.

On the other hand, if the proponent of The Same-Life Theory says that a human life is the kind of event that can be temporally gappy, and can

---

[14] Olson prefers the "Classical-Identity" characterization of the problem of personal identity, according to which the problem involves a question about the circumstances under which a thing that is a person at one time is identical to a thing (maybe a person, maybe not) that exists at a later time. And his biological approach to this problem is to say that a thing that is a person at one time and a thing that exists at a later time are identical just in case they are the same organism. Thus Olson would not build the requirement that y be a person at t_2 into the formulation of his view.

jump in a spatially discontinuous way, then he or she is free to say that when your body is disassembled in New York, your life does not end but is instead merely temporarily suspended – and that it resumes in Paris when the relevant particles are reassembled in the booth there. If he or she take this route, then he or she should also say that it is you who emerges from the booth in Paris.

Similar remarks will be true of The Same-Life Theory and the various other transporter cases we have looked at. In each such case, there will be an underlying question about the persistence conditions for the kind of event that we call a life, and the proponent of The Same-Life Theory will be free to answer that question in any one of several different ways. Moreover, depending on how he or she answers that question about the persistence conditions for lives, the proponent of The Same-Life Theory will be free to say that the person who walks out of the booth in the destination location is you, and also free to say that the person in the destination booth is not you.

We don't have any decisive argument for this claim but, for what it is worth, our intuitions tell us that a human life is not the kind of event that can be temporally gappy and spatially discontinuous in the way that would allow the proponent of The Same-Life Theory to declare any of the transporter machines a safe way to travel. So our view is that proponents of that theory should resolve never to step into any such transporter machine.

What about The Same-Life Theory and the case of Will Martinez? Well, at most one of the many Will-candidates will be such that his life is the continuation of the ten-year-old Will's life.[15] And if there is such a candidate, then it is a consequence of The Same-Life Theory that that is the one the billionaire is looking for. Otherwise, the theory entails that none of the candidates is the real Will.

Finally, consider the cases that were problematic for The Same-Soul Theory, such as the one involving you sharing a soul with a man on the other side of the world, and the example in which you have the recycled soul of Nestor from ancient times. There is no reason at all to think that your life and the life of the man on the other side of the world with whom

---

[15] Assuming that a life cannot undergo fission (see below), that is. If it can, and if Will's has, then perhaps the right thing to say is that each one of two or more of the candidates is the same person as Will.

you share a soul are the same life. (After all, even when you are asleep and unconscious, you are still alive; and similarly for your "soulmate" in the example.) Nor is there any reason to believe that your life now is the continuation of Nestor's life (even given that your soul is the same one that was connected with his body during the siege of Troy). So The Same-Life Theory does not have implausible consequences regarding the shared-soul and recycled-soul cases we have considered.

All of these results (regarding the transporter cases, the Will Martinez case, and the soul cases) strike us as eminently defensible, and we take them to provide some evidence in favor of The Same-Life Theory. There are nevertheless some interesting objections to the theory. One such objection concerns the possibility (mentioned above) of a brain-transplant case. Suppose your brain is removed from your head and placed in the body of a man called Corpo. And suppose that Corpo's brain is likewise removed from his head and placed in your body. Finally, suppose that all the while this brain-swapping procedure is taking place, both of the brains involved remain conscious, and both of the bodies remain alive.[16]

Now, the natural thing to say about such a case is that the person who comes out of the operating room looking like Corpo but thinking like you is in fact you, and that the person who comes out looking like you but thinking like Corpo is actually Corpo. In fact, consideration of how your brain and Corpo's brain (not to mention your loved ones and Corpo's loved ones) would think about the two people who emerged from the procedure makes it pretty clear that this would not really be a brain-transplant case at all. Instead, it would be a body-transplant case. For your identity would go with your brain, and Corpo's with his brain; so that what really happens in the example is that you and Corpo exchange bodies. (Or so it seems to us.)

The proponent of The Same-Life Theory must apparently say otherwise. For it looks as if the Same-Life Theorist is committed to saying that you would survive the procedure, and would come out of it looking like you

---

[16] We are oversimplifying matters here. It is not clear that the example, as described, is biologically possible. For a human body cannot remain alive without getting some regulatory input from some part of its brain. So perhaps the bodies in the example would need artificial brain stems to keep them going during the procedure. Or perhaps the two brain stems could remain with their original bodies throughout the procedure while the other parts of the brains get swapped.

but thinking like Corpo. After all, in the example your body remains alive throughout the entire process.

We suggested earlier that human lives cannot be temporally gappy and spatially discontinuous in a way that would allow the proponent of The Same-Life Theory to approve of any of the transporter machines considered above. But some people are convinced that transporter machines (at least some of them, anyway) would be a great way to travel. Meanwhile, we have just seen that The Same-Life Theory has consequences regarding the body transplant case that seem counterintuitive. It is worth noting, then, that there is another theory, loosely based on The Same-Life Theory, that seems to fare much better on both of these scores.

What is most distinctive about The Same-Life Theory, as compared to alternatives like The Same-Soul, Same-Body, and Same-Brain theories, is the emphasis it places on a certain kind of event (namely, a life), rather than a certain kind of thing (a soul, a body, and so on), in determining when personal identity is maintained. But other kinds of event might be used for this same purpose. Take, for example, the ongoing and rather complicated event that is your mental life, also known as your consciousness. This is presumably an event that has been going on since sometime before you were born, and that can be both temporally gappy and spatially discontinuous. Now consider the following theory about personal identity.[17]

> *The Same-Consciousness Theory of Personal Identity*
> If x is a person at t_1 and y is a person at t_2, then y is the same person as x iff x's conscious state at t_1 and y's conscious state at t_2 are parts of the same consciousness.

No doubt there will be many hard questions facing the proponent of this theory about exactly what kind of event a consciousness is, what it takes for such an event to persist over time, and under what circumstances it will be true that x's conscious state at t_1 and y's conscious state at t_2 are parts of the same consciousness.

---

[17] Although Locke is widely interpreted as defending some kind of memory or psychological continuity theory, he does make some remarks in chapter XXVII of Book II of *An Essay Concerning Human Understanding* that suggest that he may have actually endorsed something like The Same-Consciousness Theory.

But still, this theory does give fairly plausible results in a wide variety of cases. In general, it captures what we seem to care about when we are concerned for our survival, insofar as that concern appears to be focused mainly on our continuing to have conscious states suitably related to our present conscious states. That is, our concern about survival appears to be chiefly about our remaining conscious or, if we lose consciousness, regaining consciousness. (We also care a lot about the quality of our future conscious life, of course. But that concern is still grounded in a concern for the continuation of our consciousness.)

The Same-Consciousness Theory also seems to yield a sensible verdict in the Will Martinez case. For it is natural to think that in order for a Will-candidate to be the real Will, his current conscious states must be the proper descendants of the ten-year-old Will's conscious states. And the same goes for the body transplant case: it's natural to think that your personal identity in that case goes with your consciousness, which is why the recovering patient who looks like Corpo but thinks like you is actually you (even though it does seem as if your life goes with the other patient).

All of this seems to count in favor of The Same-Consciousness Theory. What about that theory and the transporter cases? Here the proponent of The Same-Consciousness Theory must decide what he or she thinks about the persistence conditions for the type of event known as a consciousness. Such an event can presumably be temporally gappy and spatially discontinuous, which means that the proponent of the theory need not automatically rule out the possibility that personal identity is maintained when one uses a transporter machine. But those cases certainly do raise interesting and hard questions about the persistence conditions for a consciousness. (Although it is worth noting that the same questions are raised for everyone, and not merely for the proponent of The Same-Consciousness Theory – it's just that much more rides on the answers to those questions for the proponent of that particular theory.)

One main objection that can be brought against The Same-Consciousness Theory is that it immediately gives rise to a question that its proponents cannot answer. The question is one that was noted above, namely, under what circumstances will it be true that x's conscious state at t_1 and y's conscious state at t_2 are parts of the same consciousness? If the Same-Consciousness theorist says that there are no criteria for consciousness identity, then he or she has merely replaced the mystery of personal identity with a different mystery; and if he or she attempts to give criteria for consciousness identity, then he or she is likely to be at a loss, since no one seems to be able to come up with a working theory of consciousness identity.

Here is another objection, one that works equally well against both The Same-Consciousness Theory and The Same-Life Theory. Suppose one day you begin to morph, like a character in a bad movie. Suppose the effect is that you "grow backwards" from your current state until, in a matter of just a few hours, you resemble an unborn and barely conscious human embryo.

(Of course many people, philosophers and ordinary people alike, consider such an embryo to be not a person. When such philosophers discuss the matter, they are likely to point out that such an embryo is human, and alive, and intrinsically valuable. They are also likely to say that such an embryo has a significant moral status. But still, insofar as the barely conscious embryo is not capable of reflection, or rational thought, or deliberation, and insofar as it possesses no moral concepts [such as the notions of right and wrong], it is a widely held view that such a thing is not a person.)

Now suppose that after many years in this barely conscious state, the embryo in question then grows in a way that appears normal for a human being, until it looks like a newborn baby, and then a child, and then an adolescent, and finally an adult. But suppose that from early on in this growing process the individual in question has a personality that is entirely different from the personality that you had at the beginning of the story. (And of course the individual in question has no memories of any of your experiences.)

Now, it is probably natural to say that the resulting adult person (for there is no question that the individual in question would have come to be a person, for the second time in its life) would not be the same person as you. But according to both The Same-Consciousness Theory and The Same-Life Theory, the resulting adult person in our story would be the same person as you.

Here is one last problem, which affects The Same-Consciousness Theory and The Psychological Continuity Theory alike. It is apparently possible for brain surgeons to sever the connection between the two hemispheres of a human brain in such a way that each hemisphere remains conscious, and retains the personality of the person whose brain has been divided, but ceases to have any awareness of the other hemisphere. (In fact, this has evidently been done in many actual cases, sometimes to treat patients suffering from such conditions as severe epilepsy. When this procedure is performed, the left hemisphere of the patient's brain continues to control the side of the body it always controlled [which is, oddly enough, the right side of the body], while the right hemisphere continues to control its side of the body [the left side].) So it is presumably at least theoretically possible that your brain be divided in two, and that each of the resulting hemispheres be inserted into an otherwise brainless human body, in such a way that the result is two human people, each one of which has your personality and memories, each one of which seems to have a conscious life that is the continuation of your earlier conscious life, and neither one of which is conscious of the other.

Here is why this looks like a problem for the two theories of personal identity in question. Suppose that the above scenario has occurred, and we have two human people standing before us. Call the one with the left hemisphere of your brain Lefty and the other one Righty. Now, Lefty is psychologically continuous with your earlier self, and seems for all the world to have a consciousness that is the continuation of your earlier conscious states. (We can even suppose that both hemispheres of your brain remained conscious throughout the entire procedure.) So it seems clear that proponents of both The Psychological Continuity Theory and The Same-Consciousness Theory must say that Lefty is the same person as you before the brain-splitting operation. Meanwhile, the same is true of Righty as well. So it appears that proponents of the theories in question must also say that Righty is the same person as you from before the operation. But Lefty and Righty are now two people rather than one person! After all, they are now having different thoughts and experiences, they are performing different actions, and neither one is responsible for the actions of the other. (We can further suppose that Lefty goes on to behave in a manner consistent with your earlier behavior, while Righty ends up going off the deep end and performing all kinds of terrible deeds that you would never have even considered before the split.)

This sort of example – sometimes referred to as a fission example, since it seems to involve the splitting of one person into two – has been taken by many to pose a serious challenge to theories like The Psychological

Continuity Theory. But it must be noted that the problem raised by such fission cases is really only a serious problem for a proponent of one of the relevant theories of personal identity provided that he or she is also a subscriber to the Three-Dimensionalist view of persistence (see Chapter 7). For if the advocate of, say, The Psychological Continuity Theory of Personal Identity is also an advocate of the Four-Dimensionalist view of persistence, then he or she can easily accommodate the possibility of fission cases. According to Four-Dimensionalism, a person is made up of many different momentary person-stages, each one of which corresponds to that person at a particular moment of time. Hence the metaphysician who endorses both Four-Dimensionalism and The Psychological Continuity Theory can say that Righty and Lefty are two distinct people who share certain earlier person-stages.[18]

5.7 The no-criteria approach

So far we have examined a number of different theories of personal identity that all have the following form:

> If x is a person at t_1 and y is a person at t_2, then y is the same person as x iff___.

Each of the different theories is an attempt to fill in the blank in this sentence schema so as to produce a biconditional that is both true and informative. But suppose you are convinced that each of the theories of personal identity considered above is susceptible to some counterexample or other. And suppose you take this to be good inductive evidence for the claim that every such theory is likewise susceptible to counterexample. In that case, it would make sense for you to think that the reason all of these different theories of personal identity fail is that there is no true and informative theory of personal identity. Personal identity, on this way of thinking, cannot be analyzed or explained; facts about personal identity are just brute facts – they do not obtain in virtue of any other facts.

---

[18] But it is worth noting that the Four-Dimensionalist is nevertheless committed to some counterintuitive consequences in fission cases. For she must say that prior to the fission, there are not one but instead two people located where it looks for all the world as if there is only one.

Here is one way to state this view.[19]

The No-Criteria View of Personal Identity
If x is a person at t_1 and y is a person at t_2, then if y is the same person as x, then it is a brute fact that y is the same person as x.

There are other reasons one might endorse The No-Criteria View. For example, suppose you are convinced that each person has a non-physical soul and is in fact identical to that soul. And suppose you also think that each soul is a "mereological simple" – an object with no proper parts. Finally, suppose you think, as many philosophers do, that all diachronic identity facts concerning mereological simples are themselves brute facts. Then, although you could still accept the letter of The Same-Soul Theory, doing so would be, for you, tantamount to endorsing The No-Criteria View.

Or suppose you think that each person is actually identical to a very small, physical particle that is located in that person's brain and that is a physical mereological simple. Then for similar reasons you might want to endorse The No-Criteria View.

Finally, suppose that you happen to think that all diachronic identity facts, whether concerning simples or composites, are brute facts. Then you will again have a reason to endorse The No-Criteria View.

---

[19] Merricks defends a similar view about identity over time in general in "There Are No Criteria of Identity over Time."

6 Mental states

6.1 The Mind–Body Problem

It is not far from the truth to say that *The Mind–Body Problem* is the problem of understanding the relationship between the mind and the body. But this description is misleading in two different ways. First, we should be aware that philosophers are not that interested in the relationship between the mind and *the body*, at least not the entire body. For example, there are lots of parts of the body (e.g., the appendix) that don't seem to bear any interesting relationship to our minds. Philosophers tend to focus on the relationship between the mind and the brain, the part of the body that is the (proximate) basis for what goes on in the mind. Second, it's not just mental and neurophysiological *objects*, entities like the mind and the brain, that are important. For example, there are other mental entities: mental states (e.g., John believing now that it's time for lunch), mental events (e.g., John's present pang of hunger), mental processes (e.g., John's current reflection on how best to avoid further pangs), and so forth. There are also other bodily things: brain states (e.g., the C-fibers of John's brain now firing), brain events (e.g., a signal from another part of John's central nervous system to his brain), brain processes (e.g., those processes in John's brain stem currently regulating his heartbeat), and so forth. Our preferred characterization of The Mind–Body Problem is that it is the problem of understanding the relationship between mental phenomena and the bodily basis of those phenomena.

Why is The Mind–Body Problem a *problem*? It deserves this label mainly because it is exceedingly hard to provide the desired understanding. The difficulty starts with the fact that ordinary thought and talk treat our minds and our brains very differently. Our brains have properties that we are reluctant to attribute to our minds: brains are clearly tangible objects, material substances of some kind. They are grayish in color. The average weight of an adult human brain is about 1.3 kilograms. On average, a brain is over seventy-five per cent water. An adult human brain is about 170 millimeters long. So, according to common sense, our brains are decidedly corporeal. Yet there is a strong inclination to take our minds to be incorporeal. What color is your mind? How much does it weigh? Is any percentage of it water? What's the average length of an adult human mind? All these questions probably strike you as a little odd. In fact, you are probably tempted to either dismiss these questions as confused or to answer them in ways that treat the mind as an intangible object, as some kind of immaterial substance, as not even having color, weight, chemical composition, or length. Conversely, our minds seem to have some special features that we are reluctant to attribute to our brains; Ned's belief that Paris is in France represents the world – it is about Paris – and it is correct. Is there anything in Ned's brain, a neuron, say, that is about Paris? Is there a bit of gray matter that has the property of being correct? These questions can seem just as confused as the questions about the color or the weight of human minds.

Another common-sense difference between minds and brains is the privileged access we seem to have to our own minds, but not our own brains. We have a special way of knowing facts about our minds – the process of introspection – that doesn't seem to provide us with knowledge about our brains. Indeed, introspection seems to provide us with information about our minds that is more certain than the information that our senses provide us about our brains (or any other part of the external world). We also seem to get information about our own mental life that does not seem to be available to anyone but us, and yet information about our brains is available to anyone willing and able to hammer open our skulls,[1] to perform and assess an electroencephalogram, or to analyze functional magnetic resonance imaging.

Our minds and brains definitely seem to be distinct. This common-sense judgment is reinforced by many religious traditions. For example, many theists believe that after their bodily death, minds or something much like incorporeal minds – souls – will survive even as their brains

---

[1] Admittedly, it is hard to see how *we* would get much information from hammering open *our own* skulls. So in this peculiar way we are in a *worse* position than others about knowledge of our own brains.

start to rot away with the rest of their bodies. So it looks like there are lots of considerations driving the idea that no mind is a brain and no brain is a mind. But is that right? If it is, then what really is their relationship? Surely they have *some* special relationship.

The difficulty of The Mind–Body Problem is not just that common sense says that mental phenomena and closely connected bodily phenomena are distinct. It is also that we attribute two conflicting sorts of features to mentality itself. Despite treating mentality as something incorporeal, we insist on attributing some properties to the mind that seem better suited to material substances. While it does seem odd to attribute exact spatial dimensions to a mind, we don't hesitate in assigning rough spatial and temporal locations to mental events. Your friend asks, "Where and when did you decide to go to the concert?" Your answer: "Last night, in my room, after listening to that totally groovy album." Even more importantly, we take minds to interact with the material world. Those sound waves coming from the speakers in your room caused certain changes in your brain and your decision to go to the concert, and that decision will eventually cause you and your car to be heading to the stadium. It is not surprising that what goes on in your brain has causes and effects in the material world; it is so clearly part of that world. But, if your mind is immaterial, it is really rather amazing that your mind got your car to go. Is the mind material or not? If it is not, how does it bring about changes in the material world?

A recent focus of metaphysicians has been on a particular issue about how our minds make things happen. It is sometimes known as *The Exclusion Problem*. It purports to show that, given the scientific nature of our universe, especially the apparent physical nature of our universe, there is no leftover work for our mental states to do. So our focus will be on mental states, where a mental state is understood to be the having of a mental property by an object at a time. The Exclusion Problem is especially interesting because, at first glance, it applies as convincingly to the scientifically up-to-date theories of today's metaphysicians as it does to the seventeenth-century philosophy of René Descartes.

6.2 What is Dualistic Interactionism?

For the purposes of this chapter, *Dualism* is the doctrine that there are two fundamental kinds of states in our universe, mental states and material states, that are thoroughly distinct and totally separable from each other. Let us be very clear what we mean by *thoroughly distinct*: we mean not identical, not constituted by, not having as their only parts. So, according to Dualism, no mental state is a material state, no mental state is entirely constituted by material states, no mental state has only material states as parts. Conversely, according to Dualism, no material state is a mental state, no material state is entirely constituted by mental states, no material state has only mental states as parts. Let us also be very clear about what we mean by *totally separable from*: we mean could exist without. So, it is part of Dualism that there could be a mental state (maybe something like a soul's revering God in heaven) and absolutely no underlying material states. Conversely, according to Dualism, there could be a material state (maybe something like one of the moons of Jupiter orbiting that planet) and absolutely no associated mental states. Opposed to Dualism is *Materialism*.[2] It holds that there are material states, and all mental states (if there are any) are material states or are entirely constituted by material states or only have material states as parts. It also holds that mental states are not totally separable from underlying material states; there are no free-floating mental states. According to Materialism, there are no immaterial states.

Dualistic Interactionism (DI) holds that Dualism is true, but also holds that mental states can, and sometimes do, cause material states, and material states can, and sometimes do, cause mental states. It is a view with roots back to Descartes. Sometimes DI is known as *Two-Way Interactionism*, because, according to the view, causation goes both ways, from the mental to the material and vice versa. Other versions of Dualism include a 'one-way' version of Dualism known as *Epiphenomenalism* (material states cause mental states, but not vice versa) famously held by Thomas Huxley, and a 'no-way' version known as *Parallelism* (no material states cause mental

---

[2] Strictly speaking, Dualism is opposed to *Monism*, the doctrine that there is only one fundamental kind of state in our universe. In addition to Materialism, there is another historically important sort of Monism. That is *Idealism*, the doctrine that there are mental states, and all material states (if there are any) are mental states (or are entirely constituted by mental states or have only mental states as parts). So, roughly, according to Idealism, there are no non-mental states. We have opposed Dualism to Materialism for convenience and because Idealism has fallen out of favor with most contemporary metaphysicians and so will not be considered here.

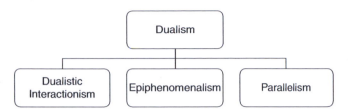

Chart 6.1: *Types of dualism*

states, no mental states cause material states) associated with Gottfried Leibniz. These two forms of Dualism veer drastically away from common sense, denying that the interaction between the mental and the material goes both ways. Neither allows that you deciding to go to the concert could have caused your car to be heading down the highway to the concert. As such, they are positions that had only limited popularity, and only had *any* popularity because of problems facing DI. In 6.3 we will consider the kind of problem for DI that can lead philosophers as brilliant as Huxley and Leibniz to adopt what are otherwise far-fetched theories.[3]

The main reasons why DI has been popular should be apparent from the way that we have introduced this chapter. Its most obvious support comes directly from our ordinary ways of thinking and talking about our own minds and brains. Given the differences in the common-sense properties of the brain and the mind discussed in 6.1, it looks as if mental states and material states should be distinct things. Even more so than that mental states and material states are distinct, it is conspicuously part of common sense that mental states sometimes cause material states and material states sometimes cause mental states. There is also no denying the other source of DI's popularity. Many have been attracted to DI because it is a view that is easily reconciled with certain widespread religions. DI, unlike any form of Materialism and unlike other standard forms of Dualism, is congenial to the possibility that we have immaterial, potentially immortal souls, ones that affect and are affected by the material world around us during our time on Earth, during that time when we are supposedly encumbered by our bodies.

---

[3] See Descartes, *Meditations on First Philosophy*, first published in 1641; Huxley, "On the Hypothesis that Animals are Automata, and Its History" (1874); and Leibniz, "New System of the Nature of Substances," first published in 1695.

6.3 DI's conflict with Physical Determinism

The conspicuousness of mental causation is the Achilles heel of DI. Trouble regarding mental causation has been raised in any number of ways,[4] but many of these ways point to a conflict between DI and science. In its simplest form, the trouble is sometimes put this way: if mental states are distinct and so dramatically different from material states, different to the point that minds have no mass, no charge or momentum, and exert no forces, different to the point that they can exist without there being any material states, then it is a mystery how anything mental could ever have any effect on any aspect of the material world. How could non-material mental states move or otherwise alter material non-mental things?

Paul Churchland puts this kind of concern in terms of a thought experiment. Pretend you are a neuroscientist who wants to "trace the origins of behavior back up the motor nerves to the active cells in the motor cortex of the cerebrum, and to trace in turn their activity into inputs from other parts of the brain, and from the various sensory nerves."[5] What do you expect to find? Presumably, you do expect to find a complex neurophysiological, chemical, and physical system. Presumably, you don't expect to find ectoplasm or a soul or anything immaterial in the causal history of your behavior. Furthermore, presumably, you don't expect the absence of such incorporeal stuff to stand in the way of your project of giving a complete explanation of human behavior.

We will reveal DI's conflict with science by providing a detailed discussion of The Exclusion Problem. The rough idea is that, if physics provides everything required for a complete account of the occurrence of all physical states, then that excludes the immaterial, mental states from playing any significant role in the causal nexus. In this section, we will see how DI conflicts with physics, assuming that physics is deterministic. In the next section, 6.4, we will show how the conflict carries over even if physics is indeterministic.

Physical Determinism states that, given the complete physical state of the universe at one time, and the physical laws of nature, the physical state of

---

[4] For a brief survey of the problems and contemporary reactions to them, see Robb and Heil, "Mental Causation."

[5] Churchland, *Matter and Consciousness*, p. 11.

the universe at all other times follows logically as a matter of necessity. This definition is not all that different from the definition of Determinism (simpliciter) that we have used throughout the book, but especially in Chapters 2 and 3. The primary difference is that Physical Determinism is only about *physical* states and physical laws. These are states and laws of the universe that are the subject matter of physics; they must be expressible in the vocabulary of physics. So, for example, conscious states of an immaterial soul, neurophysiological states, and even geological states are at least not obviously physical states. Physics does not use terms like 'soul' or 'mind', 'neuron', or 'ganglia', not even terms like 'sedimentary' or 'igneous'.[6] For the purposes of this section, assume that Physical Determinism is true.

Consider any mental state that a supporter of DI thinks has caused some material state. Without significant loss of generality, we will assume that this mental state is Harvey deciding at noon today to raise his arm and that it has caused the physical state of a certain atom (one from Harvey's arm) to increase its velocity shortly after noon. We should keep in mind that, at noon, at the time Harvey is deciding, there is a physical state of the universe that includes the physical state of Harvey's brain and body. Given the truth of Physical Determinism, the physical state of the universe at noon in conjunction with the physical laws of nature determines that the atom in Harvey's arm will increase its velocity. According to DI, Harvey deciding at noon to raise his arm and the complete physical state of the universe at noon are thoroughly distinct and totally separable states of affairs. So it intuitively appears that we have the following situation. There are two thoroughly distinct and totally separable states: Harvey deciding at noon, and the physical state of the universe at noon, both of which cause an atom of Harvey's hand to increase its velocity.

From a Dualist perspective, the natural way to understand mental causation is as involving the mental state and the underlying physical state each making its own separate contribution to bringing about the effect.

---

[6] There is potential for confusion stemming from our use of the terms 'physical' and 'material'. These are often used interchangeably in philosophical discussions. We are not using them interchangeably in this chapter. We are here using the word 'physical' more narrowly than we do the word 'material'. For a material state to also be a physical state, it must be expressible in the vocabulary of physics. So, for example, there are certain geological states that are not obviously physical states, though they clearly are material states.

The idea is that the mental and the physical work together like two men carrying a barrel too heavy for either one to carry alone. In that case, the mental state would be doing some real work. But the problem for the Dualist is that this natural way of understanding mental causation is exactly what Physical Determinism excludes. The physical state of the universe at noon (together with the laws of nature) *entails* that the atom in Harvey's hand will have an increased velocity shortly thereafter. The physical state of the universe at noon doesn't need Harvey's help. This Dualist picture is strangely extravagant, having a separate metaphysical level of states that do not seem to make a difference.

We are not saying that Harvey deciding did not cause the atom to move. There being this causal connection is consistent with Physical Determinism. However, it seems that if there is this causal connection, then it and every other case of a mental state causing a physical state must be part of a case of overdetermination. (See Chapter 2.) The deciding would be one cause of the atom increasing its velocity. The physical state of the universe at noon would be another cause of the atom increasing its velocity. The trouble is just that, since the physical state of the universe is sufficient for the effect all by itself, Harvey deciding to raise his arm wouldn't really matter. The physical level doesn't need any help from the mental level; the physical level is poised to carry the barrel all by itself. So, according to DI, the mental seems to be terribly unimportant; if this were the way our world worked, mind wouldn't matter at all. Given DI, the determinism of deterministic science entails that mental states at best cause physical effects in a superfluous way. This should give pause even to the philosopher who most longs for immortality. Surviving bodily death sounds great, but making a difference in the world is important too!

The conflict with deterministic science is the sort of argument that led some philosophers to favor Parallelism or Epiphenomenalism over DI. And it is easy to see why. For religious and other reasons, Leibniz, Huxley, and others were convinced that something like Dualism was true. Yet the conflict with science presents trouble for the claim that mental states can cause physical states. Epiphenomenalism is the view with which one is left if one drops that troublesome part of DI. Parallelism is what you get if you go a little farther, maintaining a certain symmetry, and also drop the claim that physical states can cause mental states.

6.4 DI's conflict with Physical Indeterminism

The assumption of Physical Determinism certainly appears to be important to the argument of 6.3. Maybe it is that assumption that is making
the trouble, rather than some feature of DI. That would be important.
Conceivably, the defender of DI would then be in a position to maintain
that *Physical Indeterminism* (the negation of Physical Determinism) is the
truth about our universe, that mental states could be thoroughly distinct and totally separable from all material states, and yet that mental
states still matter. Let us see if that is right. Given the success of quantum
mechanics, there may well be some reason to think that our world is physically indeterministic.

Consider the following experimental situation. A silver atom will
be released into a magnetic field and then tested to determine some of
its physical properties. With a deterministic physics, with appropriate
information about the initial conditions – the momentum of the atom,
the strength of the magnetic field, and so on – and information about
the pertinent laws of nature, one could deduce all the physical properties the atom will have in the field. With an indeterministic physics at
all like quantum mechanics, the laws together with appropriate initial
conditions will also let us deduce conclusions about the final state of the
atom. The main difference is that some of the conclusions will be probabilistic in nature. Even with a quantum-mechanics-like science, one could
deduce, say, that there is a sixty per cent chance that the atom has, say,
the property spin up. So, in one way, the relationship between the deduced
conclusions and the laws is the same. No room is left for mental states to
influence what certain of the final physical states will be; it is determined
by the physical state of the universe that the silver atom has a sixty per
cent chance of having spin up.

If rejecting Physical Determinism is going to help, a lot is going to have
to be said about how exactly it does so. Maybe this can be done. Let's suppose there are precise physical laws that govern the physical processes
that proceed from the physical state of the universe at noon on the day
that Harvey decides to raise his arm. These laws, we'll suppose, are probabilistic. So, the physical state of the universe at noon plus the laws are
sufficient for there being a certain positive probability that the atom in
Harvey's arm will experience an increase in velocity, but that probability

is not 100 per cent. Still, this physical state does obtain; his arm goes up, that atom does increase its velocity. How might the chancy element of this sequence of events be relevant? Is there some way it could leave room for Harvey deciding to cause the atom to increase its velocity without merely duplicating work to be done by the physical state of the universe at noon?

Here is the only way that seems promising: Harvey deciding to raise his arm might somehow be what made the atom increase its velocity rather than not. This physical state had some chance of obtaining and some chance of not obtaining. Maybe Harvey deciding made the difference. The deciding and the physical state of the universe at noon would both have played an important, non-redundant role. The physical state of the universe at noon lined up what the chance outcomes might be and how probable they are, while Harvey deciding makes one of these chancy outcomes obtain. We always knew the physical world would play some role in producing the physical effects of our decisions and choices. The Exclusion Problem was only a problem because it looked like the physical world wasn't leaving *any* work for the mental to do. Maybe we have found some crucial work. Introducing Physical Indeterminism at least opens the door to a causal role for the mental very much in the spirit of DI.

Or does it? Consider again our silver atom that passes through a magnetic field. The laws of nature in conjunction with the initial physical state of the experiment might tell us that there is a 0.6 probability that it will have spin up, and a 0.4 probability that it won't. Suppose someone claimed that they could affect the spin of the atom by whistling a tune in the next room. Sounds ridiculous, but let's take the claim seriously for a moment. It is important to understand that, if this guy's claim is true, then one of the laws permitting the deduction of the probability assignments is *false*. Those laws – if they are anything like quantum mechanical laws – make no mention of whistling in the next room; that is not a relevant initial condition. The deduced probability assignments imply that it is chancy whether an atom will have spin up, and they say that spin up is a bit more likely than not. If whistling could make the difference whether the atom has spin up or not, then the spin of the atom isn't really left to chance in the way the laws say it is.

It may help to think about this in terms of scientific evidence. We know what sort of evidence would support that there is a 0.6 probability of the silver atom having spin up, and a 0.4 probability of it having spin down.

Many trials of the experiment could have been run and the ratio of times the test atom has spin up to times it does not might have stayed very close to 3:2. Similarly, we know what kind of evidence would count for and against the whistler's claims and we know how to go about accumulating additional evidence. We could run more trials of the experiment, but now also keeping track of whether the whistler is whistling in the next room. If the ratio of times the test atom has spin up to times it does not stays close to 3:2 even with the whistler whistling, then we have evidence that the whistling is not making a bit of difference. If it had any causal influence on the spin of the atom (without overdetermining the direction of spin), we would expect to get a different distribution. That would also be straightforward evidence that what we thought were the laws were wrong.

Let's apply all this to Harvey. According to DI, Harvey deciding at noon to raise his arm caused an atom in his arm to increase its velocity. Let's assume that there are quantum-mechanics-like indeterministic laws that govern the physical processes that proceed from the physical state of the universe at noon and that leave open the possibility that the velocity of the atom will not increase. How might this indeterminacy be relevant to the exclusion argument? Well, it would be relevant if Harvey's mental state made the difference between the atom having an increased velocity and it not having an increased velocity. But is that how our universe works? No. The laws say that there is a certain randomness to the universe and say something quite specific about what that randomness is like. If there weren't exactly the element of randomness claimed by the theory, then the theory would say something false. If Harvey deciding made the relevant difference, then unless it does so by simply reintroducing exactly the chance of the effect predicted by the law, the law is false and so not a law at all. Physics would be wrong. Furthermore, we should expect there to be differences in the distributions of an increase in velocity and no increase in velocity depending on whether Harvey decides to raise his arm. This would amount to a difference in how electrons and other physical particles behave given the identical prior physical state depending on whether a non-physical mental state occurs. That suggests that the predictions of physics that work well away from mental states do not do so well in the vicinity of mental states. There is nothing in science that would lead us to expect that to be the case. Nothing.

Our use of the exclusion argument to reveal a conflict between DI and science is interestingly different from a lot of the arguments presented in this text. Unlike most of our other arguments, it partly turns on some claims about what actual science is like. It is important to remember that in terms of what is metaphysically possible and what is not, this could all be wrong. It is metaphysically possible that, if we ran the atom-in-the-magnetic-field experiment with someone whistling "Dixie" in the next room, the data would be different from what it is when no one whistles. Similarly, it is metaphysically possible that we would find that the laws of quantum mechanics are wrong about what goes on in our brains because of the influence of mental states. That is important to remember. But it is also important to remember two further things. First, it is the defender of DI who makes a scientific, empirical claim, the claim that immaterial states can and do cause material states, including physical states. So it is not too surprising that the arguments being considered have taken on something of an empirical air. Second, it is important to keep in mind that the assumptions being made about science and about what our world is actually like are decidedly unadventurous. That's why the argument is a real threat to DI.

Somewhat surprisingly, the issue of Physical Determinism vs. Physical Indeterminism has turned out to be pretty incidental to The Exclusion Problem. As it would be a hard thing to give up our common-sense commitment to mental causation, we should consider some Materialist alternatives to DI.

6.5 Four versions of Materialism

Materialists hold that there are material states, and that all mental states (if there are any) are material states (or are entirely constituted by material states or only have material states as parts). So, roughly, the Materialist maintains that there are no immaterial states. But there are several different forms of materialism currently defended in the literature, all with some attractions and some drawbacks. In this fifth section, we will briefly describe four versions of Materialism. The first two are *The Identity Theory* and *Functionalism*, which are both forms of *Reductive Materialism* (RM); they

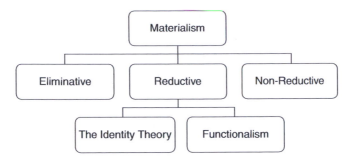

Chart 6.2: *Types of materialism*

try to characterize mental states in non-mental terms. The third is *Non-Reductive Materialism* and the fourth is *Eliminative Materialism*. In this section, we will also mention *some* well-known problems with these theories. We will not, however, consider how well or how poorly these views handle The Exclusion Problem. We are saving that issue for 6.6, after we understand these theories at least reasonably well.

6.5.1 The Identity Theory

The Identity Theory (IT) is the most straightforward way of maintaining Materialism, and holds that all mental states are nothing more than neurophysiological states.[7] So, in this spirit, one might hold:

> *S* feels pain if and only if *S*'s C-fibers are firing.
> *S* believes that Boise is in Idaho if and only if *S*'s Neuron #12 is activated.

These could also be expressed as identities between individual states:

> *S* feeling pain = *S*'s C-fibers firing.
> *S* believing that Boise is in Idaho = *S*'s Neuron #12 being activated.

Or, by indicating property identities:

> Feeling pain = having C-fibers firing.
> Believing that Boise is in Idaho = having Neuron #12 activated.

Keep in mind something that should be pretty obvious. We are taking lots of liberties here for the sake of illustration. We might as well be pulling

---

[7] See Smart, "Sensations and Brain Processes"; Lewis, "An Argument for the Identity Theory"; and Armstrong, *A Materialist Theory of Mind.*

neurophysiological terms out of a hat when pairing a belief about Boise, say, with a certain neuron being activated. We want only to illustrate how the Identity Theorist thinks about mental states. Even Identity Theorists agree that no one yet has enough knowledge of the workings of human brains to state any interesting identities. They often take the same kind of liberties that we have taken here to illustrate their view. But Identity Theorists strongly believe that as the neurosciences advance, we will discover genuine identities between mental states and neurophysiological states.

The central tenet of IT is bolstered by analogies involving many examples taken from the chemical, physical, and biological sciences. For instance, pitch is plausibly identified with oscillatory frequency. Temperature is plausibly identified with average molecular kinetic energy. These examples are taken very seriously. And, indeed, it looks like they do help us see how we'll find out what neurophysiological state each mental state is. We start with an old theory linking certain properties in certain ways. A new theory arrives on the scientific scene that matches up with the old theory in certain nice ways. For example, think of ordinary common-sense judgments about heat as a rudimentary scientific theory. It's a folk theory of heat. It turns out that this folk theory parallels elementary thermodynamics: if x is warm, x is not cold; if x has high average kinetic energy, then x doesn't have low average kinetic energy. It also turns out that, whenever something is warm it has high average molecular kinetic energy, and vice versa. Basically, average kinetic energy and temperature play perfectly parallel roles in the two theories, and that seems a good basis for identifying what we might first have thought were two different properties.

It is important to keep in mind something that is extraordinary about IT identifications/reductions of the mental to the neurophysiological. They are taken to be necessarily true, i.e., true in all possible worlds. They are not saying anything the least bit accidental about the mental states or their constitutive properties. The identity claims are really identity claims like that $2 + 2 = 4$ or that Mark Twain = Samuel Clemens; if true, they are necessarily true. If the theory is stated using biconditionals, the biconditionals are taken to be necessarily true. But, as is clear from the Identity Theorist's deferring the true (not merely illustrative) identifications to future neuroscience, nothing about the theory is supposed to be a priori true. Like Saul

Kripke's water = H_2O example, discussed briefly in Chapter 1, the identities of IT are supposed to be examples where necessary truth and a priori truth part ways. The Identity Theorists give science an important role to play in their solution of The Mind–Body Problem.

Does IT buck common sense? Remember how this chapter started. Remember why Dualism seemed so obvious. The mind and the brain, and with them everything mental and everything material, seemed to be distinct, to have different sorts of properties, to not be identical. Yet here we have a theory that has as its defining thesis that mental states are nothing more than neurophysiological states. Isn't that a problem? Take John believing that Boise is in Idaho. Because Boise is in Idaho, it is very natural to think of John's belief as a correct representation of the world. It is odd, though, to think of the current active state of a certain neuron as being a correct representation of the world. How can one state both be a correct representation of the world and also not be a correct representation of the world?

According to IT, the analogies with the other sciences suggest the best response to this worry. Surely it was once odd to think of the pitch of a sound as having the property of 440 cycles per second or oscillatory frequencies as being soothing or annoying. (Well, come to think of it, maybe that last one is *still* a little odd.) But many people think sound is oscillatory frequency. The strength of the intertheoretical identifications, including the parallel roles of pitch and oscillatory frequency in our folk theory of sound and in wave mechanics, lead people to conclude that the oddness here is something we should live with. Maybe some brain states really are representational, maybe some of these really are correct representations.

The most serious threat to IT is one you probably have not anticipated. It has to do with the limits that IT places on the kinds of material beings that can have any mental states at all. IT is overly chauvinistic in an important sense in that it rules out the possibility of there being creatures like us in having mental states, but unlike us in terms of their composition. It rules out the possibility of there being, say, silicon-based beings that have pains, beliefs, and desires though those creatures have no neurons or brains like ours. Isn't the android Data from the Star Trek television shows and movies a real possibility? He doesn't have a neurophysiology at all, but he does seem to have a lot of different mental states: he knows an awful lot, he hears sounds, and (with a special chip in place) sometimes has emotions. Why should we think that the only way something could believe that 2 + 2 = 4 is if it is in some sort of *neurophysiological* state? To put the point another way: it seems quite plausible to think that mental states are *multiply realizable*, that is, a single mental property can be realized by many different sorts of material properties. If so, it is impossible to identify any mental property with one neurophysiological property.

Was it really that important that the properties be neurophysiological? One might argue that what's really important is that they be material. Silicon chips are just as material as neurons. Maybe we should just be more open to what kinds of material states mental states might be. Fair enough, and some pretty good advice, but it misses the quandary that multiple realizability introduces. The problem is that we want to allow that a single sort of mental state can be realized both by properties of silicon chips and properties of neurons, but we also know that no mental state can be identical to both a silicon state and a neurophysiological state. How does one go about finding a material property that could be had by both Data and any of us? In the next subsection, we will consider a theory that shows us how there could be such a property.

6.5.2 Functionalism

Multiple realizability is not a problem for some theories of mental states. For example, in the mid-twentieth century, a view of the mind known as *Behaviorism* was popular. It holds that mental states are mere dispositions to behave. Being in pain was thought to be something like a disposition to say, "Ouch!" Behaviorism put not a single requirement on what made up the thing possessing the mental state; that was not considered relevant except insofar as it was pertinent to what behaviors the possessor of the mental states could perform under relevant stimulus conditions. Our next Materialist theory of mental states shares Behaviorism's lack of chauvinism.

Functionalism (FN) holds that all mental states are just functional states.[8] What are functional states? These are states definable solely in

---

[8] 'Functionalism' is a popular term. In addition to metaphysics, it comes up in all sorts of places (e.g., biology, sociology, and anthropology). Even within metaphysics, the name 'Functionalism' is sometimes used to label Armstrong's and Lewis's versions of IT.

terms of causal relationships holding among stimuli, behavior, and other mental states. Here's a (simplistic) illustrative example of an informal functional characterization of being in pain:

> S is in pain if and only if S has some state that is caused by injury, causes aggravation, and together with aggravation causes saying, "Ouch!"

Jerry Fodor gives a similar illustrative example:

> A headache, for example, is identified with the [having of a] type of mental state that among other things causes a disposition for taking aspirin in people who believe aspirin relieves a headache, causes a desire to rid oneself of the pain one is feeling, often causes someone who speaks English to say such things as "I have a headache" and is brought on by overwork, eye strain and tension.[9]

Unlike Behaviorism, FN explicitly acknowledges the importance of other mental states; they are mentioned in the informal characterizations of the mental state in question as a part of the connection between sensory stimuli and outward behavior. It matters to the Functionalist what goes on internally even though it doesn't matter what the makeup of the internal stuff is.

This distinguishing feature of FN creates a little bit of a puzzle. First, it looks like we are in danger of generating circles. For example, if it is important to refer to aggravation in the characterization of pain, then it seems that the Functionalist may want to refer to pain in the characterization of aggravation. A Functionalist might want to say:

> S is aggravated if and only if S is in some state that is caused by injury, is caused by pain, and together with pain causes saying, "Ouch!"

But then the characterization of being in pain and the characterization of being aggravated would generate a circle, thus undermining their informativeness. Someone looking for full understanding of both pain and

---

What we mean by 'Functionalism' is what we have just said that Functionalism is. It is a Materialist view about the nature of mental states. It analyzes mental states in non-mental terms by identifying them with the having of some property with a certain functional role. Don't immediately assume that our use of the name 'Functionalism' has any connection with how this name is used in other disciplines or even by other authors in metaphysics.

[9] Fodor, "The Mind–Body Problem," p. 118.

aggravation would not find it. Second, the functional characterization of, say, being in pain apparently wouldn't help to establish RM since it would include a mental term ('aggravation'). How does FN avoid the circles? How could FN really be a reductive theory of mental states?

The characterizations of being in pain and being aggravated given above present in an easy-to-understand, informal manner the intuitive idea that these two mental properties can be characterized in terms of causal relations to input, other mental properties, and output; but they don't do justice to what the Functionalist accomplishes by invoking a tiny bit of logical machinery. We need to think of the Functionalist as starting from some sort of theory about the causal powers of mental states. Here is a simplistic one in line with the functional characterizations of being in pain and being aggravated given above:

The Initial Theory
Pain is caused by injury and pain causes aggravation, and pain together with aggravation causes saying, "Ouch!"

What's simplistic about this starting point is that it is not plausible to think that this is anything like a rich enough theory about the causal powers of mental states to allow an accurate characterization of any mental properties. For the sake of illustration, we will just assume that this information is all the information FN needs.

The Functionalist can define pain and aggravation using this theory. The first step is to take the theory and drop out all the mental terms, replacing them with existentially quantified variables. That's logic speak, saying consider this theory instead:

The Ramsified Theory
There is an x and there is a y such that x is caused by injury, x causes y, x together with y causes saying, "Ouch!"

(It is called 'Ramsified' after the philosopher Frank Ramsey, who came up with the logical method we are demonstrating.[10]) Setting aside some potential ontological worries about the apparent quantification over properties – see Chapter 9 for discussion – The Ramsified Theory trivially

---

[10] See Ramsey, "Theories," published after his death in *The Foundations of Mathematics.* See also Lewis, "How to Define Theoretical Terms."

follows from The Initial Theory. This puts us in a position to define each of our two example mental properties using The Ramsified Theory:

> *S* is in pain if and only if there is an *x* and there is a *y* such that *S* has *x* and *x* is caused by injury, *x* causes *y*, and *x* together with *y* causes saying, "Ouch!"

> *S* is aggravated if and only if there is an *x* and there is a *y* such that *S* has *y* and *x* is caused by injury, *x* causes *y*, and *x* together with *y* causes saying, "Ouch!"

These characterizations of being in pain and being aggravated are just as plausible as the informal originals, though these do not generate any circles. These also make it perfectly clear that the mental states are being characterized solely in non-mental terms, because neither of these characterizations includes mental terms. (Had we started with a more sophisticated and better-supported theory, our complete folk psychology or some scientific psychological theory, it is at least plausible to think that these two definitions would also be *true*.) Thus the Functionalist avoids circularity and is able to make clear how his or her theory is reductive.

This method generalizes. Start with a theory that describes causal relations holding among mental properties, behavior, and stimuli. Functionalists will differ on whether the theory should be a scientific psychological theory or our folk psychological theory or some other. Whatever the theory, it will describe an assortment of functional roles, one corresponding to each mental property used in the initial theory. The theory can be Ramsified to then characterize each mental property as the having of a property with the corresponding functional role. In principle, FN is suited to provide reductive characterizations of all mental states.

Warning: there is still one way that FN is a rather strange sort of RM. Though it does provide a way of characterizing mental properties in non-mental terms, and so very clearly is reductive, it is admittedly a little odd what the mental states reduce to. According to FN, they don't reduce to what a Materialist might immediately think of as *underlying* states. For example, mental properties clearly don't turn out to be physical, chemical, or neurophysiological properties. According to FN, mental properties are second-order functional properties; they are the having of a first-order property with a certain causal role.[11] To see how remarkable such a view is, and to see why it can still seem a little weird to call it an RM, notice that, though mental properties turn out to be specifiable using only non-mental terms, nothing in the theory prohibits the first-order realizers of the causal roles from being ectoplasmic properties only possessed by immaterial souls! There is no requirement on the realizers themselves that they be physical, neurophysiological, or in any way material. Even a Dualist who believed in immaterial souls could identify mental properties with functional properties!

There are other issues that raise questions about FN. By way of concluding our discussion of FN, we will briefly present two of them to illustrate what else FN is up against. Readers are urged to pursue these issues further on their own.

The most famous objection to FN is John Searle's *Chinese Room Argument*.[12] Basically, the idea is to exploit Functionalism's anti-chauvinism by pointing out that, were the functional organization correct, and if the required causal connections were there, then a room with only a monolingual English speaker and a large instruction manual written in English would be counted as understanding Chinese. (The manual lists Chinese symbols but only to say in English what Chinese symbols should be jotted down in response to other Chinese symbols. The manual never says what even one Chinese symbol means.) This instruction manual is so good that Chinese answers to Chinese questions submitted to the room are exactly those one would get from a fluent speaker of Chinese. The charge is that FN gives an incorrect characterization of the mental property *understanding Chinese*, that it counts too many possible material systems as understanding Chinese. According to Searle, intuitively, neither the man in the room nor the room itself (including all of its contents) understands a word of Chinese.

Another interesting objection to FN involves *qualia*, a very special qualitative sort of mental state.[13] Consider two individuals. The first we'll call Ernie$_1$, and he is just like one of us: neurologically, there is nothing at all

---

[11] To be perfectly clear, second-order properties are ones that quantify over (i.e., assert the existence of) first-order properties.

[12] Searle, "Minds, Brains, and Programs."

[13] See, for example, Shoemaker, "Functionalism and Qualia."

abnormal about him. The second, Ernie$_2$, is in most ways like Ernie$_1$ except that he is silicon-based. So Ernie$_1$ is just like us but Ernie$_2$ is materially more like a computer than he is like a human being. Our two individuals are, however, *functionally equivalent*; their mental states stand in exactly the same causal relations to stimuli, other mental states, and behavior. In particular, both instantiate visual states when looking at an apple that stands in all the same causal relations to input, output, and other mental states. What's interesting is that the *qualitative character* of their visual experiences are inverted. What we mean by this is that when Ernie$_1$ looks at an apple, he has a visual experience with, say, a reddish qualitative character – so the apple looks red to him; but when Ernie$_2$ sees the apple, he has a visual experience with a bluish character – so the apple looks blue to him. Be careful. Outwardly, and functionally, there are no significant differences between Ernie$_1$ and Ernie$_2$. Ernie$_1$ and Ernie$_2$ will both say the same things in the same situations. Put a ripe, red apple in front of either one and that Ernie will say things like, "That apple looks nice and red to me." Neither will say, "Huh, look at that, a blue apple." The anti-chauvinism flaunted by the Functionalist when criticizing IT suggests that this kind of functional equivalence is possible. But, to the Functionalist's disappointment, with the material differences between Ernie$_1$ and Ernie$_2$, it also seems reasonable to maintain that the inverted qualia of Ernie$_2$ is a perfectly good possibility. If so, FN is in trouble. Since Ernie$_1$ and Ernie$_2$ are functionally equivalent, since they have exactly the same functional properties, they ought also to have exactly the same mental states. The problem is that, intuitively, they don't – Ernie$_2$ has a bluish visual experience and Ernie$_1$ has a reddish one.

6.5.3 Non-Reductive and Eliminative Materialism

The Chinese Room Argument and the challenge presented by inverted qualia are both interesting objections to FN and have spawned a great deal of literature from philosophers of mind and other metaphysicians. Whether they undermine FN is something about which there is disagreement. Despite the lack of agreement, we should at least consider what the prospects are for a Materialist if FN does turn out to be false.

There is a third argument that is often raised against FN, but applies equally well to all forms of RM. One primary formulation of the argument begins with another hypothetical example, this time one involving a captive scientist.[14] Mary is locked up in a black and white room. In fact, she herself is black and white. She is born, raised, and grows up here, in this small black and white world, without ever having the experience of anything of any other color. She doesn't know what it is like to see blue. Or does she? Mary, you see, is a brilliant scientist and has learned everything there is to know about blue and having bluish visual experiences. She has learned (let us suppose) that there is a single neurophysiological correlate of having a bluish visual experience, and she knows what it is. She knows the functional role of having a bluish visual experience and knows the neurophysiological correlate that plays that role. We can suppose she knows anything any Reductive Materialist might propose by way of characterizing, defining, or identifying this sort of mental state. It seems, then, that she should know what it is like to see blue, since she knows what seeing blue is. But does she know what it is like to see blue? It seems pretty clear that she doesn't. Even if Mary knew everything there was to know about human physiology (including her own) and about the functional organization of human vision, she wouldn't know what it is like to see blue. Perhaps RM is not the way to go.

The What-Mary-Didn't-Know Argument has been influential and yet also controversial. Lewis[15] points out that you don't really need the hypothetical example involving Mary. Have you ever had Vegemite? If not, nothing short of having that very sort of experience will teach you what it is like. If the taste of Vegemite would be very new to you, knowing the chemical composition of Vegemite won't help you know beforehand what the taste would be like and neither will the exact neurophysiological map of a human with some Vegemite on his or her tongue. It seems that no amount of physical information – *indeed no amount of information, period* – will teach you what any sufficiently unique experience is like. Lewis uses this observation to argue that The What-Mary-Didn't-Know Argument is not convincing. In contrast, David Chalmers finds the argument convincing.[16] He thinks that it shows that science will need to recognize consciousness as a fundamental feature of the world; the true science will

---

[14] Jackson, "What Mary Didn't Know." See also Nagel, "What Is It Like to Be a Bat?"
[15] David Lewis, "What Experience Teaches."
[16] Chalmers, *The Conscious Mind.*

include fundamental psychophysical laws governing this feature. He thinks the arguments show that consciousness is like electric charge!

Without deciding the soundness of this argument, but with reflection on it and the challenges that have been raised more specifically for IT (i.e., chauvinism) and FN (i.e., inverted qualia), we hope we have raised enough doubts about the prospects of defending RM for the reader to appreciate why a growing number of philosophers have felt pushed to either Non-Reductive Materialism (NRM) or to Eliminative Materialism (EM). NRM is the view that (i) there are mental states, and (ii) that not all mental states are definable (or identifiable) using only non-mental material terms.[17] There is not much more to say about NRM; there is not really much of a positive theory here. It indicates the limits of Materialist theorizing without doing any such theorizing. These philosophers think mental states are material states, but they do not think mental states are characterizable in non-mental material terms. They insist that what mental states exist is determined by non-mental material states of the world; possible worlds that agree on their non-mental material facts agree on all their mental facts. So, mental states are not totally separable from non-mental material ones. But this supervenience thesis, which is a standard part of all forms of Materialism, is pretty much the end of the story about the essential features of mentality. Mental facts are brute. EM[18] is not much more of a theory, maintaining only that there are *no* mental states. Unlike RM, though, EM is viewed as a theory of last resort, maintaining as it does that no one ever feels pain, that no one ever believes anything, and that no one ever decides anything. EM has the especially curious feature that it is believed only if it is false.

6.6 Dualism, Materialism, and The Exclusion Problem

In 6.5, we included almost no discussion of The Exclusion Problem within our discussion of Materialism. One reason for this is that, despite the fact that Materialists have for a long time pressed the Dualist about the nature of the causal connections between mental and physical states, these

---

[17] Davidson resists talk of states of affairs and properties, but his work is rightly regarded as central to the development of NRM. See "Mental Events."

[18] See Churchland, "Eliminative Materialism and the Propositional Attitudes."

questions were simply not thought to be a big issue for the Materialist. For Materialists, there are not two different kinds of stuff – it's all material. What could the problem be?

That was the prevailing attitude anyway, and, as a result, many important discussions and criticisms of Materialist theories developed independently of exclusion concerns. We felt it important to at least briefly present some of these concerns. Recently, however, attitudes have changed. Thanks in large measure to the careful work of Jaegwon Kim, the exclusion-style questions about mental causation and their impact for the Materialist are now a central concern.[19] Basically, the source of the renewed interest in exclusion is that two of the most popular versions of Materialism, FN and NRM, recognize the mental as a special level of material reality. We will conclude this chapter by taking another look at the different forms of Materialism, this time with our focus on their relevance to The Exclusion Problem.

IT and EM bypass The Exclusion Problem in straightforward ways. For EM, there are no mental states. So there is no need for concern about a conflict between physics and the causal contribution of mental states; no mental states, no causal contribution, and thus no threat from systematic overdetermination. Not that this is a happy resolution of the problem. Mental states don't even exist according to EM. Talk about the mental not mattering! IT's prospects for dealing with The Exclusion Problem are a bit more interesting since it accepts that there are mental states and that they are part of the causal action. Mental states are neurophysiological states. So there is not a special mental layer to worry about.[20] Our mental states have physical effects without overdetermining those effects. Though chauvinism concerns persist for IT, frustrated by a lack of fruitful alternatives, Kim, himself, has tempered his acceptance of NRM, adopting a restricted form of IT.[21]

What of FN and NRM? First consider FN. A Functionalist might be hard pressed to argue that functional properties are themselves definable in terms of physical properties, because they include the causal relation,

---

[19] Kim, *Mind in a Physical World*.

[20] We will see in just a couple of paragraphs that exclusion issues arise about causation by neurophysiological states. These issues for IT, however, don't seem quite as perilous as the issues about causation that face FN and NRM.

[21] Kim, *Mind in a Physical World*, pp. 106–11.

which is notoriously absent from physical theory. There is also the reference to stimuli and behaviors in the statement of the causal role; injury and saying, "Ouch!" are not physical properties. The causal relation and the reference to stimuli and behavior *may* be analyzable using only physical terms, but that shouldn't be taken for granted. Furthermore, and more importantly, even if these properties are so analyzable, the mental states are still another layer of reality in virtue of being second-order properties. That in itself is more than enough to get The Exclusion Problem going. Physics offers complete explanations solely in terms of particles and fields having certain first-order properties like mass and charge. Add to all this that some philosophers will resist the thought that second-order states including a causal relation can be causal for reasons having nothing to do with The Exclusion Problem (such states strike some as having too much of a logical or modal nature to cause anything – they are seen as not being oomphy enough), and it becomes clear that the Functionalist is up to his neck in worries about mental causation, overdetermination, and making a difference.[22] For NRM, the causal trouble lurking is even more transparent. Though NRM differs from DI in terms of certain claims about the separability of mental states and underlying material states, it fully agrees with DI on the issues needed to ignite The Exclusion Problem: (i) mental states cause physical states, and (ii) mental states are distinct from physical states.

The Functionalist and the Non-Reductive Materialist should probably take *some* consolation in the fact that The Exclusion Problem is not one that is peculiar to the relationship between the mental and the physical. For example, exclusion worries may arise regarding the relationship between the chemical and the physical. They may also arise concerning the neurophysiological and the physical; that's why we noted that IT does have a bit of an incidental exclusion problem to address itself. (See note 20.) Unless the prospects of identifying the chemical properties with the physical ones or the neurophysiological properties with physical properties are better than the prospects of identifying the mental properties with physical properties (and they may be – chauvinism concerns don't seem quite so serious here), exclusion issues will arise between these other levels as well. Perhaps the possibility of widespread overdetermination is a

---

[22] See Block, "Can the Mind Change the World?"

little easier to take with regard to, say, the chemical and the physical since with these levels it is not a matter of *us* mattering, but such widespread overdetermination is still somewhat undesirable. It's unlovely in a certain way: it would still mean recognizing metaphysical levels that don't make a difference.

Should the fact that The Exclusion Problem applies to NRM and FN, or the fact that it can be raised about the relationship between the chemical and the physical, be of *any* consolation to defenders of DI? We don't think so. No one believes that the chemical is totally separable from the physical. In line with that, no one thinks that the chemical and the physical make independent causal contributions to the bringing about of physical effects; whatever is going on, it is not the chemical helping to carry a barrel that the physical alone cannot. Being forms of Materialism, FN and NRM take these aspects of the chemical-physical relationship also to hold about the mental-physical relationship. DI, however, is different. Being a form of Dualism, it sees the mental as sometimes helping the physical to carry the load and allows that mental states can exist on their own. To revise DI by dropping these traditional Dualist doctrines, while it might help a little with exclusion worries, would sabotage the appeal of DI for the many drawn to either the idea that we contribute alongside the physical or the idea that we might survive our bodily deaths.

7 Time

7.1 Introduction

Space is not like time. For one thing, there is no intrinsic direction – no metaphysical grain – to any dimension of space. Instead, every spatial dimension is perfectly symmetrical. For another thing, space does not exhibit any movement or flow; unlike time, there is no dynamic aspect to the dimensions of space. And for a third thing, space is ontologically indiscriminate. It doesn't matter whether you're located right here or over there in space, since all spatial locations are equally real. Space just sits there: a gigantic, three-dimensional continuum, static and homogeneous, with nothing but their contents to distinguish one spatial region from another.

Time is different. Time has pizzazz. For starters, there is a distinctive direction to time, sometimes called time's arrow, which points always toward the future. Also, time is dynamic: each moment of time approaches inexorably from the future, enjoys its brief heyday in the spotlight of the present, and then ever after recedes serenely into the shadowy realm of the past. Not only that, but your temporal location does matter, ontologically speaking: for the past is the domain of has-beens, and the future is a land of mere potential. Only the present is truly real.

Or so it might seem. But many have thought otherwise. A large number of philosophers and scientists, especially in the last hundred years, have defended the view that time, despite appearances to the contrary, is one of four more or less similar dimensions of the universe. The direction, the passage, and the ontological inequality of time are all mere appearances, on this view, each one a function of the way we happen to perceive the world.

This issue – the degree to which time is similar to the dimensions of space – has figured prominently in recent philosophical discussions of time. And most of the people involved in those discussions have been, directly or indirectly, responding to McTaggart's famous argument against the reality of time, first published in 1908.[1] So that is where we will begin.

7.2 McTaggart's argument

McTaggart's argument has two main parts. The first is meant to show that times and events cannot possess properties like *pastness*, *presentness*, and *futurity*. The second part of the argument builds on the first part, and is designed to show that time is not real. We'll look at both parts in detail, but first we need to be clear about some important terminology that McTaggart uses in his argument.

McTaggart says there are two ways of distinguishing positions in time. In the first place, we can say that each position is *earlier than* some positions and *later than* others. For example, 2009 is earlier than 2010 and later than 2008. Distinctions of this first kind are permanent. But in the second place, we can say that each position is either *past*, *present*, or *future*; for 2008 is past, 2009 is present, and 2010 is future. Moreover, distinctions of this second kind are temporary. (Note that there are metric variants on these ways of distinguishing positions in time: *three-days-later-than*, *two-days-past*, and so forth.)

Here then is one way to generate a series of times: order the times according to whether they are past, present, or future, and also according to how far into the past or future they are. This method produces what McTaggart calls the *A series*.

And here's another way to generate a series of times: order the times according to how they stand to other times in terms of the *earlier than* and *later than* relations. This alternative method of ordering times produces what McTaggart calls the *B series*.[2]

---

[1] McTaggart, "The Unreality of Time."

[2] An odd feature of McTaggart's characterization of the A series and the B series is that they end up being identical. For a series is nothing more than some specific items in a particular order, and the A series and the B series, as defined by McTaggart, turn out to consist of the same items in the same order. Luckily for our purposes, this odd feature of McTaggart's characterization of the 'two' series does not affect the soundness of his arguments.

So much for preliminaries and terminology. We now turn to the first part of McTaggart's argument. It begins by noting that each moment in time must possess all of the different properties that generate the A series (including *futurity*, *presentness*, and *pastness*), if the A series is real. For if the A series is real, then each moment has to go from being future to being present to being past. (Not to mention all the metric variants: *being two days future*, *being one day future*, *being present*, *being one day past*, and so forth.) The argument then continues with the observation that *pastness*, *presentness*, and *futurity* (and in fact any two of the different A-series-generating properties) are incompatible properties. For no time is both past and present, or present and future, and so forth. The upshot of this first part of the argument is that the A series cannot be real.

There is a possible objection to this argument. You might object to the claim that if the A series is real, then each moment of time is past, present, and future. For you might deny that a given moment of time *is* past, present, and future (even on the assumption that the A series is real, that is). Instead, you might say, what is true of the present moment, for example, is that it *will be* past, *is* present, and *was* future.

McTaggart is well aware of this objection, however, and feels that he has a devastating reply to it. According to McTaggart, to say of the present moment that it *will be* past is to say that it is past *at a moment of future time*, and to say that it *was* future is to say that it is future *at a moment of past time*. And, as McTaggart points out, both of these additional moments (the moment of future time at which the present moment is past, and the moment of past time at which it is future) must also be past, present, and future (if the A series is real, that is). So the incompatible characteristics have merely been passed on, like a baton in a relay race, to another generation of times; and thus the contradiction remains. In fact what really happens, according to McTaggart, is that the incompatible characteristics get passed on, like an eternally multiplying series of batons in a strange relay race in which more and more runners are added to each team at each stage of the race. Which means that, instead of solving the original problem, you have actually compounded it by generating an infinite series of contradictions. And that's not good.

The second part of McTaggart's argument starts with the claim that change is essential to time. After all, Aristotle said that time is the measure of change; and in any case, without change, there would be no time. (Or so it seems, and so many people have argued.) Yet, according to McTaggart, the A series is essential to change.

To make this point, McTaggart asks us to compare his fireplace poker (which is hot on a particular Monday and cold at every other time) to the meridian at Greenwich. The meridian, says McTaggart, doesn't change in virtue of being in the UK at one latitude and outside the UK at another latitude, any more than a fence changes in virtue of being white at one end and red at another end. These aren't cases of real change, says McTaggart, and neither is the case of his poker. For it is always true that the poker is hot on that particular Monday, and it's always true that the poker is cold at all other times.

To get real change, says McTaggart, you need an A series. If you have an A series, then you have times and events changing from being future to being present to being past. So you have the poker being hot changing from being future to being present (this change is also known as the poker becoming hot), not to mention the poker being hot changing from being present to being past (also known as the poker ceasing to be hot). And if you have all of that, says McTaggart, then you have real change.

So change is essential to time, says McTaggart, and the A series is essential to change. But the A series (according to the previous argument) is unreal. So time is unreal.

7.3 The A Theory and The B Theory

There have been two main responses to McTaggart's pair of arguments. Some philosophers have accepted McTaggart's argument against the A series, while rejecting McTaggart's argument against the reality of time. These philosophers have maintained (roughly) that time is real, but consists of just the B series. They are sometimes called "B Theorists" (or "detensers" because they want to say that "tense" is not a genuine feature of objective reality).

Other philosophers have rejected both McTaggart's argument against the A series and McTaggart's argument against the reality of time. These philosophers have maintained that "A properties" are real properties of times and events – properties that change as time passes. Such philosophers are sometimes called "A Theorists" (or "tensers", because they want to say that tense is a genuine feature of objective reality).

Oddly enough, almost no one has been convinced by McTaggart that time itself is unreal.

In order to formulate The A Theory and The B Theory, let us introduce some definitions. *A properties*, if there are any, are putative temporal properties like *pastness, presentness, futurity, being one day future,* and so forth. *B relations*, on the other hand, are two-place temporal relations like *earlier than, simultaneous with, later than, one day later than,* and so forth. Now we can formulate the views as follows:

> *The A Theory*
> (i) There are genuine A properties, and (ii) the passage of time consists of each time's successive possession of different A properties.[3]
>
> *The B Theory*
> (i) There are no genuine A properties, and (ii) time does not really pass.[4]

What A Theorists and B Theorists agree on is the reality of B relations. What they disagree on is whether there are real (i.e., unanalyzable [i.e., unanalyzable in terms of B relations]) A properties, and whether time really passes. More generally, A Theorists and B Theorists disagree about the degree to which time is different from the dimensions of space, with A Theorists maintaining that time, in virtue of its passage, is sui generis among the four dimensions.

Here is how the proponent of The B Theory will respond to McTaggart's arguments. First, B Theorists already accept the conclusion of McTaggart's argument against the A series, so they are free to accept or reject the argument, depending on their views about the premises. Some B Theorists don't think McTaggart's argument against the A series is any good, but reject The A Theory anyway because they think there is some other good argument against it (like the rate of passage argument, or the argument from relativity, both of which we will discuss below).

As for McTaggart's argument against the reality of time, it's clear that the B Theorist should reject the claim that the A series is essential to change. Instead, the B Theorist should say, genuine change occurs whenever an object has a property at one time and then lacks it at another time. B Theorists can therefore safely reject the conclusion of the argument.

---

[3] See, for example, Prior, "Changes in Events and Changes in Things."

[4] See, for example, Smart, "The River of Time"; and Williams, "The Myth of Passage."

What about proponents of The A Theory? What should they say about McTaggart's arguments? Well, when it comes to McTaggart's argument against the A series, we believe that A Theorists should reject the premise that says that every moment of time must be past, present, and future, if the A series is real. For it seems to us that the A Theorist's best move is to say that we must "take tense seriously." This means, roughly, that there are fundamental and unanalyzable differences between (for example) speaking in the present tense and speaking in the past or future tenses. That is, there is a fundamental and unanalyzable difference between saying that something *is* φ and saying that it *was* φ or *will be* φ. Taking tense seriously also means maintaining that propositions have truth values at times, and can change their truth values over time. Here is the view that we will call The Tensed Conception of Semantics:

> *The Tensed Conception of Semantics (TCS)*
> (i) The verbal tenses of ordinary language (expressions like 'it is the case that', 'it was the case that', and 'it will be the case that') must be taken as primitive and unanalyzable. (ii) Propositions – the things that are true or false – have truth values *at times* rather than just having truth values *simpliciter.*

TCS also requires accepting some form of tense logic, which is basically a species of modal logic, with special operators that correspond to the various tenses of ordinary language.[5]

TCS is to be contrasted with The Tenseless Conception of Semantics:

> *The Tenseless Conception of Semantics (TLCS)*
> (i) The verbal tenses of ordinary language (expressions like 'it is the case that', 'it was the case that', and 'it will be the case that') can be eliminated through appropriate use of expressions like 'simultaneous with', 'earlier than', and 'later than'. (ii) Propositions – the things that are true or false – have truth values *simpliciter* rather than having truth values *at times.*

In any case, when we take tense seriously (i.e., when we appreciate the truth of TCS), the A Theorist should say, we can see that any moment of time that *is* present is neither past nor future (although it *will be* past and *was* future).

---

[5] For more on TCS and tense logic, see Arthur Prior, *Past, Present, and Future,* and *Papers on Time and Tense.*

Notice that when A Theorists reject the first premise of McTaggart's argument against the A series (the one that says that each moment of time must be past, present, and future, if the A series is real), they will say that they are not merely passing a contradiction along from one set of times to another, thereby generating an infinite regress of contradictions. Instead, they will claim, there is no contradiction in the first place.

As for McTaggart's argument against the reality of time, A Theorists should reject the claim that the A series is unreal, and hence the conclusion, because they reject McTaggart's argument against the A series.

Much more could be said about McTaggart's arguments, but we will turn now to another historically important argument against The A Theory.

7.4 The rate of passage argument

There is certainly something strange about saying that time passes. For we want to ask the A Theorist, "How fast, exactly, does time pass?" But it doesn't seem like there can be any good answer to this question. An answer like "One hour per hour" would be either incoherent or else completely uninformative. And if, as some have suggested, the A Theorist has to posit a second time dimension, with its own temporal units, in order to say that $time_1$ passes at the rate of one $hour_1$ per $hour_2$, then it looks like the A Theorist is committed to an infinite regress of further time dimensions, each one needed in order to account for the rate of passage of the previous one. So it appears that we have an excellent reason not to say that time passes in the first place.

Here is the argument.[6]

The rate of passage argument

(1) If it makes sense to say that time passes, then it makes sense to ask, "How fast does time pass?"
(2) If it makes sense to ask, "How fast does time pass?" then it's possible for there to be a coherent answer to this question.
(3) It's not possible for there to be a coherent answer to this question.

(4) It doesn't make sense to say that time passes.

---

[6] Smart suggests a version of this argument in "The River of Time."

Readers will of course want to make up their own minds, but for our money, this argument does not pose a serious threat to the A Theorist.[7] Here's why. To begin with, we note that the argument does indeed raise some interesting questions about how we talk about rates. Here is the main question.

(Q1)   Does rate talk essentially involve the comparison of some change to the passage of time, or can it instead involve the comparison of any two changes?

The A Theorist has options about how to answer Q1. Suppose he or she says that rate talk can involve comparing any two changes. For example, we can say that in 1989, Joe Montana's passing totals increased at the rate of twenty-one completions per game. Then the A Theorist will think that any time one gives the rate of some change in terms of some second change, one has likewise given the rate of the second change. (If, for example, we tell you that Montana's passing totals increased at the rate of twenty-one passes per game, then we have also told you that the games progressed at the rate of one game per twenty-one completions by Montana.)

Hence, on this view, whenever one gives the rate of some normal change in what is admittedly the standard way, i.e., in terms of the passage of time, then one has likewise given the rate of the passage of time in terms of the first change. For example, if we tell you that Abibe Bikila is running at the rate of twelve miles per hour, then (on this view) we have also told you that the passage of time is flowing at the rate of one hour for every twelve miles run by Bikila.

If the A Theorist takes this line then he or she should reject premise (3) of the rate of passage argument. For the A Theorist will in this case think that it is possible to state coherently the rate at which time passes, and will also think that this information is in fact given each time the rate of some normal change is described in terms of the passage of time.

(Moreover, if the A Theorist takes this line then he or she will deny that there is any need to posit a second time dimension, on the grounds that the passage of time is a change whose rate can be measured with respect to the rate of any normal change.)

Suppose, on the other hand, the A Theorist says that rate talk essentially does involve the comparison of some change to the passage of time. Then he or she faces a further question:

[7] The following evaluation of the argument is based on the defense of The A Theory offered in Markosian, "How Fast Does Time Pass?"

(Q2)   Can the passage of time be compared to itself?

Now, suppose the A Theorist answers Yes to this question. Then he or she should say that the question, "How fast does time pass?" is a sensible question with a sensible answer: time passes at the rate of one hour per hour. And if he or she takes this line, then the A Theorist should reject premise (3) of the rate of passage argument, for in that case he or she will think it is in fact possible to give a coherent answer to the question, "How fast does time pass?"

(Moreover, if the A Theorist takes this line, then he or she will again say that there is no need to posit any second time dimension with respect to which the passage of normal time is to be measured, on the grounds that the passage of time is a change whose rate may be measured with respect to itself.)

Finally, suppose the A Theorist answers No to Q2. Then he or she should accept premise (3) of the rate of passage argument. But in that case he or she will be compelled to reject premise (1) of that argument. For if the A Theorist answers No to Q2, then he or she will insist that the passage of time is the one change, among all the changes that take place in the world, of which it does not make sense to ask, "How fast does it happen?"

(Moreover, if he or she takes this line then the A Theorist will again say that there is no need to posit any second time dimension with respect to which the passage of normal time is supposed to be measured, on the grounds that the passage of time is, by its nature, a change whose rate simply cannot be measured.)

Here is what we take to be the upshot. The rate of passage argument raises some interesting questions about how we should understand talk about rates. But whichever one the A Theorist chooses from among the several coherent ways of answering those questions, there is some premise of the argument that is, according to the way he or she has answered the relevant questions, automatically false.

7.5 The argument from relativity

A different challenge to The A Theory comes from The Special Theory of Relativity (hereafter, STR). According to STR, it is argued, there is no such relation as absolute simultaneity. But if there is no such relation as absolute simultaneity, then there cannot really be any genuine A properties (such as absolute presentness or being two days past). Instead, all talk that appears to be about such properties must be analyzable in terms of B relations between things and events, just as The B Theory says.[8]

The A Theorist's best response to this argument will probably involve pointing out that for any scientific theory that seems to have metaphysical implications, we can distinguish between two versions of that theory: (i) a version that has some philosophical baggage built into it, and that does indeed have metaphysical implications; and (ii) an empirically equivalent version that has no philosophical baggage built into it, and that has no metaphysical implications. For example, in the case of STR, we can consider two different versions of STR, which can be characterized as follows:

> *STR+*
> A philosophically robust version of STR that has sufficient philosophical baggage built into it to make it either literally contain or at least entail the proposition that there is no such relation as absolute simultaneity.
>
> *STR–*
> A philosophically austere version of STR that is empirically equivalent to STR+ but that does not have sufficient philosophical baggage built into it to make it either literally contain or even entail the proposition that there is no such relation as absolute simultaneity.

Suppose we understand the argument from relativity to be concerned with STR+. Then the A Theorist can point out that although there seems to be a great deal of empirical evidence supporting STR+, that same empirical evidence supports STR– equally well. And since the A Theorist believes there is good a priori evidence favoring STR– over STR+, he or she should conclude that STR– is true and that STR+ is false.

Suppose, on the other hand, that we understand the argument from relativity to be concerned with STR–. Then the A Theorist should deny that the theory entails that there is no such relation as absolute simultaneity. For STR– will entail, among other things, that while it is physically

---

[8] The argument presented here is a variation on an argument from STR against Presentism (see below) that is discussed in Markosian, "A Defense of Presentism," and the response offered on behalf of the A Theorist borrows heavily from the same paper.

possible to determine whether two objects or events are simultaneous relative to a particular frame of reference, it is not physically possible to determine whether two objects or events are absolutely simultaneous. But this is consistent with there being such a relation as absolute simultaneity. And it is also consistent with there being such properties as absolute presentness and being two days past.[9]

7.6 "Thank goodness that's over"

Some A Theorists think that the main arguments against The A Theory fail to refute their view, either for reasons like those raised above or else for other reasons. And many such A Theorists also claim that their view, in virtue of being more intuitively plausible than The B Theory, is the default position – the presumptive winner in the case of a stand-off between the two theories. Such A Theorists will accordingly maintain that, once they have successfully dealt with whatever arguments can be given against The A Theory, no positive argument is needed in favor of their view. We leave it to the reader to decide whether this seems right, and turn now to one of the main arguments that has been offered against The B Theory.

The argument in question is suggested by Arthur Prior,[10] and it has to do with a distinction between two kinds of temporal fact, which we will call "A-facts" and "B-facts". (For the purpose of considering Prior's argument, let us adopt the simplifying assumption that facts are instantiations of universals. Among such instantiations we can include, for example, the number two being prime, and Ned's shirt being blue.) *A-facts*, if there are any, are facts involving A-properties. Putative examples would include the year 2525 being *future*, and Super Bowl XXIII being *twenty years past*. Meanwhile, *B-facts* (and everyone agrees that there are plenty of these) are facts involving B-relations. Examples would include the year 2525 being *later than* 2009, and Super Bowl XXIII being *seventeen years earlier than* Super Bowl XL.

---

[9] For more discussions of STR and the A Theory and/or Presentism, see Prior, "The Notion of the Present"; Putnam, "Time and Physical Geometry"; and Maxwell, "Are Probabilism and Special Relativity Incompatible?"

[10] See Prior, "Thank Goodness That's Over."

Now, here is the example that the argument is based on: you have an excruciatingly painful headache. Finally it ends. Then you say, as people in such situations often do, "Thank goodness that's over." End of story.

It appears that when, in the story, you say, "Thank goodness that's over," you are saying something eminently sensible. And it seems like this eminently sensible thing that you are saying involves thanking goodness for the A-fact that your excruciating headache is in the past. Not only that, but it would be pretty implausible to maintain that what you are really thanking goodness for, when you say, "Thank goodness that's over," is the B-fact that the conclusion of the headache is earlier than your utterance. For (as Prior says elsewhere) why would anyone thank goodness for that? Moreover, it has always been true that the conclusion of the relevant headache is earlier than that particular utterance. So if that is what you are thanking goodness for, would it not have been equally reasonable to say, when the headache first started, "Thank goodness the conclusion of this headache is earlier than the first utterance I will make after the headache is over"? And besides, it can't be that when you say, "Thank goodness that's over," you are really thanking goodness for the B-fact that the conclusion of the headache is earlier than your utterance, because at the time you say it, you're not even thinking about your own utterance.

Here then is the argument. When you say, "Thank goodness that's over," you are saying something sensible about a temporal fact, but you are not saying anything about any B-fact. It follows that when you say, "Thank goodness that's over," you are saying something sensible about an A-fact. And if that's true, then there are A-facts. Finally, if there are A-facts, then The A Theory is true.

Some may take this argument to be a decisive refutation of The B Theory, but we are not so sure that it is. In order to explain the best B Theory response to the argument, however, we will first have to explain Four-Dimensionalism and its rival, Three-Dimensionalism.

7.7 Three- and Four-Dimensionalism

To begin to understand the basic idea behind Four-Dimensionalism, think of our world as occupying a gigantic, four-dimensional continuum, consisting of the three dimensions of space plus the dimension of time. The physical objects in the world, on this way of thinking, are spread out in all four dimensions. Moreover, when you consider an object at a time, such as yourself at noon today, you are considering only a "temporal slice" of that object (analogous to a "spatial slice", or two-dimensional cross-section, of the object). Such a temporal slice of an object is also known as a "temporal part" of that object. But so are the various longer temporal segments of the objects: they too are "temporal parts" of the whole object, and they can be likened to the spatial segments of, say, an earthworm.

In fact, according to Four-Dimensionalism, we can extend the earthworm analogy by saying that ordinary objects like you and me are "space-time worms" made up of lots and lots of different temporal parts. Some of these temporal parts are instantaneous; they are three-dimensional cross-sections (or "time slices") of the larger object. Others are extended, and last for various subportions of the entire temporal extent of the object. But each temporal part, for as long as it lasts, occupies exactly the same region of space as the object of which it is a temporal part. And the larger object – the thing that is the person, or the chair, or whatever – is composed of all of these many different temporal parts.

On this view, the relation between you at noon today and you at noon tomorrow is not *identity*. Instead, it is the relation *being a different part of the same object*. (Like the relation between different segments of a single earthworm, or the relation between your hand and your foot.)

So much for the basic idea behind Four-Dimensionalism. Meanwhile, the basic idea behind Three-Dimensionalism is simply the denial of everything that was just said about temporal parts. According to Three-Dimensionalism, there are no such things as "temporal parts" of objects, and so, naturally, objects are not composed of any such parts. What's more, according to Three-Dimensionalism, when you consider an object at a time (such as you at noon today), you are not merely considering a part of that object. You are considering the whole object. Similarly, the relation between you at noon today and you at noon tomorrow, on Three-Dimensionalism, is not the relation *being a different part of the same object*; rather, it is simply *identity*.

Here is a way of formulating the two parties to this dispute:

x is a *temporal part* of *y* = df (i) *x* exists for a shorter span of time than *y*, and (ii) throughout *x*'s existence, *x* exactly overlaps *y*.[11]

Four-Dimensionalism
Any object that is extended in time has a different *temporal part* at each moment of its temporal extension.[12]

x is *wholly present* at moment *t* = df *x* is located at *t*, but not in virtue of having a *temporal part* at *t*.

Three-Dimensionalism
Any object that is extended in time is *wholly present* at each moment of its temporal extension.[13]

And here is how Four-Dimensionalism can help the B Theorist respond to Prior's "Thank goodness that's over" argument. Suppose the B Theorist is also a Four-Dimensionalist. Then he or she can say that there is a sense in which the thing that says, "Thank goodness that's over" is not you. It is instead a temporal part of you, namely, the temporal part of you that immediately follows the relevant headache. And that temporal part of you is indeed thankful to be later than the headache, rather than simultaneous with it. (Why is the relevant temporal part thankful that it is later than the headache? This is a good question, and one that the Four-Dimensionalist will certainly want to be able to answer. But there are available several plausible answers to this question, and the Four-Dimensionalist has the option of choosing among them. For example, it can be plausibly maintained that, as a result of natural selection, we have developed a certain bias toward the future, so that our temporal parts tend to be nearly as concerned about the welfare of their immediate successors as they are about their own welfare, but much less concerned about the welfare of their predecessors.) So the speaker who says, "Thank goodness that's over"

---

[11] Given the first condition of the above definition, it would actually be more perspicuous to attach the phrase 'proper temporal part' to that definition. Then we could understand each object to be an *improper temporal part* of itself, and we could reserve the general term 'temporal part' to cover both proper and improper temporal parts.

[12] Defenses of Four-Dimensionalism can be found in Quine, *Word and Object*; Lewis, "The Paradoxes of Time Travel," and "Survival and Identity"; Heller, *The Ontology of Physical Objects*; Hawley, *How Things Persist*; and Sider, *Four-Dimensionalism*.

[13] Defenses of Three-Dimensionalism can be found in Thomson, "Parthood and Identity across Time"; Haslanger, "Persistence, Change, and Explanation"; van Inwagen, "Four-Dimensional Objects"; and Hinchliff, "The Puzzle of Change."

really is thanking goodness for a B-fact. Which means that the premise of Prior's argument denying this is false.

If this response to Prior's "Thank goodness that's over" argument is satisfactory, then the B Theorist who also happens to be a Four-Dimensionalist has a reasonable response to Prior's argument. It is of course a further question whether this response to Prior's argument can be adapted for use by a B Theorist who endorses Three-Dimensionalism and, if not, whether there is available to the B Theorist any response to Prior's argument that is consistent with Three-Dimensionalism. Moreover, if the answer to this last question is No, then we are left with yet another question, namely, whether being committed to Four-Dimensionalism should count as a genuine cost of The B Theory or, instead, just a natural part of a general outlook according to which time is taken to be similar in many important ways to the dimensions of space. We will not attempt to answer these questions here, but will instead turn next to a consideration of two of the most influential arguments in favor of Four-Dimensionalism.

7.8 The argument from temporary intrinsics

The two arguments in question are both presented by David Lewis.[14] Here is an overview of the first one. An *intrinsic property* is a property that a thing can have all by itself, without any help from anything else. Examples would include redness and other color properties, as well as properties like being straight and other shape properties. Such intrinsic properties can be contrasted with extrinsic properties, where an *extrinsic property* is a property that a thing can have only in virtue of standing in some relation to some other thing or things. Examples of extrinsic properties would include being an uncle and being the tallest human.

Meanwhile, a *temporary intrinsic property* is what it sounds like: an intrinsic property that a thing has only temporarily. So, for example, Lewis being straight (when he is standing) or being bent (when he is sitting) would count as temporary intrinsics, in this terminology.

Now suppose Lewis first sits and then stands. While seated he displays a certain bent shape and while standing he displays a different, straightened

---

[14] For Lewis's presentation of the argument from temporary intrinsics see Lewis, *On the Plurality of Worlds*, pp. 202–5.

shape. But being bent and being straight are incompatible properties. How is it possible for Lewis to have them both? This is the problem of temporary intrinsics.

Lewis says that there are three possible solutions to this problem. The first is to say that temporary intrinsics are disguised relations. On this view, Lewis is not bent simpliciter, nor is he straight simpliciter. Rather, he is bent at some time, t_1, and straight at some other time, t_2. But, says Lewis, this makes intrinsic properties into disguised relations. And that, he says, is unacceptable: for it seems clear that apparent properties like being bent and being straight are in fact genuine intrinsic properties of the things that have them, rather than relations that those things stand in to various times.

The second possible solution to the problem of temporary intrinsics, according to Lewis, is to say that Presentism is true. Presentism says, roughly, that only present things are real. (But see 7.11 for a more detailed discussion of the view.) According to this view, each thing has only the properties that it has now. So Lewis, according to Presentism, is either bent or straight, but not both. But Lewis tells us that this proposed solution to the problem is unacceptable because Presentism is unacceptable. (For one thing, he says, it entails that there are no other times, which none of us believes.)

The third possible solution to the problem of temporary intrinsics involves the claim that to possess different temporary intrinsics is to have different temporal parts with different intrinsic properties. According to this line we can say, for example, that Lewis has a temporal part at t_1 that is bent (simpliciter) and another temporal part at t_2 that is straight (simpliciter). And there is no contradiction in saying both of these things, any more than there is a contradiction in saying that a fence has one part that is painted white and another part that is not. Moreover, if we take this line, then we can still say that temporary intrinsics are genuine properties of the things that have them, rather than disguised relations.

Since Lewis takes this last solution to the problem to be the only good one available, the upshot is supposed to be that Four-Dimensionalism must be true.

It should be clear that Three-Dimensionalists who are also Presentists will reject the premise of Lewis's argument that is the denial of Presentism. But what about the Three-Dimensionalist who does not want to commit to Presentism?

Our view is that the best option for a Three-Dimensionalist who does not want to commit to Presentism is to respond to the argument by maintaining that we need to take tense seriously. This, it will be recalled, amounts to endorsing the following semantic thesis:

The Tensed Conception of Semantics (TCS)
(i) The verbal tenses of ordinary language (expressions like 'it is the case that', 'it was the case that', and 'it will be the case that') must be taken as primitive and unanalyzable. (ii) Propositions – the things that are true or false – have truth values *at times* rather than just having truth values *simpliciter.*

If the Three-Dimensionalist endorses TCS, then he or she will say that Lewis has offered a false trilemma, and that the fourth option, the one he left out, is to say that when Lewis is standing, it is an irreducibly tensed truth that Lewis *was* bent (bent simpliciter, that is), and also an irreducibly tensed truth that Lewis *is* straight (straight simpliciter). That is, when Lewis is standing, these two sentences are both true: 'Lewis was bent' and 'Lewis is straight.' Because of the different tenses in these two sentences, such a Three-Dimensionalist will say, there is no contradiction in their both being true.

We also think it is worth noting that the Three-Dimensionalist who does not endorse either Presentism or TCS should not be reluctant to embrace the first option offered (and rejected) by Lewis. That is, such a person should not be reluctant to say that temporary intrinsics are indeed disguised relations. After all, such a Three-Dimensionalist can point out that he or she is not the only one who can be accused of biting a bullet. For while he or she must say that Lewis stands in the *bent at* relation to t_1 and the *straight at* relation to t_2, the Four-Dimensionalist must say, somewhat counterintuitively, that it is not Lewis himself who possesses the intrinsic property of being bent but, rather, the t_1 temporal part of Lewis. (And similarly with the thing that, according to Four-Dimensionalism, possesses the intrinsic property of being straight – it is not Lewis himself but, rather, a temporal part of Lewis.)

7.9 Lewis's 'patchwork' argument for person-stages

The other influential argument for Four-Dimensionalism that has been suggested by Lewis concerns the notion of a "person-stage", which is meant to be a very short-lived temporal part of a person.[15] And the argument is designed to show that all the people in our world are in fact made up of person-stages, as Four-Dimensionalism says.

Lewis's argument for person-stages begins with the claim that it is possible for a person-stage to exist all by itself. That is, it is possible for something that looks just like a normal person to pop into existence out of thin air, to last for, say, a millionth of a second, and then to pop out of existence.

("But why would such a person-stage just pop in and out of existence?" you might ask. Well, perhaps because some very powerful being causes it to do so in order to win a bet. Or perhaps for no reason at all, in a manner that many scientists and philosophers take to be consistent with some of the stranger consequences of the leading theories in quantum physics.)

The argument continues with the claim that since such a thing is possible, it is also possible for two person-stages to exist, and for one to appear to follow seamlessly from the other. Here the rationale is a kind of recombination or "patchwork" principle for possibility, according to which any possible situation can be followed by any other possible situation. The thought is that if S_1 and S_2 are both possible situations, then there is no logical or metaphysical impossibility in supposing that S_1 obtains and then is immediately followed by S_2. (Notice that this is perfectly consistent with the claim that the actual laws of nature prevent many such pairings of possible situations.)

The next step in the argument is to apply the relevant recombination principle many times over, in order to generate an entire possible world of person-stages – each one lasting for only a millionth of a second – that is qualitatively indiscernible from the actual world. This other possible world will be peopled by person-stages, but will otherwise be exactly like the actual world in its point-by-point distribution of intrinsic local qualities over space and time.

The next step of the argument involves an appeal to a certain principle about causation, according to which the pattern of causal relations in a possible world is constrained by the distribution of local qualities over space and time in that world, but not by anything else.

---

[15] This argument is from Lewis's Postscript B to "Survival and Identity," in his *Philosophical Papers*, vol. I.

And from there the argument makes an appeal to one of Lewis's favorite metaphysical theses (often called "Humean Supervenience"), according to which there are no features of any possible world except those that supervene on the distribution of local qualities and their causal relations in that world. Appealing to this thesis allows Lewis to say that the world of person-stages under consideration, in virtue of being exactly like our world in its causal relations between local matters of particular fact, is exactly like the actual world in every way.

Finally, the argument concludes that, since the actual world is in every way exactly like a world of person-stages, our world is in fact a world of person-stages. That is, we the people (in the actual world, that is) are composed of countless short-lived temporal parts.

(It is worth noting that although Lewis's argument is formulated as an argument for the actual existence of person-stages, it of course generalizes to all kinds of other stages: horse-stages, bicycle-stages, quark-stages, and so on. So it is really an argument for temporal parts in general.)

We leave it to the reader to determine whether there is any good objection to Lewis's "patchwork" argument for person-stages available to the Three-Dimensionalist, and we now turn to a consideration of what has probably been the most influential argument against Four-Dimensionalism.

7.10 Thomson's argument against Four-Dimensionalism

The argument in question is suggested by Judith Jarvis Thomson.[16] Here is the basic idea behind the argument. Consider some ordinary object, like a piece of chalk. According to Four-Dimensionalism, there are a great many temporal parts of that piece of chalk. For example, there is a one-second-long temporal part of the chalk that begins to exist at noon today, a half-second-long temporal part that begins to exist at noon today, a quarter-second-long temporal part that begins to exist at the same time, and so on.

In fact, as this example makes clear, for any persisting object and for any arbitrarily chosen, extended period of time during which that object persists, if Four-Dimensionalism is true then there will be infinitely many

[16] See Thomson, "Parthood and Identity across Time."

distinct temporal parts of that object that all fall within that period of time. Which means that if you hold a piece of chalk in your hand for even a second, infinitely many temporal parts of that piece of chalk will come into and go out of existence right there in your hand during that second. (According to Four-Dimensionalism, that is.)

That in itself might seem to a lot of people like a bad consequence of Four-Dimensionalism. (It's one thing to have some surprising objects in your ontology and quite another to have infinitely many of them, right there in your hand, popping in and out of existence in such a short period of time.) But there is more. For the alleged existence of all of these strange objects gives rise to a whole host of puzzling questions about them. Why do they keep popping in and out of existence, for example? And for any two of them that pop into existence at the same time and in the same place (such as the one-second-long temporal part of the chalk that begins at noon and the half-second-long temporal part of the chalk that also begins at noon), why does one last for longer than the other (especially considering that they are exactly alike for the entire duration of the shorter one's existence)? How does the longer-lived one know to continue existing when the shorter-lived one goes out of existence? And so on.

The argument can be formulated as a simple *modus tollens* inference. (1) If Four-Dimensionalism is true, then whenever a piece of chalk persists for any extended period of time, infinitely many distinct chalk-like objects pop in and out of existence where that chalk is located during that time. (2) It's not the case that whenever a piece of chalk persists for any extended period of time, infinitely many distinct chalk-like objects pop in and out of existence where that chalk is located during that time. Therefore, (3) Four-Dimensionalism is not true.

It's clear that Four-Dimensionalists must reject the second premise of this argument. For the Four-Dimensionalist is definitely committed to the existence of all of the relevant temporal parts. What the Four-Dimensionalist needs, then, is some account of why the relevant consequence of his or her view is not in fact a bad consequence. And part of that account should consist of finding ways of answering the allegedly puzzling questions raised by the existence of so many different temporal parts (or perhaps, in some cases, explaining why the relevant question does not really arise).

But it is worth pointing out what will be another important part of the Four-Dimensionalist's account of why we should be willing to accept the relevant consequence of Four-Dimensionalism. Any philosophical thesis must really be thought of as part of a package, containing the thesis in question and various associated theses. And no such package should be evaluated just on the basis of some one, possibly counterintuitive, consequence of that package. Instead, each such package must be evaluated in terms of all of its costs and benefits. And Four-Dimensionalism, as it is normally defended, is a part of a bigger package (including also The B Theory, The Tenseless Conception of Semantics, and Eternalism [see below]) that has many very impressive benefits, including its elegance, its theoretical simplicity, and its obvious consistency with leading scientific theories such as Special Relativity. So the Four-Dimensionalist should say, in response to the above argument, that accepting the existence of so many temporal parts of the piece of chalk is a small price to pay, considering all of the benefits associated with Four-Dimensionalism.

7.11 Presentism, Eternalism, and The Growing Universe Theory

We turn now to a different controversy in the philosophy of time, one that concerns the ontological status of non-present objects (such as Socrates and your future great-great-grandchildren). Should we include any such objects in our ontology? If so, should we include the future ones as well as the past ones, or should we restrict our ontology to just past and present objects?

The basic idea behind the view known as Presentism is that only present things are real; indeed, on this view, the difference between the present, on the one hand, and the past and the future, on the other hand, is "but one facet of the great gulf that separates the real from the unreal, what is from what is not."[17]

The dispute between Presentists and their rivals is analogous to a certain controversy in the metaphysics of modality between Actualists and Modal Realists. Actualism is the view that only actual objects exist. On this view, there are no *merely possible* objects. Modal Realism is the denial

[17] Prior, "The Notion of the Present," pp. 247–8.

of this; it is the view that some of the things that exist are not actual (they are merely possible).

One way of capturing our temporal dispute involves talk about the intensions and extensions of certain predicates. The *intension* of a predicate is the concept or property picked out by that predicate. (For example, the intension of 'is red' is the property *redness*.) The *extension* of a predicate, on the other hand, is the set of things that the predicate applies to. (So the extension of 'is red' is the set of all and only red things.) Two predicates that have the same intension are said to be co-intensive (or synonymous), and two predicates that have the same extension are said to be co-extensive. Given this terminology, it is of course possible for two predicates that are co-extensive to fail to be co-intensive. For example, the predicates 'has a heart' and 'has a kidney' are co-extensive, since they apply to all of the same things, but they are not co-intensive, since they pick out different properties.

Now consider these two predicates: 'is present' and 'exists'. Presentists and their opponents can agree that they are not co-intensive. But the Presentist's opponents also say that 'is present' and 'exists' are not co-extensive. For the Presentist's opponents think that 'exists' applies to some things that 'is present' does not apply to, such as Socrates, for example, and (perhaps) your future great-great-grandchildren.[18] The Presentist, on the other hand, says that 'is present' and 'exists' are (always and necessarily) co-extensive. Whatever 'exists' applies to, according to the Presentist, 'is present' also applies to.

So one way of capturing the issue is as a controversy over whether these expressions – 'is present' and 'exists' – are necessarily and always co-extensive. Here is another way of capturing the dispute. Let our quantifiers be completely unrestricted, so that they range over absolutely everything that there is. Then we can ask whether the following sentence is always true.

(P) Everything that exists is present.

Or, we can ask, is the following sentence sometimes true instead?

---

[18] Note: some Non-Presentists prefer to say that non-present objects exist, without existing now, where '*x* exists now' is taken to be just another way of saying that *x* is present.

(NP) Some things that exist are non-present.

Here are our official formulations of the relevant views:

Presentism
Only present objects are real.[19]

Eternalism
Past objects, present objects, and future objects are all equally real.[20]

The Growing Universe Theory
Past objects and present objects are real, but future objects are not.[21]

It is often said that Presentism is the common-sense view. But there are some rather glaring problems facing the Presentist. One such problem is that the view seems to lead to the conclusion that nothing at all really exists. After all, the present is razor-thin; it is vanishingly small. In fact, the present seems to have zero temporal extension. So it seems like the Presentist's ontology contains nothing. And that is certainly problematic.

Another worry facing the Presentist has to do with singular propositions about non-present objects. For here is a sentence that will strike the man on the street as clearly true:

(1) Socrates was a philosopher.

And yet (1) appears to express a 'singular proposition' about Socrates, i.e., a proposition specifically *about* Socrates, and one that contains Socrates (the man himself) as a constituent. But it looks like the existence (not to mention the truth) right now of a singular proposition about Socrates entails the existence of Socrates.

A third worry about Presentism has to do with relations between present and non-present objects. Isn't it true, for example, that John admires Socrates? And isn't it true that Ned stands in the *son of* relation to his father, despite the fact that Ned's father is no longer present? Moreover, don't these apparent truths commit us to saying that present objects can stand in various relations to non-present objects?

---

[19] For an example of a defense of Presentism see Prior, "The Notion of the Present" and "Some Free Thinking about Time;" and Markosian, "A Defense of Presentism."

[20] For an example of a defense of Eternalism see Sider, *Four-Dimensionalism.*

[21] For an example of a defense of The Growing Universe Theory see McCall, *A Model of the Universe.*

These apparent truths certainly seem to commit us to saying precisely that. But it looks like the Presentist has to deny that any present object can stand in any relation to any non-present object. And so it looks like the Presentist has to deny that John really stands in the *admiring* relation to Socrates or that Ned really stands in the *son of* relation to his father. And if these really are consequences of Presentism then they are certainly strange and troubling commitments of that theory.

A fourth worry about Presentism has to do with non-present times, such as the time of your birth and the time of your death. We certainly seem to talk about such times. But how can we do that if they don't exist?

There is more. Presentism is a special version of The A Theory. (For it doesn't make sense to say that only present objects exist unless you also say that presentness is a genuine, monadic property.) So any argument against The A Theory (such as McTaggart's argument, the argument from relativity, and the rate of passage argument) will also be an argument against Presentism.

The Eternalist faces none of the problems just mentioned in connection with Presentism. But what about The Growing Universe Theory? Well, it should be clear that proponents of The Growing Universe Theory will avoid the hardest versions of at least some of the problems facing Presentism. For example, proponents of The Growing Universe Theory need not worry about the accusation that they have a razor-thin ontology, since their ontology is plenty thick (and growing all the time!). Nor do they have to worry about singular propositions about past objects like Socrates, since they have such objects (and hence singular propositions about them) in their ontology. And as for the question of singular propositions about future objects (like your great-great-grandchildren), well, it is much more plausible to say that there really are no such singular propositions than it is to say the same thing with respect to past objects.

Similarly for the problem of relations between present and non-present objects: proponents of The Growing Universe Theory have all the past objects they could want for present objects to stand in relations to; and it is much more plausible to deny that present objects stand in relations to future objects than it is to deny that we stand in relations to past objects.

But some of the problems facing Presentism will translate into problems for The Growing Universe Theory. For example, proponents of The Growing Universe Theory still face the problem of how we manage to talk and think about future times, if they don't really exist. And since The Growing Universe Theory is, like Presentism, a version of The A Theory, the Growing Universe theorist must still have a response to all of the arguments against The A Theory.

7.12 Is time like space?

It may be that there are available to the Presentist (and to the proponent of The Growing Universe Theory) plausible solutions to all of the above problems.[22] Then again, it may be that there are not. But in any case, we are inclined to think that the best responses to most of the above difficulties on the part of the Presentist (or the proponent of The Growing Universe Theory) will involve some appeal to the controversial claim that time is fundamentally different from the dimensions of space. And if we are right about that, then the debate between Presentists and proponents of The Growing Universe Theory, on the one hand, and Eternalists, on the other hand, can best be seen as part of a larger debate within the philosophy of time over the extent to which time is similar to the dimensions of space. In this larger debate we can include, on the side of those who say that time is like space, B Theorists, proponents of Four-Dimensionalism, and Eternalists. And on the side of those who say that time is crucially different from space we can place A Theorists, proponents of Three-Dimensionalism, and those who endorse either Presentism or The Growing Universe Theory.

---

[22] For detailed attempts to solve these and other problems facing Presentism, see Markosian, "A Defense of Presentism."

8   Material objects

8.1 A statue and a lump

Suppose that on Monday you bring home a lump of clay and place it on your workbench. Then on Tuesday morning you carefully fashion the clay into a beautiful statue of a snowy owl, which remains in your workshop for all your friends to admire when they come over that night. But suppose that on Wednesday you wake up in a bad mood and decide that you don't like the snowy owl after all. So that morning you squash it back into an amorphous lump of clay.

This example raises several interesting metaphysical questions. Chief among them is this: how many objects are there on your workbench on Tuesday night? One plausible answer is that there is just one object there, namely, the statue. After all, most people, if asked to count the objects on the workbench at that time (most people without a metaphysical agenda, that is), would examine the situation and confidently say that there is just the statue there on the workbench.

Although "one" might seem like the common-sense answer to our question about how many objects are on the workbench on Tuesday night, there are also some good reasons to think that the right answer is "two." For it is natural to think that there is the lump of clay, which is one thing, and also the statue, which is something distinct from the lump. One reason for thinking this is that the statue and the lump have different histories. After all, the lump was brought home on Monday, when the statue didn't yet exist, and the statue came into existence on Tuesday morning, when the lump had already been around for quite a while. Also, the statue went out of existence on Wednesday morning, when you squashed it, but the lump of clay continued to exist for a long time after that.

We will return later in this chapter to the question of whether the statue and the lump are two distinct objects, but in the meantime suppose that on Tuesday night one of your friends points out that, even if the statue and the lump are one object (rather than two), the number of objects on the workbench is still many more than one. For there are in any case all of the molecules, atoms, and subatomic particles that compose the lump of clay. In fact, the number of subatomic particles alone, as your friend points out, is likely to have more than twenty digits in it. That's a big number, even without counting all of the atoms and molecules (not to mention the lump and the statue).

Suppose another friend argues that there are indeed a large number of objects on the workbench, but not quite as many as the first friend is suggesting. For, according to this other friend, all that really exists on your workbench is a swarming mass of subatomic particles. Any other putative objects, she says, including any alleged statue, lump, molecules, and atoms, are mere fictions – useful ways of talking about the many swarming particles. The ultimate reality, she insists, consists of just the fundamental particles.

Are the statue and the lump of clay two distinct objects? Is there even a statue or a lump on the workbench? Are there such objects as atoms and molecules, or does the physical world consist entirely of fundamental particles? These are some of the questions about material objects that we will be concerned with in this chapter. Others include questions about the circumstances under which two or more objects compose a further object, when an object has no parts, whether an object can gain and lose parts, and the relation between a physical object and the matter that it is made of. But our first question is even more basic than that. For we begin with the question of how to distinguish between physical and non-physical objects.

8.2 Physical and non-physical objects

We are interested in this chapter in a number of questions about physical (or material) objects. That's one main reason to want to be able to distinguish between physical and non-physical objects. Another main reason has to do with the role this distinction plays in many areas of philosophy, including The Mind–Body Problem and discussions of various forms of materialism.[1] So what exactly are physical objects?

George Berkeley said (roughly) that physical objects are the things outside of our minds that can be sensed.[2] (He also ended up arguing that there can be no such things, but his arguments for that conclusion can be divorced from his account of physical objects.)

One difficulty with Berkeley's sensational account of physical objects is that different beings have different sensory abilities, which means that this account threatens to make the notion of a physical object a relativistic one. That would be a highly undesirable result, given the crucial role played by the concept in various philosophical debates. In order to avoid this result, then, we could modify the sensational account to say that physical objects are objects that can be sensed by some sentient being or other. But if we say this then we run the risk of casting our net much too wide; for it may be possible for a disembodied mind to sense another such mind, and it may also be possible for an extremely sensitive creature to sense such seemingly non-physical entities as propositions. And there is also this objection to the sensational account: it turns the property of being a physical object into an extrinsic property of the things that have it; and yet, intuitively, being physical is an intrinsic property of physical objects.

An alternative account of the physical holds that physical objects are the objects studied by physics.[3] This appears to be a popular approach, especially among philosophers writing on physicalism. But it leads very quickly to a definitional circle if, as we suspect, the best definition of 'physics' is *the study of physical objects*.

In addition, there are a number of apparent counterexamples to the physical theory account of physical objects: numbers, equations, formulas, functions, properties, and propositions all seem to be among the objects studied by physics, but none of them strikes us as a physical object. Also, it is quite possible that some day it will turn out that the best physical theory is one that (correctly, we can suppose) posits ghosts and goddesses and other entities that we would not want to call physical objects.

---

[1] Chapter 6 discusses several versions of materialism. Our focus in that chapter was the nature of mental states.

[2] See Berkeley, *A Treatise Concerning the Principles of Human Knowledge*, Part I, section 4.

[3] See, for example, Smart, *Our Place in the Universe*, p. 79.

W. V. O. Quine has suggested that a physical object is "the aggregate material content of any portion of space-time, however ragged and discontinuous."[4] On the face of it, this proposal looks circular, since we are taking 'material' to be synonymous with 'physical'. But it may be possible to avoid this problem simply by subtracting the word 'material' from Quine's suggestion, leaving us with a proposal according to which a physical object is the content of any portion of space-time.

This proposal has some plausible consequences, but it also comes with some noteworthy metaphysical baggage. For this Quinean account entails a thesis called Universalism (see below), according to which (roughly) for any group of objects, there is a further object whose parts are the members of that group. Thus, for example, according to Universalism, there is an object whose parts are your head, the president's shoes, and a single quark from the surface of the moon. As we will see in 8.8 below, there are some interesting arguments in support of Universalism; but it is nevertheless a highly controversial thesis. Thus, the fact that our Quinean account of physical objects entails Universalism counts as a significant cost of that account.

A further problem for the Quinean view is that it may prove impossible, on that view, to distinguish between a particular physical object, such as a ball, say, and any event that is spatio-temporally coincident with that ball, such as the ball's history. What's more, on certain theories of universals, it may also prove impossible to distinguish between the ball and its various life-long properties. (Perhaps this problem is the reason Quine included the word 'material' in his statement of the view in the first place.)

Peter van Inwagen has suggested an alternative account of physical objects.[5] According to van Inwagen, there is a certain family of properties – such as being located in space, having spatial extension, persisting through time, being able to move about in space, having a surface, having mass, being made of matter, and so on – that are associated with the concept of a physical object. Van Inwagen further suggests that the latter concept is an imprecise one, and that the extent to which an object exemplifies all or most of the concepts on the associated list is the extent to which that object is a physical object.

[4] Quine, "Whither Physical Objects?," p. 497.
[5] van Inwagen, *Material Beings*, p. 17.

This common-sense account of physical objects may well be an adequate way of capturing the everyday notion of a physical object. But when it comes to the concept of a physical object that is featured in the disputes of philosophers, the common-sense account is problematic. One difficulty is that it makes the concept of a physical object a vague one, which is undesirable given the role that concept plays in numerous philosophical disputes.

Another problem for the common-sense account is that it entails that quarks, electrons, atoms, and even certain large organic molecules may not be physical objects.[6] This is bad for two reasons. First, since quarks, electrons, and so forth are all among the parts of macroscopic physical objects, this consequence of the common-sense account goes against the very plausible thesis that a physical object cannot have a non-physical object among its parts. And second, no one on either side of the debate over physicalism thinks that the existence of quarks and electrons refutes physicalism.

There may be another problem facing the common-sense account of physical objects. Imagine a possible world with very different properties and laws of nature from those in the actual world. Suppose that in this other possible world, there are point-sized objects with spatial locations that never persist through time but, instead, pop in and out of existence instantaneously. Since they don't persist, these objects of course don't move around. Suppose further that they don't have mass, or any of the other familiar properties of physical objects in this world, but instead exemplify various alien properties that nothing in the actual world ever exhibits; and suppose finally that it is these strange, alien properties that figure in the laws of nature governing this other possible world. The proponent of the common-sense account has to say that there are no physical objects in such a world (since the objects in question have almost none of the properties on the relevant list); but this seems like a strange result. For

---

[6] For as van Inwagen himself says, "one has to be very careful in ascribing any of the features in the above list to such things; and talk about the surfaces of submicroscopic objects, or about the stuffs they are made of, tends to verge on nonsense" (*Material Beings*, p. 17). It should be noted, however, that van Inwagen considers it a feature of his view, rather than a bug, that it seems to entail that quarks, etc., are not material objects.

surely the truth about this other possible world is simply that its physical objects (and laws of nature) are very different from our own.

This thought experiment involving an exotic possible world suggests a different approach to understanding physical objects. For the objects we considered in this imagined world were strange, but they were nevertheless located in space, and it is probably for that reason that we find it plausible to call them physical objects. If so, then perhaps we should say that physical objects are objects with spatial locations.[7]

The spatial location account of physical objects has some very intuitive consequences. It counts such ordinary macroscopic objects as humans, rocks, planets, and stars as physical objects. It also counts their smaller parts, including molecules, electrons, and quarks. In addition, the spatial location account declares such things as numbers, properties, functions, and sets to be non-physical, and that too seems plausible.

One worry that can be raised concerning this account, however, involves such shady objects as shadows, sensations, specters, mirror images, hallucinations, and apparitions. All of these putative objects seem to have spatial locations, but it doesn't seem right to call any of them a physical object.

A second objection to the spatial location account is that it seems to require a sharp distinction between space and time. As seen in Chapter 7, there is a sizeable movement among metaphysicians to treat the three dimensions of space and the one dimension of time as four intrinsically similar dimensions of the world; and anyone who is sympathetic to that movement will not want to make having a spatial location be the distinguishing mark of the physical. But (as also seen in Chapter 7) there is still considerable opposition to the space-and-time-are-intrinsically-alike movement, and those who take space and time to be fundamentally different will not mind the spatial location account implying as much.

Another main objection to the spatial location account concerns the possibility of spatially unextended minds that nevertheless have spatial locations. For many ordinary people, as well as such philosophers as Locke and Descartes, want to define 'mind' as roughly synonymous with 'non-physical, thinking substance'; but some who accept this definition

---

[7] This view is endorsed by Hobbes in Part II, Chapter VIII of his *Concerning Body* (contained in Hobbes, *Metaphysical Writings*), and defended in Markosian, "What Are Physical Objects?"

of 'mind', and say that they believe in minds, also believe that minds can have spatial locations.[8] (Such a person might say, for example, that your mind is currently located at a certain point inside your brain.) Anyone who likes this way of thinking about the mind will find the spatial location account of physical objects unacceptable.

There is, however, another spatial account of physical objects that might appeal to such a person. Descartes and others have suggested that what characterizes physical objects is not that they have spatial *locations* (since, it is suggested, non-physical minds can also have spatial locations) but, rather, that they have spatial *extension* (where an object is spatially extended if it occupies more than a single point in space). Endorsing this account of physical objects would allow a person to maintain, for example, that your mind is a non-physical (because unextended) object that is located at a certain point inside your brain.

The main cost of the spatial extension account of physical objects is that it entails that all point-sized things are non-physical. Thus, for example, if our current physical theories are correct, then many (perhaps even all) of the particles that compose the macroscopic objects around us are non-physical objects. For according to current theories those particles are point-sized things.

8.3 The Special Composition Question

A lot of the questions we will consider in the next two sections have to do with a branch of metaphysics called mereology, which is concerned with a cluster of issues surrounding the part–whole relation. These issues have received a lot of attention from philosophers in the last eighty years or so, and especially in the last thirty years. The main question that sparked the recent flurry of activity within the philosophical community was raised by Peter van Inwagen in *Material Beings*. Van Inwagen's book is concerned with the notion of "composition" – roughly, the forming of a whole by two or more parts. Here is how van Inwagen defines this notion.[9]

> *x overlaps y* =df there is a z such that z is a part of x and z is a part of y.

[8] See, for example, Locke, *An Essay Concerning Human Understanding*; and Descartes, *Meditations on First Philosophy*.

[9] Van Inwagen, *Material Beings*, p. 29.

The *xs compose y* = df (i) the *xs* are all parts of *y*, (ii) no two of the *xs* overlap, and (iii) every part of *y* overlaps at least one of the *xs*.

Note that the only mereological term taken as primitive in these definitions is 'part'. Note also that in keeping with tradition in discussions of mereology, van Inwagen uses 'part' in such a way that each thing is automatically a part of itself. But we can distinguish between parts in general and 'proper parts', where a proper part of *x* is understood to be a part of *x* that is not identical to *x*. (Thus the philosophical concept of a *proper part* no doubt corresponds more closely to the common-sense notion of a part than does the broader philosophical notion of a *part*.)

Now, intuitively, there are many cases in which some *xs* compose a further object. For example, it's natural to think that all of your cells compose your body, and also natural to think that four legs and a tabletop can compose a table. But it's equally plausible to think that there are many cases in which some *xs* fail to compose a further object. For example, it's very natural to think that your underwear and the Eiffel Tower do not compose anything.

If there are cases in which some *xs* compose something, and also cases in which some *xs* fail to compose anything, then it makes sense to ask, What is the general rule governing when composition occurs and when it doesn't occur? This is the question that van Inwagen raised in *Material Beings*, and that sparked the recent flurry of activity on the mereology of physical objects.

Here is a variation on van Inwagen's more precise way of asking this question.[10]

The Special Composition Question (SCQ)
What necessary and jointly sufficient conditions must any *xs* satisfy in order for it to be the case that there is an object composed of those *xs*?

It's important to understand that SCQ is not asking for an *analysis* of the concept of composition. For we already have such an analysis: it is stated in the above definition of 'the *xs* compose *y*'. Instead, SCQ is asking for some interesting, non-analytic principle about the way (if any) in which other properties and relations are (necessarily) linked up with the relation of composition. That is, SCQ is asking for a way of filling in the blank in

---

[10] For van Inwagen's characterization of the question, and an explanation of plural quantification (i.e., the use of expressions like 'for any *xs*'), see section 2 of *Material Beings*.

the following sentence schema: *for any* xs, *there is an object composed of those* xs *iff___.*

8.4 Contact and Fastening

You might think that SCQ is an easy question to answer. For example, you might think that whenever some xs are collectively in contact with one another, there is an object composed of those xs, and also that cases of composition always involve the relevant objects being in contact. Van Inwagen calls this view *Contact.*

Many people, upon first learning of SCQ, are initially drawn to this proposal. And, indeed, if you consider certain cases, such as the cells that make up your body, and the parts of your kitchen table, Contact seems to give some very plausible results. But what if you happen to bump into a stranger on the subway? Is there all of a sudden a new object that pops into existence when this happens? (An object that just as quickly pops out of existence when you and the stranger separate?) Or consider the particles that make up an atom. They are extremely small, and they're separated by relatively large expanses of empty space. So they are not in contact. But does it follow that there is no object composed of those particles? Are there no atoms after all?

These last two examples suggest both that mere contact is not enough for composition (as in the subway case), and also that genuine contact is not a requirement for composition (as in the case of the particles that compose an atom). The examples also seem to support a different relation as the key to composition: for you and the stranger on the subway are never really stuck together, whereas the subatomic particles, although not in contact with one another, are nevertheless bound together by very powerful forces. Perhaps, then, being collectively fastened together is necessary and sufficient for composition.[11] Van Inwagen calls this view *Fastening,* and, perhaps even more than Contact, it has a great deal of initial appeal.

---

[11] There may be problems with giving a satisfactory account of what it means to say that some objects are fastened together. (See in this regard van Inwagen, *Material Beings,* pp. 56–7, and Markosian, "Brutal Composition.") But let us set those problems aside.

One objection to Fastening, raised by van Inwagen, concerns the following kind of example.[12] Suppose that you and van Inwagen shake hands, and that right at that moment, your fingers and his become paralyzed in such a way that you and he are fastened together. Then according to Fastening, there is a new object in the world, composed of the two of you. But (says van Inwagen, and presumably many people will agree) this is the wrong result: we cannot increase the number of objects in the world merely by paralyzing handshakers in this way.

Advocates of Fastening will no doubt disagree, and will likely claim that there is no harm in admitting the existence of the relevant object (the thing composed of you and van Inwagen while you are stuck together), but acknowledging that we would normally ignore it when counting objects.

In any case, here is another problem for Fastening. Being fastened together is a multigrade relation that comes in degrees.[13] So which degree of fastenation among some objects is sufficient for their composing a further object? Any specific answer we give is likely to seem arbitrary; why should a degree of 0.5 (on a scale from 0 to 1), say, or 0.6478592, rather than just a tiny bit more or less, be the dividing line between cases of composition and cases of non-composition?

8.5 Nihilism

Some of the above considerations against Contact and Fastening suggest the following line of thought. You can rearrange the smallest parts of the world, piling some up over here, separating others out over there, but you cannot thereby change the total number of objects in the world, any more than you can change the number of objects that exist by rearranging grains of sand in the desert.[14] Merely sticking some small pieces together, or painting them the same color, or deciding to think of them as composing something, does not bring anything new into existence.

If this is right, then there are far fewer objects in the world than we ordinarily think. For if this is right, then it is never the case that two or

[12] Van Inwagen, *Material Beings*, pp. 57–8.

[13] A multigrade relation is one that can relate different numbers of objects. Two objects can be fastened together, but so can three objects, or four, etc.

[14] Van Inwagen makes some similar remarks, on behalf of the Nihilist (see below), in section 13 of *Material Beings*.

more objects compose a further object. Following van Inwagen, we can call this view *Nihilism*. According to Nihilism, the only material objects in the world are "mereological simples" – objects without any proper parts.

Nihilism certainly has its advantages. For one thing, unlike many other answers to SCQ, Nihilism is a clean and elegant view. For another thing, with fewer objects in your ontology, you may have fewer metaphysical problems to deal with. (For example, you won't face problems like those raised below by the example of Theseus's ship.)

Still, Nihilism does face some objections. The main one is just that the Nihilist's ontology contains too few objects. According to Nihilism, there are no atoms, molecules, rocks, dogs, chairs, planets, or stars; and that goes against what most of us believe.

There is a method for dealing with this objection, however, that is available to the Nihilist, namely, the paraphrasing approach that van Inwagen has developed in response to a similar objection to his own view (which we will consider shortly). Here's the idea. Suppose we're in a situation in which it would be natural to say that there is a chair in the corner. Then according to the Nihilist, the sentence 'there is a chair in the corner' is, strictly speaking, false. But still, the Nihilist can say, there is something in the ballpark that is true, namely, the sentence 'there are some simples arranged chair-wise in the corner'. And since we have this true paraphrase of the sentence that it would be natural to say is true, we can accommodate our intuitions on this matter, while still claiming that 'there is a chair in the corner' is (strictly speaking) false.[15]

It is an interesting question whether this paraphrasing strategy provides the Nihilist with an adequate reply to the objection that his or her ontology contains too few objects. Are our intuitions satisfied by the claim that in ordinary circumstances a sentence like 'there is a chair in the corner' is false, but may be paraphrased into a sentence that is true?

[15] There is potentially a further difficulty facing the Nihilist who opts for the paraphrasing strategy. (The difficulty is raised in Sider, "Van Inwagen and the Possibility of Gunk.") Suppose it turns out that there are no mereological simples. That is, suppose it turns out that every physical object is composed of further physical objects, so that it is "parts all the way down". Then even when it appears that there is a chair in the corner, it will never be the case that there are some simples arranged chair-wise in the corner. Perhaps the upshot is that the Nihilist may have to fall back on such paraphrases as 'there is some stuff arranged chairwise in the corner'. For more on stuff see 8.11 below.

Or is it a fatal blow to Nihilism that it entails that such sentences are always false?

In any case, here is a further objection that can be raised against Nihilism: what about you? You think, and from that it seems to follow, by Cartesian reasoning, that you exist. Yet you don't appear to be a mereological simple. So where in the Nihilist's ontology do you fit in?[16]

8.6 Van Inwagen's Proposed Answer

Consideration of this last objection to Nihilism might lead us to think as follows. What is most plausible about Nihilism is the idea that it is very difficult to increase the number of objects in the world merely by rearranging the simples that already exist. (Of course, this must be weighed against the implausibility of claiming that there are no atoms, molecules, rocks, dogs, chairs, planets, or stars.) But what is especially implausible about Nihilism is what it entails about us, namely, that we either don't exist or else are mereological simples. What is needed, then, is an answer to SCQ according to which there are a limited number of composite objects – enough to include we humans, and perhaps other things that are sufficiently like us, but not so many as to include rocks and chairs.

Van Inwagen offers such a view in response to the SCQ.[17] The basic idea behind van Inwagen's view is that there are both simples and composites, but the composites are limited to living organisms. The two main background concepts on which his view is based are the notion of a *life*, and the notion of the activity of some *xs constituting* a particular event.

A life is what you think it is: a special kind of event, of which your life is an example. Lives can be short or very long, and they tend to resemble certain other events (like hurricanes, tornados, and riots) in important respects: they persist over time, they can range over a large area, and they both take things in and expel objects that have been caught up in them.

Closely related to this last point (regarding the manner in which a life both takes in objects and also expels objects that have been caught up in

---

[16] Van Inwagen raises this objection in more detail in *Material Beings*, sections 8 and 12.

[17] Van Inwagen, *Material Beings*, especially section 9.

it) is the notion of a life (or any event, for that matter) being constituted at a time by the activity of some specific objects at that time. Thus, for example, an avalanche might be constituted, at any given time while it is occurring, by the activity of a certain group of rocks, and your life is right now constituted by the activity of a certain group of subatomic particles. (The very same particles, as it happens, that it would be natural to say compose your body right now.)

Here then is van Inwagen's view (which we will call *Van Inwagen's Proposed Answer*, or VIPA): for any xs, those xs compose a further object iff the activity of the xs constitutes a life. According to this view, there are just two kinds of physical object in the world: mereological simples and organisms.

One main objection that can be raised against VIPA is similar to the above objection to Nihilism: the view entails that there are no atoms, molecules, rocks, bicycles, or planets. And we already know from our discussion of Nihilism in 8.5 what van Inwagen's reply to this objection will be: paraphrasing, in the manner discussed above.

Meanwhile, another main objection to VIPA, having to do with the view entailing the possibility of "ontological vagueness", will be raised below. But first we'll look at another approach to answering SCQ.

8.7 The Serial Response

Contact and Fastening yield some counterintuitive results, and Nihilism is much more restrictive than common sense about the number of material objects in the world. Meanwhile, VIPA gets good results regarding living organisms, but not when it comes to inanimate objects. But perhaps the problem with all of these different views is that they fail to take into account that whether some xs compose something can depend a lot on what exactly the xs are like. For it is natural to think that the way in which some subatomic particles compose an atom is very different from the way in which some molecules form a rock or the way in which some cells compose a living body.

If we take this idea into account in formulating an answer to SCQ, we will want to identify a series of different types of object, and for each such type we will want to specify the conditions under which some objects of that type compose something (without assuming that these conditions must remain constant for all types of object).

In order for us to have a more precise way of characterizing this response to SCQ, consider the following sentence schema:

Series
Necessarily, for any non-overlapping xs, there is an object composed of the xs iff either the xs are *F1*s and related by *R1*, or the xs are *F2*s and related by *R2*, or … the xs are *Fn*s and related by *Rn*.

Now, the view in question, which we will call *The Serial Response to SCQ*, says that there is a correct answer to SCQ, but that it is an instance of Series.[18]

Perhaps the biggest objection to The Serial Response is simply that no one has yet offered a specific instance of Series in response to SCQ. It has also been suggested that The Serial Response compounds problems with standard moderate answers to SCQ. For The Serial Response first requires us to identify the different types of object (*F1*, *F2*, and so on) that are relevant to composition. And then The Serial Response requires us to find not just one relation that we can say is both necessary and sufficient for composition (and hence immune to counterexample), but one such relation for each of the types of object (the *Fn*s) that we have identified as relevant to composition.

8.8 Universalism and the argument from vagueness

We turn now to an argument that has been suggested by David Lewis and refined by Theodore Sider, and that seems to have some persuasive force against views like Contact, Fastening, VIPA, and The Serial Response to SCQ.[19] The problem, as Lewis sees it, is that we tend to think that composition is restricted to cases in which some xs are adjacent, are fastened together, contrast with their environment, and act jointly. Or anyway, the more some objects satisfy these intuitive desiderata, the more we are inclined to think they compose something.

---

[18] Compare van Inwagen's discussion of "series-style" answers to SCQ in section 7 of *Material Beings*. Compare also the view proposed by Rosenberg in "Comments on Peter van Inwagen's *Material Beings*," as well as the "Finite Serial Response" discussed in Markosian, "Brutal Composition." (The two objections that follow are from "Brutal Composition.")

[19] See Lewis, *On the Plurality of Worlds*, pp. 212–13; and Sider, *Four-Dimensionalism*, chapter 4, section 9.

But these intuitive desiderata, says Lewis, are vague; they come in degrees. Which means that if we try to use them to generate an answer to SCQ, then we will have to say that it can be a vague matter whether some particular xs compose anything. And that, says Lewis, is no good:

> The only intelligible account of vagueness locates it in our thought and language. The reason it's vague where the outback begins is not that there's this thing, the outback, with imprecise borders; rather there are many things, with different borders, and nobody has been fool enough to try to enforce a choice of one of them as the official referent of the word 'outback.' Vagueness is semantic indecision.[20]

Lewis's preferred account of vagueness is sometimes called *The Linguistic Theory of Vagueness*. Here is how VIPA, to take one example, seemingly runs into trouble with this theory of vagueness. As van Inwagen points out, in many cases it is probably an indeterminate matter whether a certain subatomic particle is caught up in a certain life. (For example, suppose you have just taken a sip of water. Then many of the H_2O molecules [and their atoms and particles] that you have just ingested will soon be incorporated into your life, but are right now in a sort of halfway state between being caught up in your life and not being caught up in your life.) So VIPA has the consequence that it can be an indeterminate matter whether a certain object is a part of a certain other object. And this means that, contrary to The Linguistic Theory of Vagueness, there can be "ontological vagueness" or genuine vagueness in the world.

According to Contact, there are (or at least can be) both cases in which some objects compose a further object and cases in which some objects fail to compose a further object. The same thing is true of Fastening, VIPA, and many other answers to SCQ. Van Inwagen calls answers to SCQ according to which there can be both cases of composition and also cases of non-composition "moderate" answers to that question, and they can be contrasted with what he calls "extreme" answers.

There are two extreme answers. One of them is Nihilism, which we have already considered, and the other one is called *Universalism* (aka *Unrestricted Composition*). According to Universalism, composition is automatic; whenever there are some (non-overlapping) xs, there is an object

---

[20] Lewis, *On the Plurality of Worlds*, p. 213.

composed of those *xs*.[21] And, as Lewis argues, considerations about vagueness seem to lead us to the conclusion that Universalism is true. (Or perhaps it would be better to say that considerations about vagueness seem to lead to the conclusion that either Nihilism or Brutal Composition [see below] or Universalism is true. For Nihilism and Brutal Composition, like Universalism, are consistent with the linguistic theory of vagueness, and with the denial of any vagueness in the world.)

In addition to allowing its proponents to reject ontological vagueness, Universalism has other advantages. Unlike some of the above answers to SCQ, Universalism is clean and elegant. And it yields no shortage of objects for the metaphysician to work with.

But is Universalism a plausible thesis? After all, it entails that there is an object composed of the Lincoln Memorial and the Taj Mahal, another object composed of you and the moon, a third object composed of your shoes plus one particular atom from Alpha Centauri, and even an object composed of one quark from the tip of the nose of each person alive right now.

In addition to the many counterintuitive consequences regarding individual cases of composition, Universalism appears to have some other metaphysically significant consequences. For example, van Inwagen has argued that Universalism entails Four-Dimensionalism (aka "the doctrine of temporal parts" and discussed in Chapter 7).[22] And one of the authors of this book has argued elsewhere that Universalism has an even stronger entailment, namely, that for any *xs* that exist at one time, and for any *ys* that exist at another time, there is a single object that is composed of those *xs* at the first time and those *ys* at the second time.[23] (So, for example, there is a single object that is composed of all of your atoms right now, and all of the atoms that will compose the next US president at noon on the day of his or her inauguration.) All of these consequences of Universalism

---

[21] The reason for the qualification that the *xs* be non-overlapping is simply that composition, as we have defined it (following van Inwagen), necessarily involves no overlap among the objects that do the composing. A related notion is that of a fusion, which is just the notion of composition without the non-overlap requirement. Thus another way to characterize Universalism is as the view that any *xs* whatsoever (i.e., whether they overlap or not) have a fusion. When so characterized, the view is normally called The Principle of Unrestricted Fusions.

[22] See van Inwagen, *Material Beings*, section 8.

[23] See Markosian, "Restricted Composition."

(assuming they are indeed consequences of the view) certainly seem to go against common sense in a big way; and for many people this is a sufficient reason to reject Universalism.

8.9 Brutal Composition

Before turning to other matters, we will consider one last response to SCQ. It involves a view that many philosophers take to be just plain crazy, although it was once endorsed by one of the authors of this book.[24] The view in question is called *Brutal Composition*. The basic idea behind this view is that there is no answer to SCQ. Sometimes some xs compose an object, and other times some xs fail to compose anything; but there is no systematic rule governing when composition does and does not occur. Whenever some xs compose something, it is just a brute fact that they do so, and whenever some xs fail to compose something, that too is a brute fact.

Now, we must be a little bit careful about the way we formulate this view. It cannot simply say that there is no answer to SCQ, since there exist such true but trivial answers to our question as this one:

> *Trivial*
> Necessarily, for any xs, there is an object composed of the xs iff there is a y such that (i) the xs are all parts of y, (ii) no two of the xs overlap, and (iii) every part of y overlaps at least one of the xs.

(Trivial is trivial because it follows trivially from our definition of 'the xs compose y'.)

What is wanted in an answer to SCQ is something that, in addition to being true, is non-trivial. But Brutal Composition should not even be formulated as the claim that there is no non-trivial answer to SCQ. For besides being trivial, there is another way in which an answer to SCQ could be defective: it could fail to be systematic. Consider some infinitely long English sentence that simply goes through every single possible arrangement of some xs, and specifies, for each one, whether composition occurs in that case or not.[25] Such a brute force "answer" to SCQ would not be a

---

[24] See Markosian, "Brutal Composition."

[25] Don't literally consider such a sentence. (That would take forever, and you're supposed to be reading a book here.) Just consider in the abstract the fact that there are such sentences.

real answer to the question, since it would tell us nothing about why composition occurs, and that is really what students of SCQ want to learn.

If we take facts to be instantiations of universals, some of which obtain in virtue of other facts, and if we understand a brute fact to be one that does not obtain in virtue of any other fact or facts, then we can understand Brutal Composition as a two-part thesis consisting of (i) the claim that there is no true, non-trivial, and finitely long answer to SCQ; and (ii) the claim that whenever some xs compose a further object, it is a brute fact that they do so.

One reason a person might endorse Brutal Composition is dissatisfaction with each of the available answers to SCQ. When we first learn about SCQ, we are likely to think, "What a great question! That's just the kind of thing that it makes sense for a philosopher to puzzle over." And we are also likely to feel certain that there must be an answer to such a straightforward and gripping question. But after studying the matter for some time, and finding that each proposed answer to the question comes at a high cost in counterintuitive consequences, some may feel that although it was correct to think that SCQ is a great question, it was a mistake to think that it must have an answer. Some facts have to be brute facts – why not compositional facts?[26]

Here is another possible reason for endorsing Brutal Composition. It's natural to think that for every possible world, there will be certain brute facts about that world (in addition to a large number of further, non-brutal facts). And it's also natural to think that the brute facts about a world will include such facts as the total number of physical objects that exist in that world. But if the total number of objects in a world is a brute fact about that world, then it seems to follow that either Nihilism or Brutal Composition is true. For if Universalism is true, then the total number of objects in a world is determined by the number of mereological simples in that world; and if Fastening is true, then the total number of objects in a world is determined by a combination of the number of simples plus the number of cases in which some simples are fastened together; and similarly for other moderate answers to SCQ. Meanwhile, we have already seen that Nihilism has the implausible consequence that either we are simples or else we don't exist

---

[26] For a more detailed version of this argument, and a general defense of Brutal Composition, see Markosian, "Brutal Composition."

at all. So it seems to follow, from the assumption that the total number of objects in a world is a brute fact about that world, that Brutal Composition is true.

For many people, the main objection to Brutal Composition may be just that it is so initially implausible to them. Such people are likely to feel that a question as clear and as philosophically compelling as SCQ must have a real answer. People who find Brutal Composition to be intuitively untenable may also be motivated by the idea that compositional facts are not the right kind of facts to be brute facts.

Another objection to Brutal Composition has been offered by Theodore Sider. Here is a version of Sider's argument.[27] Suppose Brutal Composition is true, and consider (a) a case in which some objects fail to compose anything, and (b) a case in which some objects do compose something. Now connect (a) to (b) with a series of cases, each one of which is extremely similar to its neighbors in any non-mereological respect (spatial proximity, degree to which the xs are fastened together, degree to which the activity of the xs constitutes a life, and so forth) that might be taken to be relevant to whether composition occurs. (The only limit on how similar adjacent members of the series will be to one another is how long we are willing to make the series. Since we are doing the relevant work in our imaginations, then, let the series be as long as is needed to make adjacent members so similar that we human beings, even with the help of our best precision instruments, could never tell them apart.) The result is a virtual continuum of cases in which every two adjacent cases are nearly indiscernible from one another. And yet somewhere in this series there will be a pair of adjacent cases such that in one member of the pair composition occurs and in the other one it does not. (This follows from the fact that (a) is a case of composition and (b) is not.) In short, Brutal Composition entails that there can be two cases that are arbitrarily alike with respect to any (non-mereological) factors that might be taken to be relevant to whether composition occurs, but such that in one of the cases composition occurs and in the other it does not. Sider and others take this to be a reason to reject Brutal Composition.

---

[27] The argument appears in chapter 4, section 9 of Sider, *Four-Dimensionalism*. For a reply to Sider's argument, see Markosian, "Brutal Composition."

8.10 A question about simples

SCQ is a question about groups of objects and the circumstances under which the members of a group are parts that form a whole. Here is another mereological question, in this case about individual objects: under what circumstances is a physical object a mereological simple? That is, when does an object *not* have proper parts? More precisely: what necessary and jointly sufficient conditions must any *x* satisfy in order for it to be the case that *x* is a mereological simple? We will refer to this as *The Simple Question*.[28]

Note that (as with SCQ and the notion of composition) The Simple Question is not asking for an *analysis* of the concept of mereological simplicity. For we already have such an analysis: a mereological simple is an object without proper parts. Instead, The Simple Question is asking for some interesting, non-analytic principle about the way (if any) in which other concepts are (necessarily) linked up with the concept of being a mereological simple.

Before we consider different possible answers to The Simple Question, we should note that it is a substantive issue whether there even are any mereological simples. That is, we must not overlook the possibility that, as it happens, every physical object has proper parts. If every physical object has proper parts, then the parts (being physical objects themselves) would have parts, which would have parts, and so on; in which case every material object in the world would count as what David Lewis has called "atomless gunk."[29] Can we know in advance that this is not the case? Some philosophers (including Democritus and Aristotle) have suggested that we can, because it is a necessary truth that there must be some simples that all other objects are composed of.[30] But other philosophers (including Lewis and Sider) have suggested otherwise.[31]

---

[28] Van Inwagen raises essentially the same question with his "Inverse Special Composition Question" (roughly, under what circumstances is an object composed of two or more parts?); see *Material Beings*, pp. 48–9. For more on The Simple Question, see Markosian, "Simples."

[29] See Lewis, *Parts of Classes*, p. 20.

[30] See, for example, Aristotle, *On Generation and Corruption*, 316a13–b16 (translated and quoted in Barnes, *Early Greek Philosophy*, pp. 211–12).

[31] See Lewis, *Parts of Classes*, chapter 1, and Sider, "Van Inwagen and the Possibility of Gunk."

Although philosophers have disagreed on whether it is possible for a world to contain no mereological simples at all, it is generally agreed that it is at least possible for there to be some simples in the world. And The Simple Question is asking about the necessary and jointly sufficient conditions under which this possibly exemplified concept – that of a mereological simple – is in fact exemplified.

One natural answer to this question is that a physical object is a mereological simple iff it is point-sized. (Where a point-sized material object is one that has a spatial location, and possibly such other properties as mass, charge, spin, and so on, but that has zero spatial extension.) Call this *The Pointy View of Simples*.

The Pointy View certainly seems plausible, especially in its claim that being point-sized is sufficient for being a mereological simple. But suppose there are pointy objects, and suppose it is possible for two of them to be colocated. (After all, they're really small, so it's not as if they will crowd each other out.) Finally, suppose that two colocated pointy objects can compose a third object. Then the third object will be point-sized, but it will not be a simple.

Questions can also be raised about The Pointy View's claim that being point-sized is necessary for being a simple. Suppose that in 1,000 years we will have reached a final physics – a physical theory that is apparently the ultimate and true theory of everything. And suppose that according to this theory, there are some fundamental building blocks, called simplons by the scientists, that all objects in the universe are made of. Suppose these simplons are tiny, perfectly spherical, spatially continuous bits of matter, each of which is one trillionth the size of the next smallest particle. Suppose, moreover, that simplons are physically indivisible, that each one is utterly homogeneous, and that two simplons can never come into contact with each other. Finally, suppose that simplons are the smallest objects that figure in any way in the ultimate physical theory of the scientists.

Now, in our scenario, the simplons are of course not point-sized (since they are spherical). So according to The Pointy View of Simples they are not mereological simples. But this seems like a strange consequence of The Pointy View, for several reasons. For one thing, it is strange to think that a homogeneous, perfectly spherical, and spatially continuous object such as a simplon has parts, when there is nothing to distinguish one putative part of it from another. It's also strange to think that a simplon has parts when it is physically indivisible. And for a third thing, many will find it strange to think that the physicist, who posits no smaller parts of a simplon, must yield to the metaphysician (the proponent of The Pointy View, that is), who insists that the simplon – despite all appearances to the contrary – does in fact have infinitely many smaller parts (each of which is itself a physical object).

A second view about mereological simples, perhaps supported by the simplon example, is that simples are objects that it is physically impossible to divide. Call this *The Physically Indivisible View of Simples*. According to this view, which was endorsed by the ancient Greek philosopher Democritus, what makes an object a mereological simple is that the laws of nature prevent it from being divided into smaller parts.[32] Democritus envisioned small objects, each one invisible to the naked eye, of varying shapes and sizes. He called these little things 'atoms' (meaning uncuttable in his language), for he took them to be unbreakable and undividable. Democritus reckoned that some of these atoms must be smooth and round, so that they tend not to adhere to each other, while others must be rough, or crooked, or shaped in such a way that they could easily glom onto one another to form larger clumps that would be perceptible to the naked eye. And he took these atoms to be the basic building blocks of all other physical objects in the universe.[33]

The Physically Indivisible View of Simples certainly gives some very plausible results in a lot of cases. It entails that a computer is not a mereological simple, for example, since it can be divided into many smaller parts, and also that a quark is a simple (assuming, with current science, that a quark cannot be divided into any smaller pieces). But there nevertheless are problems with the view.

Imagine a ring that is made of some material that is physically unbreakable. That would be a simple, according to The Physically Indivisible View. So far, no problem. But now imagine a trillion such rings that are interlocked, so as to form an enormous chain that goes all the way around the planet. Because each link in the chain is physically indivisible, the chain

---

[32] See Barnes, *Early Greek Philosophy*, pp. 206–12.

[33] That is actually a misleading way to put Democritus's view, for he was also a Nihilist about composition. So he thought the world consisted of nothing but "atoms and the void."

is, too. And that means that, according to The Physically Indivisible View, the chain will count as a mereological simple. But this is clearly the wrong result, for the chain has a trillion parts, namely, the individual rings of which it is made.

Or think of an intricately designed bomb, made of a thousand bits of plastic, metal, and so on, that is rigged in such a way that the removal (or even the slightest rearrangement) of any of those bits will, as a matter of physical necessity, result in the bomb exploding, which in turn will result in the complete annihilation of the entire bomb. It would be physically impossible to divide this bomb, so The Physically Indivisible View will yield the verdict that the bomb is a mereological simple. But again this seems like the wrong result.

Both a long chain of physically indivisible rings and the bomb in the above example are at least *metaphysically* divisible; i.e., even if the laws of nature prevent them from being divided, it is at least metaphysically possible that they should be divided. And perhaps that is why these objects are not simples. Perhaps we should say that something is a mereological simple iff it is not just physically but *metaphysically* impossible to divide it. Call this *The Metaphysically Indivisible View of Simples*.

Here's one objection to The Metaphysically Indivisible View of Simples. It seems clear that any extended object will be metaphysically divisible (even if it is not physically possible to divide it). So it looks like The Metaphysically Indivisible View of Simples will entail that non-extended (i.e., point-sized) objects will be the only things that are mereological simples. So it appears that The Metaphysically Indivisible View of Simples turns out to be equivalent to The Pointy View of Simples, in which case it will be subject to the same objections (including the simplon objection) as the latter view.

And here is a second objection to The Metaphysically Indivisible View of Simples. Consider a point-sized object. Call it Poindexter. Intuitively, The Metaphysically Indivisible View of Simples is supposed to yield the result that Poindexter is a mereological simple, since it seems to be metaphysically indivisible. But is Poindexter really metaphysically indivisible? Is it not metaphysically possible for Poindexter, like you, to grow in size? (Of course if Poindexter did grow in size, then it would no longer be point-sized; but that is no reason to think that Poindexter, in virtue of being point-sized now, has to be essentially point-sized. After all, we don't think that you are essentially your current size.) And if it is metaphysically possible for

Poindexter to grow in size, then is it not also metaphysically possible for Poindexter first to grow and then to be divided in half? If such a thing is metaphysically possible (and it is hard to see why it would not be), then neither Poindexter nor any other point-sized object will be metaphysically indivisible; which means that The Metaphysically Indivisible View will entail that there could never be any mereological simples.

Perhaps the proponent of The Metaphysically Indivisible View will modify the view so that it says that x is a mereological simple iff it is metaphysically impossible to divide x without first changing its current intrinsic properties. That would make Poindexter a mereological simple, since it would have to grow before it could be divided.

But this modification to The Metaphysically Indivisible View will have unwanted consequences. For the shape of any object is presumably among its intrinsic properties, and dividing any object (even a stick of butter) will always involve changing its shape. So the proposed modification will end up entailing that every object (including a stick of butter!) is automatically a simple.

Let's backtrack a little bit. Perhaps what was most forceful about the simplon example above was the implausibility of saying that the metaphysician knows better than the physicist whether a simplon has any smaller parts. This suggests that we should consider the following view about simples (where we understand "fundamental particles of physics" to be objects that, according to the ultimate physics, do not have any proper parts): x is a mereological simple iff x is a fundamental particle of physics.

One objection to this view, which we can call *The Fundamental Particle View*, is that there may end up not being any fundamental particles in the ultimate physics, in which case there would be no simples, according to the view. (But a similar objection can be raised against any of the views of simples considered here, with the exception of MaxCon [see below]. And in any case a proponent of the view will no doubt reply that it is indeed possible that everything is atomless gunk.)

A more serious objection concerns the difficult issue of whose job it is – the physicist's or the metaphysician's – to tell us whether simplons are mereological simples. On the one hand, there does seem to be something inappropriate about the metaphysician positing parts of simplons that the physicist does not countenance. But on the other hand, insofar as the physicist's theory says that simplons have no proper parts, that theory *is* a metaphysical theory; so perhaps it does make sense to turn to the meta-physician to tell us about the mereology of simplons.

Here's one final objection to The Fundamental Particle View. Suppose that in some other possible world, the ultimate physics says that the fundamental particles are large chains, like the one in the above example that stretched all the way around the world. That is, suppose that with respect to this other possible world, the best physical theory is one that posits such chains but does not mention any rings that the chains are made of. Then according to The Fundamental Particle View, those chains (in the imagined world) would be mereological simples. And this, as noted above, seems like the wrong result.

So far we have considered one view (The Pointy View of Simples) according to which the key to whether an object is a mereological simple lies in its topological properties, as well as several views (the various Indivisible Views and The Fundamental Particle View) according to which some non-topological factor is crucial. Another topological theory about mereological simples that has been discussed in the literature is *The Maximally Continuous View of Simples*, or MaxCon.[34] Here is the idea behind MaxCon. Some objects are spatially continuous and some are not. When an object is spatially continuous, and when the region it occupies is not a part of some larger, spatially continuous, matter-filled region, then that object is said to be "maximally continuous". And according to MaxCon, x is a mereological simple iff x is a maximally continuous object.[35]

Simplons will count as simples, according to MaxCon, since they are spherical (and hence spatially continuous). And point-sized objects would also qualify, since they too are spatially continuous. But computers, chains of physically indivisible rings, and the hyper-explosive bomb in the above example would not count as mereological simples on MaxCon.

We considered above (in connection with The Pointy View of Simples) an objection to the idea that being point-sized is a sufficient condition for being a mereological simple. The objection involved the possibility of two point-sized simples being colocated at a time when they happen to compose a third object, which is also point-sized, but which, intuitively, is not

---

[34] MaxCon is defended in Markosian, "Simples."

[35] In what follows we will ignore the distinction between being maximally continuous and being merely spatially continuous.

a simple. Since MaxCon, like The Pointy View of Simples, entails that the third object in the imagined scenario is a mereological simple (because it is a maximally continuous object), this objection will work just as well against MaxCon as it does against The Pointy View.

Another objection to MaxCon, and perhaps one that is likely to have more takers, targets a different consequence of the view, namely, that it is possible for there to be a spatially extended object that is a mereological simple. In order to appreciate the relevant objection, consider a large, spherical object that is spatially continuous. Let it appear to have a top half that is blue and a bottom half that is red. Now, the natural thing to say about this sphere is that it does have a top half, which is blue, and also a bottom half, which is red. But the MaxConner cannot say this, for according to him or her, the sphere is a mereological simple, without a top half or a bottom half.

It is worth noting that any view of simples that, like MaxCon, entails the possibility of spatially extended, mereological simples (including The Physically Indivisible View, The Fundamental Particle View, and The Brutal View [see below]) can be subjected to some variation on this objection.

In any case, it looks as if the MaxConners, if they want to stick with their view, must choose among four different options, each of which can be criticized: (1) deny that it is possible for a maximally continuous object to be heterogeneous; (2) claim that although the sphere has such spatially indexed properties as blue-at-region-R1 and red-at-region-R2, there is nothing in the example that has the property of being plain old blue or plain old red; (3) insist again that nothing in the example has the property of being plain old blue or plain old red, but maintain that the sphere has a certain blue + red "color distribution property" that is akin to the property of being polka dotted; or (4) claim that what is plain old blue in the example is a certain portion of *stuff*, rather than any *thing*, and similarly with what is plain old red. This last option will involve positing some stuff, in addition to the thing that is the sphere, and maintaining that the stuff that the sphere is made of is distinct from the sphere itself.

We will have more to say in the next section on questions about things and stuff, but first there is one more response to our question about simples that must be mentioned. This last response is modeled on Brutal Composition as a response to The Special Composition Question. Here the idea is that there are simples, and there are composites, but there is no true (and non-trivial) account of which things are simple and which are composite. When something is a mereological simple, that is not the case in virtue of some other fact or facts about the thing; it is just a brute fact that that object is a simple. And similarly for things that are composite.

This *Brutal View of Simples* will face objections analogous to those faced by Brutal Composition, including a continuum-style argument. In addition, there is this objection. Suppose it turns out that there are point-sized objects that are physically indivisible and that are fundamental particles of physics, according to the ultimate physical theory. Then we can ask the proponents of The Brutal View whether these objects are mereological simples; and it seems as if they face a dilemma. If they say that the point-sized, physically indivisible, fundamental particles of physics are not mereological simples, then they not only go against common sense on this matter, but must also posit some mysterious proper parts of these objects. And if the proponents of The Brutal View of Simples say that the point-sized, physically indivisible, fundamental particles of physics are mereological simples, then they must insist that this is not the case in virtue of their being point-sized, or indivisible, or fundamental, or even all three of these things. And that too seems to go against common sense.

8.11 Things and stuff?

We have already seen that philosophers who believe in the possibility of spatially extended mereological simples may have a good reason to posit the existence of *stuff* in addition to *things*. And we will shortly examine another possible reason for positing stuff. Indeed, some philosophers have suggested that our ontology of the physical world should include stuff only, without any things at all. But before we can address these issues, we must first get clear on what exactly stuff is, and how we should understand the alleged distinction between things and stuff.

So what is stuff? There are several, importantly different ways for the stuff theorist to answer this question, but here is what seems to us to be the most promising way. The concept of *stuff* is one of those fundamental concepts – like the notions of a *thing*, and of *space*, and of the relation of *occupation* that can hold between a thing and a spatial location – that is best taken as primitive (i.e., incapable of analysis or definition). But we can nevertheless say a bit more to help shed some light on the concept.

To begin with, stuff is also known as matter (and is sometimes called material). Moreover, stuff is what things are made of. For example, there is your bicycle, which is a thing, and then there is the matter that your bicycle is made of, which is some stuff.[36] It has also been suggested that we can find some clues about the distinction between things and stuff in our ordinary language. In general, our talk about things usually involves the use of count nouns like 'quark', 'dog', and 'star'; while our talk about stuff tends to involve the use of mass nouns such as 'plastic', 'water', and 'wood'. When we say, "There are two dogs in the yard," we take ourselves to be talking about things; whereas when we say, "There is some water on the floor," we mean to be talking about stuff. A closely related point is that it is natural to count things (three rocks, twelve computers), but not to count stuff (four golds?); instead, we tend to measure stuff (four ounces of gold, five gallons of milk).

Just as different things can exemplify very different properties (as in the case of a quark, a hydrogen atom, and a planet), so too can different stuffs exemplify very different qualities (as in the case of some water, some gold, and some marble). This raises a question about how the stuff theorist ought to think about different kinds of stuff: Are the differences among different kinds of stuff (such as gold and water, or quark stuff and electron stuff) to be thought of as fundamental differences with ontological significance, or are they just interesting differences within a single ontological category (like the differences between such things as quarks and electrons)? Some of the early, influential stuff theorists, like the pre-Socratic philosopher Anaxagoras, apparently favored the former approach, but as far as we can tell, there is nothing built into the notion of stuff that requires this answer to the present question. In other words, we think that there is nothing to stop the stuff theorist from saying that stuff is stuff, and that all stuff belongs to a single ontological category, even though some stuff is different from some other stuff.

In any case, on the conception of stuff that we have in mind, the stuff theorist will say that whenever a region of space is filled, it is filled by

---

[36] The stuff theorist must be careful not to confuse two different relations that correspond to the phrase 'made of'. One is a relation between a thing and some other things, as when we say, "the house is made of the bricks." But the other one, the stuff theorist ought to say, is a relation between a thing and some stuff, as when we say, "the statue is made of the clay."

some matter (also known as stuff). Some matter-filled regions are also occupied by things, and some are not.[37] When a matter-filled region is occupied by a thing, that is because there happens to be a thing that is made of the relevant matter. But since not every portion of matter is such that there is a thing made of that portion of matter, there will also be matter-filled regions that are not occupied by any thing. For example, the kind of stuff theorist that we have in mind might say that there is a portion of matter consisting of the matter that your body is made of right now together with the matter that the Eiffel Tower is made of, and also that there does not happen to exist any object (right now, anyway) that is made of that particular, spatially disconnected portion of matter. Thus, although the sum of the region you occupy right now with the region occupied by the Eiffel Tower right now is a matter-filled region, there is nevertheless no object that occupies that exact (spatially disconnected) region.

Perhaps we have said enough about what stuff is. The real question is, what can stuff do for you? Why would a person want to posit stuff? And we have already seen that one reason for positing stuff is that you might have an independent reason for believing in the possibility of extended mereological simples, in which case appealing to stuff can help you deal with problems like the one raised by the solid, indivisible sphere considered above that seemed to have a blue top half and a red bottom half.

Here is another reason for positing stuff. Suppose that in ancient Greece there was a statue, *Discobolus*, made of gold. Suppose that after many years of being admired by art aficionados, *Discobolus* fell into the hands of a philistine, who had it melted down and turned into a large golden shield that survives to this day. Then the natural thing to say is that the stuff *Discobolus* was made of, namely, the relevant portion of gold (i) survived the destruction of *Discobolus*, (ii) continues to exist today, and (iii) is now the stuff that the gold shield is made of.

---

[37] We are here taking the relation of occupation between a thing and a region to require a "perfect fit", so that a thing can occupy only one region at a time. In particular, on this conception of occupation, a thing does not occupy any proper subregion of the region that it occupies, and it likewise does not occupy any region that it does not "fully" occupy. In short, a thing and the region it occupies, in this sense, must always be exactly the same size and shape.

But if the gold survived being melted and *Discobolus* did not, then the gold cannot be identical to *Discobolus*. And for similar reasons the gold cannot be identical to the shield.

Perhaps it will be suggested that what is really going on in this case is that there is this one object, call it *Goldie*, that first "constitutes" *Discobolus* and then later "constitutes" the shield, and that *Goldie* is a thing rather than being some stuff. (We will consider in 8.13 the idea that one object can constitute a distinct but spatially coincident object, as this claim entails.) Such a suggestion may or may not have some plausibility when it comes to certain kinds of case, but is less plausible in a case like the present one, where it requires maintaining that *Goldie* continues to exist as a material object even when in melted, liquid form. And the suggestion becomes even less plausible if we change the details of the story so that the gold in question is not only melted but also divided into a million tiny droplets of gold that are for a long time scattered all over the universe before eventually being reunited and rearranged into a solid shield. For then it is even more counterintuitive to say that *Goldie* – a single material object – continues to exist throughout the story. (Who ever heard of an object that consists of a million tiny droplets of liquid gold scattered all over the universe?)

If considerations such as these persuade us to have an ontology that includes stuff, in addition to things, then we will no doubt want to say that every object is made of some portion of stuff, and that no object is ever identical to the portion of stuff that it is made of. We will also probably want to say that a given object is typically made of different portions of stuff at different times.

Of course, the main objection that can be raised against such a dualist ontology of both things and stuff will be one based on the principle of ontological parsimony, according to which one should always keep one's ontological commitments to a minimum. This kind of principle has always been popular among metaphysicians, both for methodological reasons (the fewer categories you have in your ontology, the lower your risk of positing non-existent entities or stuffs) and aesthetic reasons (many philosophers just prefer a leaner, meaner ontology). But falsely denying the existence of some type of entity (or stuff!) is also bad, and even granting that we should not believe without positive evidence, isn't it also true that we should believe in the face of (overall) positive evidence?

We'll return to the question of whether one ought to include stuff in one's ontology in 8.14. But, first, two digressions.

8.12 The Problem of Identity over Time for Physical Objects

Legend has it that in ancient Greece there was a merchant named Theseus who had a ship.[38] One day, while Theseus's ship was in dry dock, a plank was replaced. The plank that was removed from the ship was set aside for later use. ("Reduce, re-use, recycle," the ancient Greeks always said.) The next day a plank from a different part of the ship was replaced, with the old one again being set aside, and so on for a thousand days in a row, until, by the end of the thousand days, every single plank of the ship had been replaced. (We'll assume for the sake of simplicity that the ship was made of exactly 1,000 planks, and no other parts.) Not only that, but as the planks were taken out of the ship, they were carefully arranged together in the adjacent dry dock in such a way that they gradually came to compose a ship with exactly the same blueprint as the ship with which Theseus began, the end result being that each of the original planks was back in its original position with respect to all of its fellow planks.

When this procedure was completed, according to the legend, Theseus was puzzled. "Which one is my ship?" he wondered. "Is it the one in the original dry dock but with all the new planks, or is it the one with all the original planks but in the new dry dock?"

It's not an easy question to answer. On the one hand, it might seem obvious that Theseus's ship remained in the same place while it was gradually refurbished. After all, that's what we would probably say about the case if there had been no recycling of planks going on – if, say, each plank removed from the ship had been immediately destroyed. But on the other hand, it's natural to think that Theseus's ship was slowly moved, plank by plank, from one dry dock to another. For that is no doubt what we would say if there had been no replacement planks going into the original dry dock.

The story of the ship of Theseus raises a difficult question about mereological change: how much gaining and losing of parts is consistent with a

---

[38] The story as presented here is different in various ways from the actual legend.

material object's continued existence? This is a special instance of a more general question: How much change of any kind is consistent with a physical object's continued existence? This more general question is a question about the *persistence conditions* for physical objects. Here is a slightly more precise way of asking the question: *If* x *is a physical object at* t_1 *and* y *is a physical object at* t_2, *then under what circumstances is* y *identical to* x? The problem raised by this question is analogous in certain ways to The Problem of Personal Identity discussed in Chapter 5. We'll refer to our current problem as *The Problem of Identity over Time for Physical Objects.*

It's always a good idea, when tackling a philosophical problem, to begin with something close to the common-sense view of the matter, and then to see what kind of theory emerges from that conventional wisdom. In this case, common sense seems to say that the persistence conditions for physical objects are such that it very often does happen that a physical object survives the gain or loss of several (or even quite a few) of its parts, and likewise that an object can, at least in some cases, survive quite dramatic changes in other, non-mereological respects.

What then should we say is required for the continued existence of a physical object? One factor that philosophers have sometimes focused on in this regard is spatio-temporal continuity. Another such factor is sameness of substantival kind. (Where an object's substantival kind is, roughly, the one kind, among the many exemplified by that object, that would be the best answer to the question, 'What is it?' as applied to that object. Thus, for example, *human being* might be your body's substantival kind, and *piece of furniture* might be the substantival kind of a particular chair.)

Combining these two factors (spatio-temporal continuity and sameness of substantival kind), we might try the following "moderate" account of identity over time for physical objects. If x is a physical object at t_1 and y is a physical object at t_2, then y is identical to x iff (i) there is the right kind of spatio-temporal continuity between x at t_1 and y at t_2, and (ii) x's substantival kind at t_1 and y's substantival kind at t_2 are the same.[39]

One objection that might be raised against this moderate account concerns its claim that spatio-temporal continuity is necessary for a physical object's persistence. For you might think that this requirement is inconsistent with any mereological change at all. Whenever an object loses a

[39] For a defense of a variation on this view see Quinton, *The Nature of Things*, chapter 3.

part, for example, you might think that the object must undergo a discontinuous change in its shape: one instant it has the larger shape that includes the soon-to-be-lost part, and the next instant it has the smaller shape that does not include that part.

But perhaps it can be replied that this objection is based on a misunderstanding of what spatio-temporal continuity amounts to. After all, even if, for example, a tree instantaneously loses a limb, so that it undergoes a discontinuous change in its shape at the moment the limb ceases to be a part of it, still, the region of space-time occupied by the tree will normally be continuous in the traditional sense: from any point in that region we can trace a path to any other point in the region without ever leaving the region.

Another objection that might be raised against the spatio-temporal continuity requirement in our moderate account of identity over time for physical objects concerns the possibility of genuinely discontinuous motion by a physical object. It is sometimes said that in quantum theory, the smallest particles are capable of moving instantaneously from one position to another. And there may be less exotic examples of discontinuous motion as well: if you take your bicycle apart and ship the pieces in separate containers across the country, where it is reassembled, then it is natural to think that your bicycle not only went out of existence for a while but also moved from point A to point B without being located at any point in between. (Not that this is the only plausible thing to say about the bicycle example. For another popular school of thought has it that your bicycle continues to exist, as a scattered object, while disassembled. And, provided the bike is not always disassembled, this is consistent with it occupying a continuous region of space-time.)

A third kind of objection to the spatio-temporal continuity requirement involves the possibility of time travel (which is often thought to involve occupying a discontinuous path through space-time). If you are convinced that time travel is at least metaphysically possible, then you should probably not make spatio-temporal continuity a necessary condition for a physical object's continued existence.

There may also be problems with requiring sameness of substantival kind. One possible counterexample would be a caterpillar that changes into a butterfly. (But it is no doubt open to the proponent of our moderate theory to maintain that the substantival kind of the caterpillar/butterfly is really whatever biological species it instantiates.) Other possible counterexamples would include the (fictional but presumably nevertheless metaphysically possible) case of a man who turns into a wolf, the case of a car that transforms into a robot, and the case of a helicopter that is slowly transformed into a windmill.

Meanwhile, there may also be a problem with making the combination of sameness of substantival kind and spatio-temporal continuity sufficient for the continued existence of a physical object. Suppose that you have a favorite rock sitting on your desk, and that at midnight tonight a very powerful being, for no particular reason, annihilates that rock, so that it literally disappears into thin air. But suppose also that a second very powerful being, who has no knowledge of either the first being or your rock, decides, purely on a whim, to create a brand-new rock out of thin air; and suppose that, as luck would have it (and this would admittedly be a rather large coincidence), the second creature's rock comes into existence at just the moment that your original rock goes out of existence, in exactly the location vacated by your rock, and with all of the same intrinsic properties possessed by your rock at the time of its annihilation. Then we will have a case in which your original rock and the rock on your desk after midnight will satisfy both the spatio-temporal continuity condition and the sameness of substantival kind condition; but it seems as if the rock on your desk after midnight is not the same thing as the rock on your desk before midnight.

This last example might be taken to show that we need to add a condition to our moderate account of identity over time for physical objects. Maybe we need to say something about the object not suffering too dramatic a mereological turnover all at once. Thus, we might try the following revised version of our moderate account. If x is a physical object at t_1 and y is a physical object at t_2, then y is identical to x iff (i) there is the right kind of spatio-temporal continuity between x at t_1 and y at t_2, (ii) x's substantival kind at t_1 and y's substantival kind at t_2 are the same, and (iii) at no time between t_1 and t_2 does x suffer an instantaneous loss of more than fifty per cent of its total parts.

It might strike some readers that the basic structure of this revised moderate account is promising, but that the percentage in the last condition is wrong. Some will prefer to say that an object cannot suffer an instantaneous loss of more than 33.33 … per cent of its total parts, or that an object cannot suffer an instantaneous loss of more than twenty-five per cent of its total parts, or even that an object cannot suffer an instantaneous loss of *as much as* fifty per cent of its total parts (thus making fifty per cent not the upper limit of mereological change that is consistent with persistence but, rather, the lower limit of mereological change that is inconsistent with persistence).

In fact, once we consider all of the different "percentage options" available to the proponent of the revised moderate account of identity over time for physical objects, the existence of so many options may itself seem like a problem. For with so many options, it begins to look as if the choice among them must necessarily be an arbitrary one. Why should two possible cases that are alike in every way except that they differ by only the tiniest amount in their percentages of mereological change (we're talking a difference that shows up only in, say, the trillionth place after the decimal point) differ in such an important matter as whether they involve genuine persistence?

We will leave it to readers to come up with further potential problems for this revised version of our moderate theory of identity over time for physical objects. Meanwhile, it is worth noting the existence of some alternative approaches to The Problem of Identity over Time for Physical Objects. One such alternative will be to say that different kinds of physical object have different persistence conditions. It might be thought, for example, that a bicycle can survive disassembly, the shipment of its former parts across the country, and subsequent reassembly, but that a human being cannot. Similarly, it might be thought that a bar of gold can survive being melted into a liquid form and then cooled back into a bar, but that various other solid objects cannot survive any such ordeal. (One problem with this pluralistic approach, however, is that it requires that we identify what the different relevant kinds are, as well as what the persistence conditions are for each kind; and hence the pluralistic approach seems to make our task harder rather than easier.)

Another approach to our problem, no doubt motivated by such puzzling examples as the ship of Theseus, takes a hard line against persistence through mereological change. According to this view, called *Mereological Essentialism*, it is an essential feature of each object that it has exactly the parts that it has. Since no physical object can ever gain or lose a part, on this view, as soon as the first plank is removed from Theseus's ship, the old ship goes out of existence. In its place is a brand-new (though perhaps old-looking) ship that is one plank smaller than the old ship. Moreover, according to Mereological Essentialism, when the replacement plank is fitted into place, yet another new ship comes into existence. And similarly for virtually every macroscopic object in the world: in each case, what appears to be a persisting object that occasionally gains or loses a small number of parts is in fact a series of distinct objects, each of which pops in and then out of existence in a short span of time.[40] (Because of what goes on at the microscopic level, the rate at which macroscopic objects pop in and out of existence is truly astonishing, if Mereological Essentialism is true.)

Yet another approach to our problem involves taking the most liberal line possible regarding persistence through mereological change. This approach combines Universalism in response to The Special Composition Question with the thesis (mentioned briefly above in connection with Universalism) that for any xs that exist at one time, and for any ys that exist at another time, there is a single object that is composed of those xs at the first time and those ys at the second time. If we take this liberal line on persistence, then we will say that there is a "mereologically constant" object composed of just the original planks from Theseus's ship, and that this object gradually moves from one dry dock to the other during the plank-replacing procedure; and also that there is a "mereologically variable" object that is composed, at each time during the procedure, of just the planks arranged ship-wise in the original dry dock.

One problem with this liberal line regarding persistence, however, is that it also entails that there is an object composed of (i) the original planks at the beginning of the procedure, (ii) half of the original planks and half of the replacement planks at the end of the procedure, and (iii) all of your cells right now. (And that's just one of countlessly many such examples, each one sounding crazier than the previous one.) In short, if

---

[40] This is how it is on the most frequently discussed version of Mereological Essentialism, anyway. According to another version, which combines Mereological Essentialism with Universalism (see above), replacing a plank from a ship does not cause the ship to go out of existence but, instead, merely causes it to become a scattered object, and to cease being a ship. On this version of the view, the only way to cause an object go out of existence is to annihilate one or more of its parts. But also on this version of the view, no object is ever a ship (or a rock, or a human, or an instance of any other familiar kind) for more than a fraction of a second.

we take the liberal line on persistence, then we will have to admit into our ontology an enormous number of strange objects that common sense would never recognize.

Another problem with the liberal line on persistence is that it raises such difficult questions as how it ever happens that two different people manage to refer to the same object in a conversation.[41]

Here is one final response to The Problem of Identity over Time for Physical Objects: there is no answer to our question about the persistence conditions for physical objects. On this view, when an object x that exists at t_1 is identical to an object y that exists at t_2, it is always just a brute fact that x is identical to y. Not only that but, according to this view, there just isn't any true statement of necessary and jointly sufficient conditions for the persistence of a physical object; there are no "criteria of identity over time" for material things.[42]

It should be clear from our discussion that The Problem of Identity over Time for Physical Objects is a difficult one. Every possible solution comes with some significant cost or other. We will come back to this point in 8.14.

8.13 The return of the statue and the lump

Recall our original example from the beginning of this chapter, involving a statue of a snowy owl and the lump of clay that it is made of. We'll call the problem raised by this kind of example *The Problem of Material Constitution*. Let's take a closer look at this problem.

It is natural to say that on Tuesday night, when the statue sits proudly on your workbench, there are two different, "coincident" objects there, since (as was noted above) it seems as if the statue is a new thing that was created that morning, while the lump of clay is a much older object that has been around for a long time. But there is an obvious objection that can be raised against this "two objects" or "coincident entities" account: we know that it's not possible for two things to be in one place at the same time, as the statue and the lump of clay would be if they were distinct; so it

---

[41] For a discussion of this reference problem see Quine, "Identity, Ostension, and Hypostasis".

[42] For a defense of the "no criteria" view see Merricks, "There Are No Criteria of Identity over Time."

must be that there is really only one thing there, which is capable of going by two different names.

Some philosophers who endorse the coincident objects view think that there is a perfectly adequate reply to this objection.[43] What we know, they say, is that there cannot be two different objects *of the same kind* in one place at a single time. So, for example, there cannot be two statues, or two lumps of clay, in the same place at the same time. But the statue and the lump are different kinds of object: in particular, the lump of clay is the kind of object that can survive being squashed and that can "constitute" a less hardy thing like a statue, while the statue is the kind of object that cannot survive being squashed and that can be "constituted by" a more durable thing such as a lump.

The coincident entities theorists who make this reply will face some hard questions about how it is determined what kind a particular object is. In addition, they will face a further objection to the coincident entities view. How, they are likely to be asked, can two objects like the statue and the lump of clay have such different temporal properties as *came into existence ten hours ago* and *existed for many days*, given that they are currently in the same place, with exactly the same parts, and with all the same non-temporal properties? What grounds the alleged difference in their temporal properties? For that matter, how can they be of different kinds, given that (again) they are in the same place and have all the same parts and all the same non-kind properties?

A good move for the Coincident Objects Theorists to make in response to this objection might be to appeal to Four-Dimensionalism (see Chapter 7), and to claim that the lump is in fact simply the statue plus some additional temporal parts. For then they can say that the reason the statue has the temporal property *came into existence ten hours ago* while the lump has the temporal property *existed for many days* is that the statue has no temporal parts earlier than ten hours ago, while the lump does. And the reason for this difference is that the statue *just is* the fusion of one particular group of temporal parts, while the lump *just is* the fusion of a different group of temporal parts.

---

[43] The father of this reply to the objection is Locke. See Book II, chapter xxvii of *An Essay Concerning Human Understanding.*

Perhaps this appeal to temporal parts will allow the Coincident Objects Theorist to solve the problem with respect to the alleged differences in temporal properties between the statue and the lump. But there is a different problem lurking nearby.

Allan Gibbard describes a case involving a lump of clay that comes into existence already in the form of a statue, that exists for a time without changing its shape or any other notable properties, and that is then completely annihilated, so that lump and statue both come into and go out of existence together.[44] The Coincident Objects Theorist cannot argue that in Gibbard's case the lump and the statue are distinct because they have different temporal properties (for they don't have different temporal properties). But the Coincident Objects Theorist will presumably want to argue that the statue and the lump in this case nevertheless *are* distinct, on the grounds that they have different modal properties. For it is very natural to think that the lump could survive being squashed, while the statue could not.

But now the Coincident Objects Theorist will have trouble explaining how two distinct things could differ with respect to their modal properties, given that they are located in the same place, are composed of all the same parts (including even the same temporal parts), and have all the same non-modal properties. What grounds the alleged difference in the modal properties of the statue and the lump?

8.14 All stuff all the time?

We have seen that there are various problems that fall under the general heading of "the metaphysics of material objects" (including those raised by SCQ and The Simple Question, together with The Problem of Identity over Time for Physical Objects and The Problem of Material Constitution). We have also seen that none of these problems is easy to solve.

At this point it becomes tempting to take a radically different approach to all of these issues. Instead of trying to solve a host of seemingly intractable problems, why not simply get rid of them? Why not banish *physical things* from our ontology altogether, and instead go with a pure-stuff ontology? If there are no material objects, then there is no question about which material objects are mereological simples, there is no question

---

[44] Gibbard, "Contingent Identity."

about when several physical objects compose a further object, there is no problem about the persistence conditions for material objects, and there is no problem of material constitution for them, either.

An ontologist who does away with material objects altogether and instead posits only stuff will no doubt have some explaining to do, for physical things certainly play a prominent role in our everyday conception of the world. There are a number of different ways the pure-stuff ontologist's explanation could go. Here is one such way.

The world is filled with stuff, spread out in irregular and frequently changing patterns. Various properties are instantiated by various portions of stuff, so that, for example, *being red and apple-shaped* is instantiated by a certain portion of stuff over here and *being yellow and banana-shaped* is instantiated by a different portion of stuff over there. Although there are no bananas, in the sense that there are no things that are bananas, there are plenty of cases of some stuff arranged banana-wise. Similarly for apples, and ships, and all the other putative objects that are countenanced by common sense. In general, whenever it would be correct to say, for example, "Here is a banana," what makes it correct to say that is not the presence of a thing that is a banana but, rather, the presence of some stuff arranged banana-wise.

Since there are no physical objects, there are no problems about the mereology of physical objects. So there is no need to worry about questions like The Special Composition Question or The Simple Question. Likewise, there is no Problem of Identity over Time for Physical Objects, even though we sometimes seem to speak truly when we say things like, "Here is the same bike that you bought from Ted two years ago." In such a case, what is literally true is something like this: here is an episode of bicycleness, and this episode of that property has been going on since two years ago when that sales-event involving you and Ted occurred.[45]

As for statues and lumps, well, there are of course no objects that are statues or lumps; but there are often cases of some stuff arranged lump-wise, and even cases of some stuff that is arranged both lump-wise and statue-wise. And in a typical one of those cases, the episode of lumpiness is longer lasting than the corresponding episode of statuehood (and could

---

[45] For more on episodes of properties, see 4.2.

survive traumas like being squashed that the episode of statuehood could not).

That, at any rate, is one way the pure-stuff ontologist's explanation could go. But however they fill in the details of their objectless ontology, the main objection they will face is simply that their view is too counter-intuitive, insofar as it entails that, strictly speaking, there are no quarks, atoms, molecules, bricks, houses, computers, or stars.

There is another substantial objection to the pure-stuff ontology, and it hits a little bit closer to home. Where, we can ask the pure-stuff ontologist, do you fit into your own ontology? There appear to be four main options: (i) you are a non-physical object – some kind of conscious mind or soul; (ii) you are some stuff; (iii) you fit into some other ontological category besides thing or stuff; and (iv) you don't exist.

The last option is seemingly refuted by Cartesian reasoning (you think, and therefore you exist), whereas the first option, although it may have a lot going for it, will be rejected by anyone who is a materialist. Meanwhile, option (ii) seems to be the most natural fit for anyone who is a materialist; but there may be problems with saying that you are some stuff.

The main problem is simply that you do not seem to be made of the same stuff from one moment to the next. Heraclitus is famous for saying that you cannot step into the same river twice. And it is not just the river that he was worried about. He also worried about you. For Heraclitus conjectured – correctly, as it turns out – that the matter that makes up your body (or what appears to be your body) is constantly changing. So exactly which stuff should the pure-stuff theorist identify with you? The stuff that you seem to be made of right now, the stuff that you seemed to be made of at noon yesterday, or some other specific portion of stuff? It seems that any possible answer will be wrong almost all the time.

The pure-stuff theorist could try saying that you are, at any given time, identical to the stuff that it seems your body is made of at that time. But if so they will have to give up the transitivity of identity, since they'll be committed to saying that for two times, t_1 and t_2, and two portions of stuff, s_1 and s_2, you are identical to s_1 at t_1 and you are identical to s_2 at t_2, even though s_1 is never identical to s_2.

What about option (iii)? It's not as outlandish as it initially sounds. For some philosophers (and perhaps most Buddhists) already believe, for independent reasons, that you are in fact not a physical thing or some stuff but, rather, an event. If we combine this idea with the pure-stuff ontology, we get the view that you are an event (presumably a "person-event" or a "human-event") that happens to involve different portions of stuff at different times. This idea could be extended to various other kinds of "object" as well; the pure-stuff ontologist could say that atoms, rocks, mountains, and chairs are all events of one kind or another, each one involving different portions of stuff at different times.

We suggested above that one advantage of a pure-stuff ontology is that it allows its proponent to dismiss certain otherwise difficult metaphysical problems such as The Problem of Identity over Time for Physical Objects and those raised by SCQ and The Simple Question. But are matters really that simple for the stuff ontologist? Won't there be stuff analogues of all the same problems?

The answer is yes and no. There is, for example, an interesting question about the circumstances under which a portion of stuff has no proper parts; but The Simple Question for Portions of Stuff is, arguably, much easier to answer than its counterpart for things. For it is natural to think that a portion of stuff is a simple iff it is point-sized; and although we won't have the space here to defend this claim, we think that The Pointy View of Simple Portions of Stuff is less susceptible to counterexample than its thing counterpart. Similar remarks apply to Universalism and Mereological Essentialism for Portions of Stuff. So it may turn out that the pure-stuff ontologist can defend a theory of stuff that includes stuff analogues of The Pointy View of Simples, Universalism, and Mereological Essentialism, but without anything like the counterintuitive consequences of the thing versions of those theses.

8.15 Many hard questions

Are a statue and a lump of clay one object or two? Under what circumstances do a swarming bunch of subatomic particles compose a larger object? Do particles ever compose anything, or is there nothing more to the world than a plurality of mereological simples? Speaking of mereological simples, what must an object be like in order for it to have no proper parts? And if subatomic particles do sometimes compose larger objects, then what about those larger objects? Under what circumstances do some of them compose a further object? If there are circumstances under which some objects do compose a further object, then how much mereological change can those composite objects survive? Finally, what about the relationship between a physical object and the matter that it's made of? Are they two or one? Come to think of it, does the world even really contain any physical objects, or is it really all just a bunch of stuff?

These are among the surprising and sometimes bewildering questions that arise as soon as one considers the metaphysics of the ordinary physical objects that populate our world.

9 Properties

9.1 The One-Over-Many Problem

In Plato's dialogue *Meno*, Socrates says to Meno: "[T]ell me what virtue is in the universal; and do not make a singular into a plural, as the facetious say of those who break a thing, but deliver virtue to me whole and sound, and not broken into a number of pieces."[1] Socrates wants to know what virtue is, and his plea for it to be presented whole and sound was to make clear that he did not want descriptions of behaviors that make certain kinds of people virtuous (e.g., the virtue of a man is to order the state), and that he was not looking for a list of virtues (e.g., wisdom, humility, piety, temperance, and so on). Socrates wanted to know the common nature of all virtues. He wanted to know about *virtuehood*, about whatever it is that makes wisdom, humility, and other virtues be virtues. In *Meno*, Socrates briefly makes similar queries about color and shape. He wanted to know what makes "red" and "green" colors and what makes "round" and "oblong" shapes. In other dialogues, Socrates makes similar requests about the nature of some individual virtues. For example, in *Euthyphro*, he considers piety. What is it that makes pious things pious? In *Charmides*, the focus is temperance. What is it that makes temperate things temperate?[2] Questions of this sort are at the heart of *The One-Over-Many Problem*.

Plato was interested in at least two different aspects of the question, "What is virtue?" In *Meno*, he was primarily interested in the conceptual matter just described. Socrates wanted Meno to give him some illuminating characterization of virtuehood. (They consider the proposal that virtue is the power of governing and that virtue is the desire and power

---

[1] *The Dialogues of Plato*, vol. II, p. 35. Plato wrote *Meno c.* 380 BCE.
[2] A standard source for *Euthyphro*, *Charmides*, and all of Plato's dialogues is *The Collected Dialogues of Plato*.

of attaining good.) The same was true of Plato's discussions of color, shape, piety, and temperance. But, in *Meno* and other works, Plato was also concerned with a less conceptual and more ontological issue. Instead of an account of what it is to be a virtue, he can be understood as interested in the *entity* virtuehood, in how it exists (if it does exist). Parallel questions can be asked about the existence of temperance, piety, red, green, color, and shape. Plato was doing some ontology.

Our goal in this chapter is to introduce you to one emblematic ontological issue. That issue is the existence of *properties*. Properties are something like qualities, features, characteristics, or attributes. Wisdom and humility are as good examples as any; they are characteristics of many people. Red, green, oblong, and round are all good additional examples. Virtuehood is another one. Among the examples just mentioned, virtuehood is notable in that it is a second-order property;[3] it is a property of properties – it is a property of wisdom and a property of humility. Color and shape are good additional examples of second-order properties since they are properties of red and round respectively. At certain key junctures, *relations* will be an important part of our discussion. Relations are just like properties except that they characterize two or more things in relation to one another. Possession is an example of a relation; Brooks Robinson possesses sixteen Gold Gloves. Between-ness is another relation: New York City is between Boston and Philadelphia. Our ontological issue is this: Are there such things as properties and relations? If there are, what are these entities like?

9.2 Universals

9.2.1 Multiply instantiable properties and relations

When Socrates instructs Meno to tell him "what virtue is in the universal; and do not make a singular into a plural," Socrates is presupposing

---

[3] In English, prima facie, 'virtue' is used as a name (cf., 'Mother Teresa displays virtue') for the property of *being virtuous*, the first-order property expressed by 'is virtuous' in 'Mother Teresa is virtuous'. The English translation of Plato quoted above, in the specific passage there quoted, instead uses 'virtue' as a name for *virtuehood* or the property of *being a virtue*, the second-order property expressed by 'is a virtue' in 'Humility is a virtue'. When it is especially important to make clear that our interest is the second-order property, and not so important that we stick to the exact wording of the quotation, we will use 'virtuehood' instead of 'virtue'.

that there is something (virtuehood) that makes virtues virtues. He also adopts certain assumptions about what this thing is like. First, though Socrates sometimes refers to properties as ideas, it is clear that properties can't be mental ideas that depend for their being on human minds. Humility being a virtue obtains even if no one has ever conceived of virtue. Virtuehood must be something *objective*. Second, it is also clear that virtuehood can be instantiated by many things. There are many virtues, even though there is only one thing that makes them all virtues. Virtuehood is *multiply instantiable*. This is the characteristic that distinguishes *universals* from *particulars*. Universals can be instantiated by many particulars; particulars are not instantiated by more than one thing.[4]

In this section, we consider two traditional stances that treat properties as universals. Moved by the Socratic questions, a common thread in these two views is an all-at-once, very general answer to The One-Over-Many Problem. It is intended to apply whenever a property is predicated of (i.e., attributed to) some entity.

Predication via Universals
a is *F* if and only if *a* instantiates *F*-ness,

where '*F*-ness' is understood to name a universal. Offered as an account of predication, the thought is that not only is Socrates wise because he instantiates "wise-ness" (wisdom), but also that he is bald because he instantiates "bald-ness" (baldness). This account needs to be supplemented with clauses to handle relational predications. For two-place predication, we need:

a R*s* *b* if and only if *a* and *b* (in that order) instantiate *R*-ing,

where '*R*-ing' stands for a two-place relation, understood to be a universal. Accordingly, Brooks possesses the 1970 Gold Glove, because Brooks and

---

[4] Arguably, there are properties that cannot be multiply instantiated. If it is a property at all, then *being Barack Obama* is an example; Barack Obama is the only thing that could ever possibly have this supposed property. Believers in universals who want to count this as a property will see it as a special case without much metaphysical significance. That it can't be multiply instantiated has nothing to do with the nature of the kind of entity it is, with the fact that it is a property. That it can't be multiply instantiated is completely dependent on what specific property it is, with it being the property of being Barack Obama and not a commonly instantiated property like the property of being hungry.

that Gold Glove (in that order) instantiate the relation of "possess-ing" (possession).[5]

Predication via Universals is offered as an account of predication. It does not, however, come pre-packaged with an ontological view about what universals exist or about what exactly these universals are like. In this section, we focus on two representative ontological views. The first we'll call *Platonism*, because it is in the spirit of Plato's ontology. The second is *Aristotelianism*, so named for its similarities with Aristotle's views.

9.2.2 Platonic universals

Platonism begins with the assumption that there is a universal correspond-ing to every meaningful predicate. You may already have been making this assumption based on the Socratic questions discussed in 9.1. This assump-tion stems naturally from a very intuitive semantic theory that identifies the meaning of some natural-language terms with a corresponding univer-sal. On this theory, wisdom is (at least) part of the meaning of the predicate 'is wise', temperance is part of the meaning of 'is temperate', and so on.

To even think of any property independently of the thing or things that have it requires a tiny bit of theoretical reasoning. It is a very straight-forward matter to think of Socrates without baldness; you just think of him with a full head of hair. It is a different and much less straightfor-ward matter to think of the baldness independent of Socrates. In this way, all properties are *abstract* in the weak sense that they are "got before the mind by an act of abstraction."[6] Because of the assumption that there is a universal corresponding to every meaningful predicate, Platonic uni-versals also turn out to be abstract in a strong sense. Consider 'is iner-tial'. It is certainly a meaningful predicate, part of standard statements of Newtonian physics. So inertiality exists, even though nothing is inertial. There are less scientific examples. No unicorns exist, but the predicate 'is a unicorn' is meaningful. So, whatever universal 'unicorn' means must

---

[5] Henceforth, we will not bother to state any of the clauses required for an account of predication to handle relational predications. We leave that as an exercise for the interested reader.

[6] Campbell, "The Metaphysics of Abstract Particulars," p. 478. Campbell's paper (and several other of the works referenced in this chapter) can be found in Mellor and Oliver's edited anthology, *Properties*.

be an uninstantiated one. Uninstantiated universals and, for the sake of a uniform ontology, all other universals must live a special sort of existence. They must exist in something like the way numbers do (assuming that numbers exist), not in space and with no beginning or end in time. Thus, in addition to being objective and multiply instantiable, Platonic universals are abstract in the sense that they are non-spatial and atemporal.

9.2.3 Concerns about Platonic universals

Parsimony

If the truth of a theory demands that some object exist, and that object doesn't really exist, then the theory is false. Obviously, that would be a bad feature of the theory. Less obviously, if the truth of a theory demands the existence of something that is inordinate enough to make one wonder whether it really exists, then that is not good either. (Maybe you've heard of Ockham's razor.) Some opponents of Platonism are suspicious of Platonic universals precisely because they are somewhat extraordinary. They are abstract in two ways: they are abstract in that they come before the mind by an act of abstraction and they are abstract in the sense that they are non-spatial, atemporal things. So, according to Platonism, while you might run into a pious preacher at a revival meeting, you won't see piety there (literally speaking, that is). Others go further and argue that the abstractness of Platonic universals makes them unknowable. They hardly seem to be the sort of thing that could be an object of perception. It is hard to see how they could stand in any causal connection with the rest of the world. How could we know what they are like or when they are instantiated? How could we refer to them? How could they be what some of our words mean?

Generality

Traditionally, one primary reason for believing in Platonic universals is the supposed explanatory value of the resulting account of predication. The problem is that, when coupled with Platonism, Predication via Universals faces two knock-down objections.

First, there are meaningful predicates that don't express any property. Consider the predicate 'is non-self-instantiating'. Ned is non-self-instantiating. Indeed, he is never instantiated by anything, and so certainly he never self-instantiates. Nevertheless, is it true that Ned is non-self-instantiating if and only if Ned instantiates non-self-instantiation, as is implied by Predication via Universals? Well, it is only if the property non-self-instantiation exists. But this is one property that definitely doesn't exist because, if it did, it would be self-instantiating if and only if it were not self-instantiating, and that is a contradiction. Any proposition of the form 'P if and only if not-P' is necessarily false no matter what proposition P is.[7]

Second, we are going to have to be careful about the instantiation relation. Consider the fact that John instantiates temperance. Remembering what Predication via Universals says about relational predications, this account tells us that John *instantiates* temperance if and only if John and temperance (in that order) *instantiate* instantiation. There lies the trouble. This account is circular. The verb 'to instantiate' is used in the statement of what is to be explained and in what is supposed to do the explaining.

So, Predication via Universals can't be fully general; it can't apply to all predications, unless one is prepared to accept contradictions as true and to endorse a circular account of the predication of instantiation. The natural response to make to these objections is to restrict the application of this account of predication. Platonists can deny that there is a property corresponding to every predicate and then restrict Predication via Universals to good effect, denying that there is an instantiation relation, denying that there is a property of non-self-instantiation, and restricting the application of the account to predications involving predicates with a corresponding universal. The Platonist can still accept that it is true that John instantiates temperance and that Ned is non-self-instantiating, but he or she should maintain that predications involving the predicate 'instantiates' and 'is non-self-instantiating' are primitive predications, ones that are not given an account. They should be taken to be brute.

This sort of revision is important to the dialectic. We were led to Predication via Universals and to Platonism by the seemingly obligatory Socratic questions about the One (virtue, color, shape …) and the Many (virtues, colors, shapes …). But what should we now think about those questions? Are they really obligatory? They seem just as obligatory when

---

[7] This a well-known version of Russell's Paradox. For more on Russell's Paradox, see Irvine, "Russell's Paradox."

posed about instantiation or non-self-instantiation as they do when posed about virtue, and yet now the Platonist seems forced to say that when the questions are posed about instantiation or non-self-instantiation, they don't need answers! Once one restricts Predication via Universals in the natural way, "What is instantiation?" and "What is non-self-instantiation?" don't demand an answer beyond that predications of instantiation and non-self-instantiation are brute matters of fact. As a result, upon reflection, it is natural to start to wonder whether any of the Socratic questions really demand an illuminating answer.

9.2.4 Aristotelian universals

There is a more severe way of pulling back from the full generality of Predication via Universals, a way that is in the spirit of Aristotle's ontology.[8] To appreciate what we have called Aristotelianism, let yourself feel the pull of Socrates's central question in *Meno*, assume there is a need to explain why virtues are virtues, and go along with Plato in thinking that the universal virtuehood is part of that explanation. But don't assume that every meaningful predicate expresses a universal. Instead, postulate only the universals needed to account for the *true* predications.

Since nothing is inertial and there are no unicorns, don't posit inertiality or unicornhood. Don't posit any uninstantiated universals. This has an advantage: we are not pushed to thinking of universals as non-spatial and atemporal. So we needn't think of there being Plato's Heaven, a separate realm of forms, containing universals that are sometimes instantiated here and there by various objects and events scattered about space and time. Rather, we can see a universal's existence as with, and only with, the things that instantiate it. Being so tied to concrete particulars allows universals to stand in causal relations. Thus, Aristotelian universals are less mysterious than Platonic universals. They are only abstract in the weak sense that all properties are. Aristotelianism is significantly more parsimonious than Platonism.

---

[8] Passages from Aristotle suggesting elements of this view include *Categories* 5, 2a34–2b6, *De Interpretatione* 7, 17a38–40, and *Metaphysics* Book VII, 13,1038b9–12, all of which can be found in *The Basic Works of Aristotle*.

David Armstrong is responsible for a surge in the popularity of Aristotelianism. He takes the Aristotelian stance to an extreme. Yes, he denies that there are any uninstantiated properties, denies that there is a property of non-self-instantiation, and denies that there is an instantiation relation. In answering The One-Over-Many Problem, however, he doesn't even assume that there is virtue, color, shape, or wisdom. Armstrong doesn't immediately assume a corresponding universal exists even for the most ordinary predicates. "[I]t is the task of total science, conceived of as total enquiry, to determine what universals there are."[9] Armstrong's is an a posteriori approach. See what properties science commits us to, then worry about how to account for the many ordinary predications we commonly take as true.

9.2.5 Concerns about Aristotelian universals

The primary attraction of Aristotelianism is that universals are spatially and temporally embedded in our universe, not a separate world of being. Still, it retains one of the limitations of Platonism. Because of the paradoxical nature of non-self-instantiation and the threat of a circular account of instantiation, an Aristotelian is in no better position to give a fully general account of predication than is the Platonist. Furthermore, by bringing the universals back down to Earth, Aristotelian universals have a mysterious feature not had by Platonic universals. According to the Aristotelian, this electron's charge and that electron's charge are not *two* instantiations of charge; this electron's charge literally is *the very same thing as* that electron's charge, even if the two electrons are a million miles apart. It is surprising (some might say absurd) that one thing, the property charge, can simultaneously be wholly present in two places at one time.

9.3 No universals

9.3.1 Sets, tropes, and austerity

Can we get by without any universals in our ontology? Maybe. *Set Nominalists* and *Trope Nominalists* acknowledge properties but maintain that they are not universals. *Austere Nominalists* deny that there are any properties.

---

[9] Armstrong, *Nominalism and Realism*, p. xii.

9.3.2 Set Nominalism

Some accounts of predication minimize the differences between properties and particulars. They identify properties with a special kind of particular. The first account of this sort is:

> *Predication via Sets*
> *a* is *F* if and only if *a* is a member of *F*-ness,

where '*F*-ness' names a set. Plato is wise because he is a member of wiseness (wisdom), which is taken to be the set of wise things. So, wisdom is a particular and not a universal; strictly speaking, sets are not instantiated by any member or by anything else – they are not multiply instantiable. Predications of membership are typically taken to be brute.[10] Set Nominalists can deny that there exist any universals, instead treating every property as a special sort of set.

One nice feature of Set Nominalism is that, in virtue of their theoretical good-standing, sets and set membership somehow seem less mysterious than universals and instantiation. This is due to sets being used to great advantage by mathematicians, logicians, and others. The identity conditions of sets are also well understood: *S* and *T* are the same set if and only if *S* and *T* have exactly the same members.

Unfortunately, there is a straightforward problem with Set Nominalism. Here is how it is reported by David Lewis:

> The usual objection to taking properties as sets is that different properties may happen to be coextensive. All and only the creatures with hearts are the creatures with kidneys; all and only the talking donkeys are flying pigs, since there are none of either. But the property of having a heart is different from the property of having a kidney, since there could have been an animal with a heart but no kidneys. Likewise the property of being a talking donkey is different from the property of being a flying pig.[11]

Why are we telling you about a theory that is subject to such devastating counterexamples? We do so because, if one is willing to expand one's ontology in an extreme way, Set Nominalism becomes a viable theory. Indeed,

---

[10] Lewis is an exception. In *Parts of Classes*, he analyzes membership in a set in terms of the *part of* relation.

[11] Lewis, *On the Plurality of Worlds*, p. 51.

this was Lewis's theory. Lewis believed that much more exists than just what actually exists. For Lewis, whatever possibly exists exists. So, what about those items on our does-not-exist list from Chapter 1, including Vulcan, Pegasus, and Atlantis? Lewis thought that they all belong on the does-exist list, just not on any Actually Exists list. What this expanded ontology brings are just the consequences Lewis wants. The property of having a heart is different from the property of having a kidney, because some possibly-but-not-actually existing animals have a heart and no kidneys, others have kidneys but no heart. Being a talking donkey is different from being a flying pig, because there are possible talking donkeys that are not flying pigs.

Set Nominalism has its attractions. Universals are a little strange in virtue of being multiply instantiable; our familiarity with talk of sets and the membership relation from standard mathematics makes sets seem less strange. Furthermore, the supposed abundance of sets of possibilia make them pretty well suited for being the meanings of predicates; in this regard, they are more like Platonic universals than Aristotelian universals. But these features of Set Nominalism are won only at an ontological price. Sets are not ontologically innocent; they are abstractions, and they are something that exists over and above their members. Even more daunting, the Set Nominalist has to see reality as including entities like Pegasus that, prima facie, only possibly exist, thereby accepting loads of material objects that we cannot perceive and that cannot stand in any causal relation to us. Besides the ontological price, we should also keep in mind that the usefulness of sets of possibilia for semantics is somewhat limited by the fact that predicates that are necessarily satisfied (e.g., 'is wise or not wise' and 'is angry or not angry') turn out to be synonymous. The same goes for predicates that necessarily are not satisfied (e.g., 'is wise and not wise' and 'is angry and not angry').

9.3.3 Trope Nominalism

There is another way of taking properties to be particulars. On this view, like the Aristotelian one, there are no uninstantiated properties. Unlike the Aristotelian view, this one can deny the existence of universals, taking all properties to be *tropes*, to be abstract particulars (in the weak, abstraction sense of 'abstract'). Tropes are things like Plato's wisdom and Socrates's wisdom. They are properties, but they are not multiply instantiable – they are not universals. Plato's wisdom is not Socrates's; no matter how similar they might be, they are two things, not one.

Predication via Tropes
a is F if and only if *a* has F-ness,[12]

where 'F-ness' names a trope. Socrates is wise because he has wisdom, because a certain named trope is his. *Modest* Trope Nominalism stops there, taking the having of a trope by a particular as brute.[13]

Stopping there, however, stops short of incorporating some distinctive and clever features of Trope Nominalism as it is famously advanced by Donald Williams and others.[14] These *Ambitious* Trope Nominalists maintain that there is a special relationship that holds between two tropes that are tropes of a single thing; such properties are *compresent*. Remarkably, the Ambitious Trope Nominalist uses this relation to say what the single things are: each one is a set of compresent tropes.[15] Furthermore, Ambitious Trope Nominalists have wanted to say something similar about what the Platonist takes to be universals, things like wisdom (wisdom simpliciter, not Socrates's or Plato's or anyone else's). They do so in terms of a second special relation that holds between two tropes. Wisdom is the set of all wisdoms; it is the set of tropes that *match* or (wholly) resemble some wisdom trope. Whether one trope matches or is compresent with another is not a matter for further account; such facts are taken to be brute. Within this framework, what the Ambitious Trope Nominalist says about predication is:

Predication via Sets of Tropes
a is F if and only if *a* intersects F-ness,

where 'F-ness' names a set of matching tropes. As is standard, intersection is defined in terms of set membership. So, seen as offering a philosophical

---

[12] We use the word 'has' instead of the word 'instantiates' to help emphasize the difference between Predication via Universals and Predication via Tropes. Some Trope Nominalists think only universals can be instantiated.

[13] Ehring, in *Causation and Persistence*, and Heil, in *From an Ontological Point of View*, each adopt something like Modest Trope Nominalism to bolster their attempts to solve metaphysical problems.

[14] Williams, "On the Elements of Being: I." Also see Campbell, "The Metaphysics of Abstract Particulars."

[15] We are simplifying a bit by identifying non-abstract particulars with a *set* of compresent tropes. They might be better identified with a *mereological sum* of their compresent tropes. See Chapter 8 for more on mereology.

account of predication, what this tells us is that Socrates is wise because Socrates, a set of compresent tropes (which includes a baldness trope and a wisdom trope among many others), shares a member with wisdom, a set of matching tropes (which includes that wisdom trope of Socrates, a wisdom trope of Plato, and lots of other wisdom tropes). What we have here is a theory that weaves together a theory of non-trope particulars with a theory of predication.

Part of the motivation for Trope Nominalism is what is seen as the extravagance of theories of universals. Trope Nominalists differ on exactly what tropes exist. Some hold that a thing's tropes include a distinct trope corresponding to each predicate the thing satisfies. Others take a stance in the spirit of Armstrong's theory of universals by holding that things have only the tropes that science tells us they have. Regardless, even Armstrong's view of universals is more extravagant in an important respect than the stingiest Trope Nominalisms. All theories of universals maintain that there are multiply instantiable properties, entities that are simultaneously instantiated by many different, spatially separated particulars. There need be no such thing according to the Trope Nominalist. In addition, Trope Nominalists find evidence of particularized properties in common sense: the bridge collapsed because of the weakness in the cable. (Discussion of apparent reference to particularized properties will be taken up in 9.5.) Sets of matching tropes might even play some role in semantic theory.

What is the downside to Trope Nominalism? Well, certain predications still will be taken as brute, be they predications of non-self-having, having, compresence, matching and/or set membership. And we still have an ontology of properties that are abstract particulars in the weak sense of 'abstract'. You might think that this minimizes the ontological extravagances, but there is an even more abstemious approach still to come.

9.3.4 Austere Nominalism

The Austere Nominalist can deny that there exist properties.[16] There is no need for universals, tropes, or properties as sets. The Austere Nominalist

---

[16] We take the term 'Austere Nominalist' from Loux, *Metaphysics*, p. 60. Loux has published many excellent books and articles on the ontology of properties, including the edited anthology *Universals and Particulars*.

refuses to give an account of predication, rejecting The One-Over-Many as a pseudo-problem.

Given how we have set up this chapter, Austere Nominalism may seem like an extreme view. It might appear that the Austere Nominalist is denying some perfectly obvious truths, like that Socrates is wise or that wisdom is a virtue. There might be such extreme views, maybe even some motivated by ontological considerations, but Austere Nominalism need not be so radical. When defended, it is usually advanced in a level-headed, common-sense way. Here's a passage from W. V. O. Quine that is indicative of how it has been advanced:

> One may admit that there are red houses, roses, and sunsets, but deny except as a popular and misleading manner of speaking, that they have anything in common … That the houses and roses and sunsets are all of them red may be taken as ultimate and irreducible.

And a bit later:

> We may say, e.g., that some dogs are white and not thereby commit ourselves to recognizing either doghood or whiteness as entities. 'Some dogs are white' says that some things that are dogs are white; and, in order that this statement be true, the things over which the bound variable 'something' ranges must include some white dogs, but need not include doghood or whiteness.[17]

There is no one thing (no universal, no set) that makes Plato and Socrates wise. Nor are there two things (two tropes) that do so. Plato is wise and Socrates is wise, and each of those facts is taken to be a brute fact. The Austere Nominalist is prepared to take *all* predications as primitive.

Sometimes Austere Nominalism is called *Ostrich Nominalism*, but this name was introduced (as far as we know) by Armstrong to poke fun at the view for ignoring the demand for an account of predication.[18] It is, however, difficult to see why there should be such needling, because, as we have seen through our consideration of non-self-instantiation and the threat of giving a partly circular account of predication, all the standard accounts of predication need to take some predications as primitive,

---

[17] From Quine, "On What There Is," pp. 29–30 and p. 32. Also see Sellars, "Grammar and Existence: A Preface to Ontology."

[18] Armstrong, *Nominalism and Realism*, p. 16.

including some of their own theoretical apparatus (e.g., predications of instantiation or set-membership). Everyone refuses to answer a Socratic One-Over-Many question when it is applied to some bit of predication.[19] What is distinctive about the Austere Nominalist is that he or she is prepared to take lots and lots of ordinary predications as basic.

9.4 Explanatory success?

What opens the door for Austere Nominalism is that all the accounts of predication that we have considered leave some predications unexplained. Nevertheless, it is not easy to step through this door even once it is opened. Many philosophers resist Austere Nominalism because it appears to miss out on some illumination. *With Austere Nominalism, it looks as if no predications get explained.* At least with the other four basic theories we have considered (Platonism, Aristotelianism, Set Nominalism, and Trope Nominalism), we do get somewhere. Adopting the position that there are properties gives us *some* explanatory advantage. Doesn't it?

This assessment misrepresents the debate between the Austere Nominalists and our other ontologists. It does so in two ways. First, Austere Nominalism isn't in as bad a position as it seems. Second, the other four ontologies are not in as good a position as it seems. The first point can be made briefly. The second is a little more involved.

As for the first point, the Austere Nominalist needn't and probably won't take *all* predications as brute. He or she might hold, say, that *a* is a bachelor as *a* is a man that never married. He or she can engage in the sort of conceptual understanding that Plato attempts in his early dialogues. The Austere Nominalist can endorse that *a* is temperate if and only if *a* avoids excesses. In principle, accounts could also be given for virtue, piety, color, shape. All the Austere Nominalist refuses to do is to give a fully general account of predication, an analysis of the locution '*a* is *F*'. Some, even many, predications are open to explanation.

As for the second point, let's reconsider Set Nominalism. It can be tempting to think that it includes a circular account of predication. This

---

[19] This point is forcefully made by Devitt in "'Ostrich Nominalism' or 'Mirage Realism',", and by Lewis in "New Work for a Theory of Universals," pp. 353–4.

can be tempting because it is easy to think of the account of predication as holding:

Circular Predication via Sets
a is *F* if and only if *a* is a member of the set of all *x* such that *x* is *F*.

But that's not right. This account specifies the set of *F*s within the account of predication. That's blatantly circular; 'is *F*' is used on both sides of the 'if and only if'. The account is supposed to be telling us what makes something *F* and then uses that notion in the explanation. Instead, the (genuine) Set Nominalist specifies the set of *F*s independently of giving his account. He or she identifies the set of *F*s, naming it '*F*-ness' and uses the name in the account. So, letting *F*-ness be the set of all *x* such that *x* is *F*, what Predication via Sets actually says is what is given in 9.3: *a* is *F* if and only if *a* is a member of *F*-ness. Thus, letting 'wisdom' name the set of wise things, Socrates is wise because he is in that set, because he is a member of wisdom. The circular variation says that Socrates is wise because Socrates is in the set that includes everything that is wise; in short, he is wise because he is wise.

An interesting question to ask is whether Predication via Sets is much of an improvement over the Circular Predication via Sets. We think this is an important question that has not received enough attention. Yes, the actual statement of Predication via Sets is not circular. It tells us that what makes something *F* is its standing in the membership relation to an entity. The account itself doesn't use *F* to specify what that entity is. That's done separately from the account. But, being non-circular is not the same as being illuminating. How big an improvement the actual account is over its circular variation depends on whether we have some (perhaps direct) independent access to the entity *F*-ness – the set of *F*s. What is needed is some way of determining what the members of that set are without first determining what things are *F*. For example, if the Set Nominalist could *point* to the set or *describe* it without using the predicate 'is *F*', then the interest of the account would improve dramatically. If there is not such access, if our only access to the set of *F*s is our being told that it is the set of things that are *F*, then it is hard to see what understanding there is to be gained from even the non-circular statement of Predication via Sets.

Though it is not as obvious, this same issue arises with each of the accounts of predication that we have considered.

> What philosophers who propose the existence of universals do is to propose a general reason which looks informative because it shifts to another level, but unfortunately is not. It merely marks time: but marking time can look very like marching if only the movements of the performers are watched, and not the ground which they profess to be covering.[20]

In each account, 'F' appears in both the explanandum (i.e., what is to be explained) and the explanans (i.e., what is to do the explaining). In each case, the occurrence of 'F' in the explanans is as part of a name for some entity, either a name for a Platonic universal, an Aristotelian universal, a set of possibilia, a set of tropes, or a trope. 'F' is not being used as part of the predicate 'is F'; that would make the account circular. Nevertheless, how explanatory the account is depends on whether we have some access to the named entity that is independent of our judgments of what things are F. There should be some way of determining what the named entity is and whether a stands in the right relation (be it instantiation or set membership) to the entity without first determining whether a is F. For example, if someone points to the universal F-ness or describes this universal without using the predicate 'is F', then the prospects for an informative explanation improve. If there is not this access, if our only access to the named entity is our being told that it is what makes all F things F, then nothing has been gained.

Plato thought we did have special access to the realm of forms. He thought we could know piety and temperance, without determining what things were pious and what things were temperate. According to Plato, prior to our births, our immortal souls were acquainted with the forms – piety and temperance included – and, after our births, we are able to *recollect* the forms. Needless to say, Plato's is an extreme view. One needn't be quite so metaphysically adventurous. For example, Bertrand Russell thought we know universals *by acquaintance*, by learning to abstract the F-ness that observed particular Fs have in common.[21] Aristotelians and Trope Nominalists are even in a position to argue that their properties can be identified ostensively (roughly, by pointing), because, arguably, Aristotelian universals and tropes can be perceived. So there may be a way to make one or more of the accounts of predication illuminating. Our point is that there is still work to be done. Regarding the explanation of

---

[20] Pears, "Universals," p. 220.
[21] Russell, *The Problems of Philosophy*, p. 73.

predication, the playing field between the Austere Nominalist and the others is more level than it might first have appeared.

The accounts of predication go beyond what are, strictly speaking, the associated ontological views. The cores of the ontological views are about what exists, they say what belongs on the does-exist list. For example, the central claim of Platonism is that there exist Platonic universals. Given the work that needs to be done in order for the accounts of predication to be explanatory, they are best seen as philosophical theories made possible by the associated ontology, not as the sole foundation of arguments in favor of that ontology. In a way, this is fortunate for the Platonist, the Aristotelian, the Set Nominalist, and the Trope Nominalist. It is part of the reason that all these property ontologies continue to have their supporters. As we will see in the next section, these ontologies are interesting apart from what they say about predication and the One-Over-Many. So, endorse your favorite account of predication if you have some reason to believe in the needed entities. Just be very careful if your only reason for adopting that ontology is the supposed explanatory value of the account of predication.

9.5 Some common-sense truths

The One-Over-Many Problem is not the only ontological issue that has pre-occupied metaphysicians interested in the question of whether properties exist. That issue is really just one example of how some philosophers found properties appealing in the service of advancing a philosophical account. In this section, we consider several common-sense truths that seem rather directly to commit us to properties.

Here are some examples:

(1) Socrates has wisdom.
(2) Plato and Socrates have wisdom in common.
(3) Plato and Socrates have something in common.
(4) Humility is a virtue.

Sentences (1)–(4) seem true. In each case, the apparent source of the commitment to properties is obvious: (1), (2), and (4) all include what appears to be a name (either 'wisdom' or 'humility') referring to some kind of property. Sentence (3) includes the quantifier 'something' that appears to quantify over properties.

With the possible exception of the Modest Trope Nominalist, the friends of properties considered above are in a good position to accept these sentences as true. Indeed, these examples (or ones like them) are often cited as part of an argument for the existence of properties. The Platonist will not be ashamed to admit there exist such things as wisdom and humility, and hold that wisdom at least is one property Plato and Socrates both instantiate. Friends of Aristotelian universals can take exactly the same stance – so long as they are not too stingy about the sorts of universals that exist.[22] The Set Nominalist with his or her ontology of possibilia is also in good shape. For the Set Nominalist like Lewis, sentence (1) is true because having wisdom is a matter of being a member of wisdom, which is the set of all possible things that are wise. Sentences (2) and (3) are made true by Socrates and Plato both being members of this set. Sentence (4) is true because humility, the set of all possible humble things, is a virtue. The Ambitious Trope Nominalist can take a stance that is similar to the Set Nominalist's: sentence (1) is true because having wisdom is a matter of intersecting wisdom, the resemblance set of wisdom tropes. Sentences (2) and (3) are made true by Socrates and Plato both intersecting this set. Sentence (4) is true because humility, the set of all humility tropes, is a virtue. Modest Trope Nominalists need to postulate something to serve as the reference of 'humility' and 'wisdom' or resort to some sort of paraphrase. (As we will see in a bit, the Austere Nominalist may have some suggestions.)

Trope Nominalists offer some other common-sense truths that seem to reveal a commitment to tropes:

(5) The weakness of the cable caused the collapse of the bridge.[23]

The trope theorist takes sentences like (5) at face value. The weakness in the cable of that bridge exists, and is a distinct thing from the weakness in the cable of any other bridge.

---

[22] A philosopher like Armstrong should be agnostic (or even skeptical) about whether there is a universal of humility or one of wisdom. He shouldn't assume that 'is humble' or 'is wise' are part of the formulation of *science*, which for Armstrong is the gatekeeper for what exists. To keep sentences (1)–(4) all true, such an Aristotelian will have to scramble at least a bit (i) to find something to be the reference of 'wisdom' and 'humility' and to be a value of the quantified variable in (3); or (ii) to find instead suitable paraphrases of one or more of these sentences.

[23] Campbell, "The Metaphysics of Abstract Particulars," p. 480.

For the Aristotelian and the Set Nominalist, the weakness in the first cable *is* the weakness in the other cable – there is just the one thing, either the universal weakness or the set of possible weak things. So, it is not immediately clear how the Aristotelian and the Set Nominalist can avoid the bizarre consequence that it is true that the weakness in a cable on a bridge, perhaps 5,000 miles away, caused this nearby bridge to break. The Platonist may have a way out since he or she might be willing to take the different instantiations of a universal to be different things, but this only expands the Platonist's already rich ontology to include not only abstract universals, but also more concrete instantiations of these universals. Perhaps the best move for the Aristotelian, the Platonist, and the Set Nominalist would be to paraphrase (5) as saying that it is the fact that the cable in that bridge instantiates weakness, not the weakness itself, that caused the bridge to collapse. There may, however, still be lingering worries that this paraphrase is committed to another sort of entity, a *fact*. One might also have a more specific concern about the viability of this option for the Platonist and the Set Nominalist. How could a fact about a particular *instantiating an abstract universal* or *being a member of* a *set of possibilia* make anything collapse?

What of the Austere Nominalist? Hoping to deny that there are any properties, the Austere Nominalist needs to say something about sentences (1)–(4) and the Trope Nominalist's favorite, sentence (5). There is an easy paraphrase for (1) and for (2):

(1′) Socrates is wise.
(2′) Socrates is wise and Plato is wise.

So far, so good. There is something similarly simple for the Austere Nominalist to say about (5):

(5′) The bridge collapsed because the cable in that bridge was weak.

Taken at face value, (5′) commits us to nothing but the bridge and the cable.[24] So, really, it is sentences (3) and (4) that make the most immediate trouble for the Austere Nominalist.

---

[24] Some philosophers following Quine would not be satisfied with this rendering of (5) as it is not clear how (5′) could be adequately represented in the symbolic language of predicate logic. The connective 'because' can't be introduced into this language except in trivializing ways. But, ultimately, Quine's insistence that there be

There is the option of denying that (3) and (4) are true. Perhaps these sentences are, strictly speaking, false. In a way, they do seem to assert exactly what the Austere Nominalist wants to deny. Sentence (3) says that there is *something* Plato and Socrates share, and sentence (4) seems to imply that a certain other thing, *humility*, exists and is a virtue. How could these things help but be anything besides some kind of property? And isn't that exactly what the Austere Nominalist says is not on the does-exist list? Remember what Quine said: "One may admit that there are red houses, roses, and sunsets, but *deny except as a popular and misleading manner of speaking, that they have anything in common*" (our emphasis). The viability of digging in one's heels by rejecting (3) and (4) depends on just how prepared one is to give up these common-sense truths.

There may not seem to be much at stake here. What trouble could we get in by denying that Socrates and Plato have something in common, so long as it is true that they are both wise? That humility is a virtue hardly seems to be a bedrock datum that should be preserved at all cost, especially given that one is not denying either that, say, Mother Theresa is humble or that she is virtuous. We think that there is much at stake here. Denying (3) and (4) should not be done without careful consideration. This is especially clear regarding sentence (3). The Austere Nominalist's trouble with (3) is that there is a quantifier that apparently ranges over properties. There are lots of other similar and very important sentences. In particular, a lot of what is said in mathematics in terms of sets and functions can be said without sets and functions if we use quantifiers like the one found in (3) instead. If it should turn out that this quantification is nominalistically harmless, then this is potentially an ontological boon for those who like austere ontologies. So though we won't get into too many details, let us spend a little time looking for possible paraphrases of (3). What we find will suggest a paraphrase of sentence (4).

One thing to notice about (3) is that it seems to follow trivially from (2′). How could Socrates and Plato both be wise and yet not have something in common? What's remarkable is that (2′) is consistent with Austere Nominalism. So, (2′) is consistent with Austere Nominalism though one

such a representation stems from a somewhat distant issue about our ability to use and understand natural language; it doesn't directly have to do with what (5′) says exists.

of its trivial entailments is not. How can that be?[25] How could a sentence entailed by a sentence that doesn't entail that there exist properties entail that there exist properties? Despite appearances, maybe, just maybe, that Plato and Socrates have something in common *doesn't* do that.

The question is whether we need to see (3) as saying that there exists some entity such that Socrates has it and Plato has it. If we simply interpret the natural-language quantifier 'something' in the manner used in elementary logic classes then the answer to this question is no. But, back in Chapter 1, we already had a case involving a quantification in natural language that decidedly should not be treated this way: 'The average American family has 1.81 children.' Normally, a definite description like 'The average American family' is interpreted as involving quantification as 'There exists a family, it is American, it is average and nothing else is a family, American, and average.' (The phrase 'and nothing else ...' preserves the uniqueness implication of use of the definite article 'the'.) But, as we saw in Chapter 1, there is a straightforward way of avoiding ontological commitment to such a bizarre entity. The quantifiers of natural language need not get an automatic identification with the quantifiers of predicate logic. We should be open to the idea that sentences including natural-language quantifiers, even very simple ones like (3), might be open to understandings that do not bear any commitment to properties. There are various ways to proceed here but, as illustration, we will briefly discuss work by George Boolos and also work by Augustin Rayo and Stephen Yablo.[26]

Boolos suggests that (2) is equivalent to: 'There are some wise things such that Plato and Socrates are among them.' Then sentence (3) is equivalent to: 'There are some things such that Plato and Socrates are

---

[25] This puzzle is laid out nicely by Hofweber, in "Innocent Statements and Their Metaphysically Loaded Counterparts." Schiffer calls inferences like the one from (2′) to (3) a *something-from-nothing transformation*; see pp. 61–71 of *The Things We Mean*. He takes these transformations to reflect conceptual truths – in our case the conceptual truth that, if Socrates is wise and Plato is wise, then there is a property that Socrates has and Plato has. Schiffer accepts that properties exist but holds that they have no interesting or deep nature not determined by the practices constitutive of the concept of a property.

[26] Boolos, "To Be Is to Be a Value of a Variable (or to Be Some Values of Some Variables)" and "Nominalistic Platonism;" Rayo and Yablo, "Nominalism through De-Nominalization."

among them.' What is interesting is that these paraphrases seem not to commit one to the existence of properties, just to things that could amount to nothing more than Socrates, Plato, and some other ordinary particulars.

Rayo and Yablo paraphrase sentence (3) differently from Boolos. They think of (3) as saying that Socrates and Plato are the same way. Even better, to avoid being sucked into thinking that there are such entities as *ways*, they can paraphrase (3) as:

(3′) Socrates is somehow and Plato is likewise.

We can also give a parallel paraphrase of (2): 'Wise is somehow Socrates and Plato are.' One thing that is nice about (3′) is that 'somehow' and 'likewise' don't even appear as if they are quantifying over any entity. They don't replace a name or description; they replace the word 'wise' in 'Socrates is wise' and in 'Plato is wise', respectively. There is no temptation to think that there need be any property (not a trope or set of tropes, not a universal, not a set of possibilia) for an assertion made by (3′) to be true.

We have yet to try an Austere Nominalist paraphrase of sentence (4). The usual place to begin is to suggest, 'Everything humble is virtuous.' Two criticisms are often made of this idea. First, it is usually pointed out that, though humility is a virtue, not everything humble is virtuous. After all, some things have their humility outweighed by their more numerous or more serious vices with the consequence that, though they are humble, they are not virtuous. We are not sure this criticism is a good one; it may depend on a particular reading of 'virtuous' (virtuous in an all-things-considered sense) rather than on another perfectly good reading (virtuous in an in-some-manner-or-to-some-extent sense). Nevertheless, even if our suspicion is right, there is the second criticism. Consider:

(6) Red is a color.

If one is tempted to paraphrase (4) as 'Everything humble is virtuous,' one should also be tempted to paraphrase (6) as 'Everything red is colored.' So far, so good. By parity of reasoning, one should then paraphrase

(7) Red is a shape

as 'Everything red is shaped.' That's the problem. Though (4) and (6) are true, (7) is false. Its paraphrase, if it really is a good paraphrase, should be false as well. Unfortunately, for the Austere Nominalist, it's not false. It's true; everything red is shaped.[27]

Taking our cue from Rayo and Yablo, here are some suggestions for better paraphrases of (4), (6), and (7):

(4′) If something is humble, then it is virtuous in a humble way.
(6′) If something is red, then it is colored in a red way.
(7′) If something is red, then it is shaped in a red way.

Notice that the first two are clearly true and now the third is clearly false. To be shaped in a red way, red must be a manner in which the red thing is shaped. But red is never a manner in which an object is shaped. Round, square, oval, triangular, each of these could be a manner in which an object is shaped, but red couldn't. Really, the only thing not to like about (4′), (6′), and (7′) is that they look as if they are ontologically committed to ways. As before, that can be fixed by recognizing that a way or a manner in which something is virtuous or colored or shaped is *somehow* it is virtuous or colored or shaped.

(4″) If something is humble, then humble is somehow it is virtuous.
(6″) If something is red, then red is somehow it is colored.
(7″) If something is red, then red is somehow it is shaped.[28]

Notice that humble is somehow all humble things are virtuous even if not all humble things are virtuous. Red is not somehow all red things are shaped even though red is somehow all red things are colored.[29]

We have gone on about how the Austere Nominalist might handle some classic cases from the ontology literature. We think this is justified, not because we think Austere Nominalism is obviously the correct theory, but *because it has the least ontology with which to work*. That is important because the paraphrases open and appealing to the Austere Nominalist

---

[27] Jackson, "Statements about Universals," p. 427.

[28] Arguably, all these could be put just a little bit differently without using the word 'somehow'. For example, (6″) might be rephrased as: 'If something is red, then it is redly colored.'

[29] Is there a problem stemming from uninstantiated properties? On this manner of paraphrase, it seems that inertiality will (incorrectly) turn out to be a shape simply because nothing is inertial. Certainly this requires further investigation, but we take some consolation that matters generally get messy whenever vacuous truths are involved. (For more on being vacuously true, see Chapter 3.)

are open to and might also be appealing to other ontologists. For example, in order to resist commitment to tropes or property instantiations or facts, a Platonist about universals might adopt (5′) as a paraphrase of (5). For another example, the Modest Trope Nominalist might adopt (4″) as a paraphrase of (4), apparently avoiding the need for humility, understood to be a universal or to be a set of matching tropes.

9.6 Ontological decisions

We have briefly described five basic ontologies: Platonism, Aristotelianism, Trope Nominalism, Set Nominalism, and Austere Nominalism. The first four nicely organize:

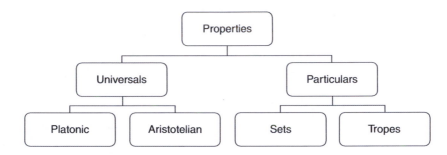

Chart 9.1: *Property ontologies*

The fifth, Austere Nominalism, in contrast to these four, denies that there are any properties. Each view has its own virtues and vices. Austere Nominalism minimizes the ontology of properties but seems bound to include many brute predications. Each of the others has fewer primitives, though they differ from each other and from Austere Nominalism on how simple and how familiar their primitives are. How much brute predication a theory has, and how mysterious or enlightening these predications are, must be weighed against how much inordinate ontology the theory takes on. And, of course, these considerations must not be weighed only relative to the role the ontology plays in a theory of predication or in the preservation of common-sense truths. They must be weighed relative to our entire corpus of knowledge.

Bibliography

Aristotle, *The Basic Works of Aristotle*, ed. Richard McKeon (Random House, 1941).

Armstrong, David, *A Materialist Theory of Mind* (Routledge & Kegan Paul, 1968).

  Nominalism and Realism (Cambridge University Press, 1978).

  What Is a Law of Nature? (Cambridge University Press, 1983).

Ayer, A. J., *The Foundations of Empirical Knowledge* (Macmillan, 1940).

Barnes, Jonathan, *Early Greek Philosophy* (Penguin Books, 2001).

Beauchamp, Tom and Rosenberg, Alexander, *Hume and the Problem of Causation* (Oxford University Press, 1981).

Bennett, Jonathan, *Events and Their Names* (Hackett Publishing Company, 1988).

Berkeley, George, *A Treatise Concerning the Principles of Human Knowledge*, ed. Kenneth Winkler (Hackett Publishing Company, 1982).

Bird, Alexander, *Nature's Metaphysics* (Oxford University Press, 2007).

Blackburn, Simon, "Hume and Thick Connexions," *Philosophy and Phenomenological Research* **50** (1990, supplement), 237–50.

Block, Ned, "Can the Mind Change the World?," in George Boolos (ed.), *Meaning and Method: Essays in Honor of Hilary Putnam* (Cambridge University Press, 1990).

  "What Is Functionalism?," in Ned Block (ed.), *Readings in Philosophy of Psychology, vol. I* (Harvard University Press, 1980).

Boolos, George, "Nominalistic Platonism," *Philosophical Review* **94** (1985), 327–44.

  "To Be Is to Be a Value of a Variable (or to Be Some Values of Some Variables)," *Journal of Philosophy* **81** (1984), 430–49.

Campbell, Keith, "The Metaphysics of Abstract Particulars," *Midwest Studies in Philosophy* **6** (1981), 477–88.

Carroll, John, "Anti-Reductionism," in Helen Beebee, Christopher Hitchcock, and Peter Menzies (eds.), *Oxford Handbook of Causation* (Oxford University Press, 2009).

Laws of Nature (Cambridge University Press, 1994).

"The Humean Tradition," *Philosophical Review* **99** (1990), 185–219.

Chalmers, David, *The Conscious Mind* (Oxford University Press, 1996).

Chisholm, Roderick, "Human Freedom and the Self," in Chisholm, Roderick, *On Metaphysics* (University of Minnesota Press, 1989). (Originally published as The Lindley Lecture by the Department of Philosophy, University of Kansas, 1964.)

"Law Statements and Counterfactual Inference," *Analysis* **15** (1955), 97–105.

"The Contrary-to-Fact Conditional," *Mind* **55** (1946), 289–307.

Churchland, Paul, "Eliminative Materialism and the Propositional Attitudes," *Journal of Philosophy* **78** (1981), 67–90.

Matter and Consciousness (MIT Press, 1988).

Davidson, Donald, "Causal Relations," *Journal of Philosophy* **64** (1967), 691–703.

Essays on Actions and Events (Oxford University Press, 1980).

"Mental Events," in Lawrence Foster and J. W. Swanson (eds.), *Experience and Theory* (University of Massachusetts Press, 1970); reprinted in *Essays on Actions and Events*.

"The Individuation of Events," in Nicholas Rescher et al. (eds.), *Essays in Honor of Carl Hempel* (D. Reidel Publishing Company, 1970).

Descartes, René, *Meditations on First Philosophy*, ed. John Cottingham (Cambridge University Press, 1996).

Devitt, Michael, "'Ostrich Nominalism' or 'Mirage Realism'," *Pacific Philosophical Quarterly* **61** (1980), 433–9.

d'Holbach, Paul-Henri Thiry (Baron), "The Illusion of Free Will," from *The System of Nature*, in Daniel Kolak and Raymond Martin (eds.), *The Experience of Philosophy* (Oxford University Press, 2002). First published in 1770.

Dretske, Fred, "Epistemic Operators," *Journal of Philosophy* **67** (1970), 1007–23.

Dretske, Fred and Snyder, Aaron, "Causal Irregularity," *Philosophy of Science* **39** (1972), 69–71.

Eells, Ellery, *Probabilistic Causality* (Cambridge University Press, 1991).

Ehring, Doug, *Causation and Persistence* (Oxford University Press, 1997).

Fischer, John Martin, *Moral Responsibility* (Cornell University Press, 1986).

Fodor, Jerry, "The Mind–Body Problem," *Scientific American* **244** (1981), 114–23.

Frankfurt, Harry, "Alternate Possibilities and Moral Responsibility," *Journal of Philosophy* **66** (1969), 829–39.

Gibbard, Allan, "Contingent Identity," *Journal of Philosophical Logic* **4** (1975), 187–221.

Goodman, Nelson, *Fact, Fiction, and Forecast* (Harvard University Press, 1954; 2nd edn. 1983).

  "The Problem of Counterfactual Conditionals," *Journal of Philosophy* **44** (1947), 113–28; reprinted in *Fact, Fiction, and Forecast*.

Hall, Ned, "Causation and the Price of Transitivity," in John Collins, Ned Hall, and Laurie Paul (eds.), *Causation and Counterfactuals* (MIT Press, 2004).

Haslanger, Sally, "Persistence, Change, and Explanation," *Philosophical Studies* **56** (1989), 1–28.

Hawley, Katherine, *How Things Persist* (Oxford University Press, 2001).

Heil, John, *From an Ontological Point of View* (Clarendon Press, 2003).

Heller, Mark, *The Ontology of Physical Objects* (Cambridge University Press, 1990).

Hinchliff, Mark, "The Puzzle of Change," *Philosophical Perspectives* **10** (1996), 119–36.

Hobart, R. E., "Free Will as Involving Determinism and Inconceivable without It," *Mind* **43** (1934), 1–27.

Hobbes, Thomas, *Metaphysical Writings*, ed. Mary Whiton Calkins (Open Court, 1989).

Hofweber, Thomas, "Innocent Statements and Their Metaphysically Loaded Counterparts," *Philosopher's Imprint* **7** (2007), 1–33.

Hume, David, *An Inquiry Concerning Human Understanding* (Bobbs-Merrill Educational Publishing, 1955).

Huxley, Thomas, "On the Hypothesis that Animals are Automata, and Its History," *Fortnightly Review* **16** (1874), 555–80.

Irvine, A. D., "Russell's Paradox," in Edward N. Zalta (ed.), *Stanford Encyclopedia of Philosophy* (Fall 2008 edn.), http://plato.stanford.edu/archives/fall2008/entries/russell-paradox/.

Jackson, Frank, "Statements about Universals," *Mind* **86** (1977), 427–9.

  "What Mary Didn't Know," *Journal of Philosophy* **83** (1986), 291–5.

Jaki, Stanley, "The Early History of the Titius–Bode Law," *American Journal of Physics* **40** (1972), 1014–23.

Kant, Immanuel, *Critique of Pure Reason*, trans. Norman Kemp Smith (St. Martin's Press, 1929).

Kim, Jaegwon, "Events as Property Exemplifications," in Myles Brand and Douglas Walton (eds.), *Action Theory* (D. Reidel Publishing Company, 1976).

  Mind in a Physical World (MIT Press, 1998).

  "Noncausal Connections," *Noûs* **8** (1974), 41–52.

Kripke, Saul, *Naming and Necessity* (Harvard University Press, 1980).

Lange, Marc, *Laws and Lawmakers* (Oxford University Press, 2009).

Leibniz, Gottfried Wilhelm, *Philosophical Essays*, ed. and trans. Roger Ariew and Daniel Garber (Hackett Publishing Company, 1989).

"New System of the Nature of Substances," in *Leibniz's 'New System' and Associated Contemporary Texts*, ed. and trans. R. S. Woolhouse and Richard Francks (Oxford University Press, 1997).

Lewis, C. I., *An Analysis of Knowledge and Valuation* (Open Court, 1946).

Lewis, David, "An Argument for the Identity Theory," *Journal of Philosophy* **63** (1966), 17–25; reprinted in *Philosophical Papers*, vol. I.

"Are We Free to Break the Laws?," *Theoria* **47** (1981), 113–21; reprinted in *Philosophical Papers*, vol. II.

"Causation," *Journal of Philosophy* **70** (1970), 556–67; reprinted in *Philosophical Papers*, vol. II.

"Causation as Influence," in John Collins, Ned Hall, and Laurie Paul (eds.), *Causation and Counterfactuals* (MIT Press, 2004).

Counterfactuals (Harvard University Press, 1973).

"How to Define Theoretical Terms," *Journal of Philosophy* **67** (1970), 427–46; reprinted in *Philosophical Papers*, vol. I.

"New Work for a Theory of Universals," *Australasian Journal of Philosophy* **61** (1983), 343–77.

On the Plurality of Worlds (Blackwell, 1986).

Parts of Classes (Blackwell, 1991).

Philosophical Papers, vol. I (Oxford University Press, 1983).

Philosophical Papers, vol. II (Oxford University Press, 1986).

"Survival and Identity," in Amélie Rorty (ed.), *The Identities of Persons* (University of California Press, 1976); reprinted in *Philosophical Papers*, vol. I.

"The Paradoxes of Time Travel," *American Philosophical Quarterly* **13** (1976), 145–52; reprinted in *Philosophical Papers*, vol. II.

"What Experience Teaches," in William Lycan (ed.), *Mind and Cognition* (Blackwell, 1990).

Locke, John, *An Essay Concerning Human Understanding, vol. I* (Dover Publications, 1959). First published in 1690.

Loux, Michael, *Metaphysics: A Contemporary Introduction* (Routledge, 2002).

Loux, Michael (ed.), *Universals and Particulars* (University of Notre Dame Press, 1970).

Mackie, John, *The Cement of the Universe* (Clarendon Press, 1974).

Markosian, Ned, "A Compatibilist Version of the Theory of Agent Causation," *Pacific Philosophical Quarterly* **80** (1999), 257–77.

"A Defense of Presentism," in Dean Zimmerman (ed.), *Oxford Studies in Metaphysics, vol. I* (Oxford University Press, 2003).

"Brutal Composition," *Philosophical Studies* **92** (1998), 211–49.

"How Fast Does Time Pass?," *Philosophy and Phenomenological Research* **53** (1993), 829–44.

"Identifying the Problem of Personal Identity," in Joseph Campbell and Michael O'Rourke (eds.), *Topics in Contemporary Philosophy, vol. VI, Time and Identity* (MIT Press, forthcoming).

"Restricted Composition," in John Hawthorne, Theodore Sider, and Dean Zimmerman (eds.), *Contemporary Debates in Metaphysics* (Blackwell, 2008).

"Simples," *Australasian Journal of Philosophy* **76** (1998), 213–26.

"What Are Physical Objects?," *Philosophy and Phenomenological Research* **61** (2000), 375–95.

Maslen, Cei, "Causes, Contrasts, and the Nontransitivity of Causation," in John Collins, Ned Hall, and Laurie Paul (eds.), *Causation and Counterfactuals* (MIT Press, 2004).

Maxwell, Nicholas, "Are Probabilism and Special Relativity Incompatible?," *Philosophy of Science* **52** (1985), 23–43.

McCall, Storrs, *A Model of the Universe* (Clarendon Press, 1994).

McTaggart, J. M. E., "The Unreality of Time," *Mind* **17** (1908), 456–73; reprinted in Robin Le Poidevin and Murray McBeath (eds.), *The Philosophy of Time* (Oxford University Press, 1993).

Mellor, D. H. and Oliver, Alex (eds.), *Properties* (Oxford University Press, 1997).

Menzies, Peter and Price, Huw, "Causation as Secondary Quality," *British Journal for the Philosophy of Science* **44** (1993), 187–205.

Merricks, Trenton, "There Are No Criteria of Identity over Time," *Noûs* **32** (1998), 106–24.

Nagel, Thomas, "What Is It Like to Be a Bat?," *Philosophical Review* **73** (1974), 435–50.

Olson, Eric, *The Human Animal* (Oxford University Press, 1997).

Parfit, Derek, *Reasons and Persons* (Oxford University Press, 1984).

Pears, David, "Universals," *Philosophical Quarterly* **1** (1951), 218–27.

Plantinga, Alvin, *The Nature of Necessity* (Oxford University Press, 1974).

Plato, *The Collected Dialogues of Plato*, ed. Edith Hamilton and Huntington Cairns (Princeton University Press, 1961).

The Dialogues of Plato, vol. II, trans. B. Jowett (Oxford University Press, 1924).

Popper, Karl, *The Logic of Scientific Discovery* (Basic Books, 1959).

Price, Huw, "Causal Perspectivalism," in Huw Price and Richard Corry (eds.), *Causation, Physics, and the Constitution of Reality: Russell's Republic Revisited* (Oxford University Press, 2007).

Prior, Arthur N., "Changes in Events and Changes in Things," in *Papers on Time and Tense*.

Papers on Time and Tense (Oxford University Press, 1968).

Past, Present, and Future (Oxford University Press, 1967).

"Some Free Thinking about Time," in Jack Copeland (ed.), *Logic and Reality* (Clarendon Press, 1996).

"Thank Goodness That's Over," in Prior, Arthur N., *Papers in Logic and Ethics* (Duckworth, 1976).

"The Notion of the Present," *Stadium Generale* **23** (1970), 245–8.

Putnam, Hilary, "Time and Physical Geometry," *Journal of Philosophy* **64** (1967), 240–7.

Quine, W. V. O., "Identity, Ostension, and Hypostasis," *Journal of Philosophy* **47** (1950), 621–33.

Methods of Logic (Henry Holt and Company, 1950).

"On What There Is," *Review of Metaphysics* **2** (1948), 21–38.

"Whither Physical Objects?," in Robert Cohen, Paul Feyerabend, and Marx Wartofsky (eds.), *Boston Studies in the Philosophy of Science, vol. XXXIX* (D. Reidel Publishing Company, 1976).

Word and Object (MIT Press, 1960).

Quinton, Anthony, *The Nature of Things* (Routledge & Kegan Paul, 1973).

Ramsey, Frank, *The Foundations of Mathematics* (Routledge & Kegan Paul, 1931).

Rayo, Augustin, and Yablo, Stephen, "Nominalism through De-Nominalization," *Noûs* **35** (2001), 74–92.

Ree, Paul, "Determinism and the Illusion of Moral Responsibility" (English translation by Stefan Bauer-Mengelberg of chapters 1–2 of *Die Illusion der Willens Freiheit*, originally published Berlin, 1885), in Paul Edwards and Arthur Pap (eds.), *A Modern Introduction to Philosophy*, 3rd edn. (Free Press, 1973).

Reid, Thomas, *Essays on the Active Powers of Man*, in *Inquiry and Essays*, ed. Ronald Beanblossom and Keith Lehrer (Hackett Publishing Company, 1983). First published in 1788.

Robb, David and Heil, John, "Mental Causation," in Edward N. Zalta (ed.), *Stanford Encyclopedia of Philosophy* (Fall 2008 edn.), http://plato.stanford.edu/archives/fall2008/entries/mental-causation/.

Rosenberg, Jay F., 1993, "Comments on Peter van Inwagen's *Material Beings*," *Philosophy and Phenomenological Research* **53**, 701–8.

Russell, Bertrand, "On Denoting," *Mind* **14** (1905), 479–93.

"On the Notion of Cause," *Proceedings of the Aristotelian Society* **13** (1912–13), 1–26.

The Problems of Philosophy (Dover Publications, 1999).

Schaffer, Jonathan, "Causation and Laws of Nature: Reductionism," in John Hawthorne, Theodore Sider, and Dean Zimmerman (eds.), *Contemporary Debates in Metaphysics* (Blackwell, 2008).

"Overlappings: Probability-Raising without Causation," *Australasian Journal of Philosophy* **70** (2000), 40–6.

"Trumping Preemption," *Journal of Philosophy* **97** (2000), 165–85.

Schiffer, Stephen, *The Things We Mean* (Clarendon Press, 2003).

Searle, John, "Minds, Brains, and Programs," *Behavioral and Brain Sciences* **3** (1980), 417–24.

Sellars, Wilfrid, "Grammar and Existence: A Preface to Ontology," *Mind* **69** (1960), 499–533.

Shoemaker, Sydney, "Causal and Metaphysical Necessity," *Pacific Philosophical Quarterly* **79** (1998), 59–77.

"Functionalism and Qualia," *Philosophical Studies* **27** (1975), 291–315.

Sidelle, Alan, *Necessity, Essence, and Individuation: A Defense of Conventionalism* (Cornell University Press, 1989).

"On the Metaphysical Contingency of Laws of Nature," in Tamar Szabó Gendler and John Hawthorne (eds.), *Conceivability and Possibility* (Oxford University Press, 2002).

Sider, Theodore, *Four-Dimensionalism* (Oxford University Press, 2001).

"Van Inwagen and the Possibility of Gunk," *Analysis* **53** (1993), 285–9.

Smart, J. J. C., *Our Place in the Universe* (Blackwell, 1989).

"Sensations and Brain Processes," *Philosophical Review* **68** (1959), 141–56.

"The River of Time," *Mind* **58** (1949), 483–94; reprinted in Antony Flew (ed.), *Essays in Conceptual Analysis* (St. Martin's Press, 1966).

Stace, Walter T., "The Problem of Free Will," in Joel Feinberg and Russ Shafer-Landau (eds.), *Reason and Responsibility*, 11th edn. (Wadsworth, 2002); from Stace, *Religion and the Modern Mind* (J. B. Lippincott Co., 1952).

Thomson, Judith Jarvis, "Parthood and Identity across Time," *Journal of Philosophy* **80** (1983), 201–20.

"People and Their Bodies," in Jonathan Dancy (ed.), *Reading Parfit* (Blackwell, 1997).

Tooley, Michael, *Causation* (Oxford University Press, 1987).

Tooley, Michael, "The Nature of Laws," *Canadian Journal of Philosophy* **7** (1977), 667–98.

Unger, Peter, "The Uniqueness in Causation," *American Philosophical Quarterly* **14** (1977), 177–88.

Van Fraassen, Bas, *Laws and Symmetry* (Clarendon Press, 1989).

Van Inwagen, Peter, *An Essay on Free Will* (Oxford University Press, 1983).

   "Four-Dimensional Objects," *Noûs* **24** (1990), 245–55.

   Material Beings (Cornell University Press, 1990).

Ward, Barry, "Humeanism without Humean Supervenience: A Projectivist Account of Laws and Possibilities," *Philosophical Studies* **107** (2002), 191–218.

Williams, Donald, "On the Elements of Being: I," *Review of Metaphysics* **7** (1953), 3–18.

   "The Myth of Passage," *Journal of Philosophy* **48** (1951), 457–72.

Woodward, James, *Making Things Happen* (Oxford University Press, 2003).

Index

3210518R00148

Printed in Great Britain
by Amazon.co.uk, Ltd.,
Marston Gate.